American Literature in Context to 1865

Literature in Context

Literature in Context is an important new series that provides readers with relevant historical knowledge that deepens their understanding of American and British literature. Each accessible volume discusses the issues and events that engaged writers and provides original and useful readings of important literary works that demonstrate how context contributes to meaning.

American Literature in Context to 1865
Susan Castillo

American Literature in Context from 1865 to 1929
Philip R. Yannella

American Literature in Context after 1929
Philip R. Yannella

American Literature
in Context *to 1865*

Susan Castillo

A John Wiley & Sons, Ltd., Publication

This edition first published 2011
© 2011 Susan Castillo

Blackwell Publishing was acquired by John Wiley & Sons in February 2007. Blackwell's
publishing program has been merged with Wiley's global Scientific, Technical, and Medical
business to form Wiley-Blackwell.

Registered Office
John Wiley & Sons Ltd, The Atrium, Southern Gate, Chichester, West Sussex, PO19 8SQ,
United Kingdom

Editorial Offices
350 Main Street, Malden, MA 02148-5020, USA
9600 Garsington Road, Oxford, OX4 2DQ, UK
The Atrium, Southern Gate, Chichester, West Sussex, PO19 8SQ, UK

For details of our global editorial offices, for customer services, and for information about how
to apply for permission to reuse the copyright material in this book please see our website at
www.wiley.com/wiley-blackwell.

The right of Susan Castillo to be identified as the author of this work has been asserted in
accordance with the UK Copyright, Designs and Patents Act 1988.

Library of Congress Cataloging-in-Publication Data

Castillo, Susan P., 1948–
    American literature in context to 1865 / Susan Castillo.
        p. cm.
    Includes bibliographical references and index.
    ISBN 978-1-4051-8864-7 (alk. paper) – ISBN 978-1-4051-8863-0 (pbk. : alk. paper)
1. American literature–History and criticism.   2. National characteristics, American, in
literature.   3. Literature and history–United States.   4. American literature.   I. Title.
    PS88.C43 2010
    810.9′973–dc22

                                                                            2009050846

A catalogue record for this book is available from the British Library.

Set in 10.5/13pt Minion by Toppan Best-set Premedia Limited
Printed and bound in Malaysia by Vivar Printing Sdn Bhd

1   2011

To Paul and Cristina

Contents

Preface

In my life as an academic, I have always believed that it is vitally important for scholars to make their work available to the widest possible audience. This book is aimed at such an audience, ranging from advanced undergraduates to intelligent general readers. In writing it, my aim has been to provide an overview of American literature in its historical context up to the end of the American Civil War in 1865. The scope of such an undertaking means that, of necessity, readers should look elsewhere for studies in greater depth of individual authors and historical moments.

What I have tried to do in this book is open windows through which readers can look more closely in the future should they wish to do so. Although my approach has been broadly chronological, I have not adhered to a rigid chronological scheme. The main reason for this choice is that there has been in the past a tendency to map histories of American literature onto exceptionalist ideology, which would contend that America is a country unlike any other, divinely directed and unfolding toward perfection. In my view, this perspective is intellectually untenable. Here, in contrast, I have tried to convey the splendid untidiness and exuberant vitality of American literature, and the ways in which many different voices with different agendas have clamored to be heard.

Note

Key texts, terms, and people in the book are denoted in bold type.

Acknowledgments

This book would never have been written without the support of the following friends and colleagues. Some read drafts, others provided suggestions for bibliography, and still others kept me anchored to the earth; many combined all three roles: Anna Ballard, Naona Beecher-Moore, Janet Beer, Michael Bibler, Manuel Broncano, Bonnie Craig, Michele Costa, Marcie Ferris, William Ferris, Sarah Ficke, Rebecka Fisher, Janet Floyd, Susan Forsyth, Cristina Garrigos, Paul Giles, Kathryn Gray, Richard Gray, Michael Green, Trudier Harris, Andrew Hook, Nathaniel Hook, John Howard, Hsinya Huang, Peter Hulme, Alice Jenkins, John Kasson, Joy Kasson, James Mackay, Polina Mackay, Denis Macdermot, Heidi Macpherson, Tim Marr, Bill Marshall, Christina Matteotti, Penny McCarthy, Sharon Monteith, Marina Moskowitz, Judie Newman, Simon Newman, Theda Purdue, Ivy Schweitzer, Alison Stanley, Eena Taylor, Helen Taylor, Linda Toocaram, Brian Ward, Susan Wedlake, Betty Wood, and Duncan Wu. Any inaccuracies or infelicities are, needless to say, entirely my own. I am deeply grateful for your generosity and friendship.

Thanks are due to the School of Humanities, King's College, for giving me the semester's leave which enabled me to complete this project, and to the staff at the British Library, especially Carole Holden. I am grateful to the British Library for permission to produce the images contained in this book, and to Emma Bennett of Wiley-Blackwell for believing in this project, and for her support and encouragement. To Jenny Roberts, the best of copy-editors, thanks for her eagle eye and her intelligence.

Finally, my greatest debt is to my family on both sides of the Atlantic: to my American family, to my daughter's partner Liam, and to my son Paul and my daughter Cristina, to whom this book is dedicated.

Susan Castillo, London, August 2009

Timeline of Texts and Historical Events

Texts	Historical Events
Indigenous peoples of the Americas transmit both oral and written texts, the latter in pictograms. Performative genres include speeches, songs, stories, and plays.	
	1492. Christopher Columbus reaches the Bahamas.
	1494. Second voyage of Columbus.
	1498. Columbus's third expedition reaches the South American mainland.
	1500. Indigenous populations of the Americas are decimated by European diseases such as smallpox.
	1504. Columbus's fourth and final voyage.
	1509–1547. Henry VIII's reign.
	1514. Bartolomé de las Casas petitions the Spanish monarchy on behalf of Native Americans.
	1519–20. Cortés and his forces conquer the Aztec kingdom of Montezuma.
	1531. Beginning of the cult of Our Lady of Guadalupe.

Texts	Historical Events
	1539. First printing press in Mexico.
1542. Álvar Núñez Cabeza de Vaca, *The Relation of Álvar Núñez Cabeza de Vaca.*	
	1547–53. Edward VI's reign.
1552. Bartolomé de las Casas, *The Very Brief Relation of the Devastation of the Indies.*	
	1553–58. Mary Tudor's reign.
	1558–1603. Reign of Elizabeth I.
1568? Bernal Díaz del Castillo, *The True History of the Conquest of New Spain.*	
	1584. Walter Ralegh arrives with an expedition to Roanoke, and names the new territory Virginia for the Virgin Queen.
1588. Thomas Harriot, *A Brief and True Report of the New Found Land of Virginia.*	1588. The Spanish Armada is defeated.
	1603–25. Reign of James I (of England), VI (of Scotland).
	1603–13. Samuel de Champlain founds the city of Quebec.
1604. James I, "Counter-Blaste to Tobacco."	1607. Jamestown is established in Virginia.
1610. Gaspar Pérez de Villagrá, *Chronicle of New Mexico.*	1619. Twenty African indentured servants arrive in Jamestown.
	1620. The *Mayflower* reaches Plymouth Harbor.

Texts	Historical Events
1624. John Smith, *The General History of Virginia, New England, and the Summer Isles.*	1625–49. Reign of Charles I.
1630. John Winthrop's sermon, *A Model of Christian Charity* (published in 1838), describes the Puritan vision of the City upon a Hill.	1630. The Great Migration of English Puritans, led by John Winthrop, establishes the Massachusetts Bay Colony.
1630–50. William Bradford's journal *Of Plymouth Plantation* (published 1856).	1637. The Pequot War.
1637. Thomas Morton, *New England Canaan.*	
	1638. Anne Hutchinson is exiled from Massachusetts Bay at the height of the Antinomian controversy. 1641–51. The English Civil War.
1643. Roger Williams, *A Key into the Languages of America.*	
1650. Anne Bradstreet, *The Tenth Muse.*	
	1649. Charles I executed.
	1651–53. The English Commonwealth. 1653–59. Oliver Cromwell's Protectorate.
1662. Michael Wigglesworth, *The Day of Doom.*	1660. Parliamentary monarchy is restored under Charles II. 1660–85. Reign of Charles II.

Texts	Historical Events
1673–1729. Samuel Sewall's *Diary*.	1675–78. King Philip's War.
	1676. Bacon's Rebellion.
	1680. The Pueblo Revolt.
	1685–1688. Reign of James II.
1682. Mary Rowlandson's *Narrative*.	1682. William Penn draws up a Frame of Government for Pennsylvania.
c. 1685. Edward Taylor, *God's Determinations*.	
	1689–1702. Reign of William and Mary.
	1692. The Salem Witch Trials.
1702. Cotton Mather, *Magnalia Christi Americana*.	
1704–05. Sarah Kemble Knight's *The Private Journal of a Journey from Boston to New York* (published 1825).	
	1713. The War of the Spanish Succession is marked by the Treaty of Utrecht.
	1714–27. Reign of George I.
	1715. First Jacobite Rebellion in Scotland.
	1718. New Orleans is founded by the French.
	1726–56. The "Great Awakening."
1728. William Byrd, *History of the Dividing Line* (published 1841).	1727–60. Reign of George II.
	1745. Second Jacobite Rebellion in Scotland.

Texts	Historical Events
1755. *Some Account of the Fore Part of the Life of Elizabeth Ashbridge.*	1755–63. The French and Indian Wars.
1760. Briton Hammon's *Narrative.*	1760–1820. Reign of George III.
1764. James Grainger, *The Sugar Cane.*	1764. The British Parliament passes the Sugar Act. 1765. Parliament passes the Stamp Act.
1768. Samson Occom, *A Short Narrative of My Life.*	1770. The Boston Massacre.
1771–1790. Benjamin Franklin writes his *Autobiography* (Part I published 1818).	
1773. Phillis Wheatley, *Poems on Various Subjects.*	1773. The Boston Tea Party.
1774. John Woolman, *The Journal of John Woolman.*	1775–83. The War of Independence.
1776. Thomas Paine, *Common Sense.*	1776. The Declaration of Independence.
1777. William Robertson's *History of America.*	
1778. Lemuel Haynes, *Liberty Further Extended.*	
1782. J. Hector St. John de Crèvecoeur, *Letters from an American Farmer.*	

Texts	Historical Events
	1783. The Treaty of Paris marks the end of the War of Independence.
1786. Philip Freneau, *Poems*.	
1786. Thomas Jefferson, *Notes on the State of Virginia*. Royall Tyler, *The Contrast*.	
1787–88. The Federalist Papers.	1787. The US Constitution is adopted.
1789. Olaudah Equiano, *The Interesting Narrative of the Life of Olaudah Equiano*.	1789. George Washington becomes America's first President. 1789–99. The French Revolution.
1790. Judith Sargent Murray, *On the Equality of the Sexes*.	1791. Toussaint L'Ouverture leads a successful slave revolt in St. Domingue.
1791. Susanna Rowson, *Charlotte: A Tale of Truth*.	
1794. Hannah Webster Foster, *The Coquette*.	
	1797. Prince Hal delivers his Charge to the African Lodge.
1798. Charles Brockden Brown, *Wieland*.	1803. The Louisiana Purchase.
	1812–14. The War of 1812.
1820. Washington Irving, *The Sketch Book*.	1819. The US acquires Florida. 1820. The Missouri Compromise.

Texts	Historical Events
	1821. Sequoyah invents the Cherokee syllabary.
1823. James Fenimore Cooper, *The Pioneers*.	
1826. Elias Boudinot, *A Letter to the Whites*.	
1827. Catherine Maria Sedgwick, *Hope Leslie*.	
	1828. Andrew Jackson is elected to the Presidency.
1829. William Apess, *A Son of the Forest*. David Walker's *Appeal*.	
	1830. Indian Removal Act passed by Congress.
	1831. William Garrison founds the abolitionist newspaper *The Liberator*. Nat Turner's slave revolt.
	1832. The Nullification controversy.
1833. William Apess, *An Indian's Looking-Glass for the White Man*. 1836. Ralph Waldo Emerson, "Nature," Angelina Grimké, *Appeal to the Christian Women of the South*.	

Texts	Historical Events
1837. Ralph Waldo Emerson, "The American Scholar." Catherine Beecher, "An Essay on Slavery and Abolitionism, with Reference to the Duty of American Females."	
1838. Edgar Allan Poe, *The Narrative of Arthur Gordon Pym.*	1838. The Trail of Tears.
1839. Edgar Allan Poe, *The Fall of the House of Usher.*	1839. John O'Sullivan coins the term "Manifest Destiny."
1841. James Fenimore Cooper, *Deerslayer.* Ralph Waldo Emerson, "Self-Reliance."	
1844. Ralph Waldo Emerson, "The Poet."	
1845. Margaret Fuller, *Woman in the Nineteenth Century.* Edgar Allan Poe, *The Raven.* Frederick Douglass, *Narrative of the Life of Frederick Douglass.* Les Cenelles publish the first anthology of Francophone African-American poetry.	1845. The United States annexes Texas.
1846. Herman Melville, *Typee.*	1846–48. The Mexican War.
	1848. Seneca Falls convention on women's rights.
1850. Nathaniel Hawthorne, *The Scarlet Letter.*	1850. The 1850 Compromise. The Fugitive Slave Law.

Texts	Historical Events
1851. Nathaniel Hawthorne, *The House of Seven Gables.* Herman Melville, *Moby-Dick.* Harriet Beecher Stowe, *Uncle Tom's Cabin.*	
1852. Nathaniel Hawthorne, *The Blithedale Romance.* 1853. William Wells Brown, *Clotel: Or, The President's Daughter.* 1854. Thoreau, *Walden.* 1855. Walt Whitman, *Leaves of Grass.*	
	1857. The Supreme Court rules, in the Dred Scott decision, that African-Americans are not citizens of the United States.
1859. Harriet Wilson, *Our Nig.*	1859. John Brown leads an attack on the US arsenal at Harper's Ferry.
1860–65. Emily Dickinson writes several hundred poems. 1861. Harriet Jacobs, *Incidents in the Life of a Slave Girl*	1860. Abraham Lincoln is elected to the Presidency. 1861. Southern states secede from the Union, forming the Confederate States of America. War breaks out with an attack on Ft. Sumter. 1861–65. The Civil War. 1863. The Emancipation Proclamation. 1865. Abraham Lincoln is assassinated.

Chapter 1

The Arrival of the Europeans

Introduction

When **Christopher Columbus** and his men landed in the Caribbean after a long and arduous voyage, they were dazzled at the beauty of the islands they encountered and fascinated by the people who inhabited them. **Bartolomé de las Casas**, a Dominican friar who accompanied Columbus's expedition, provides a vivid and evocative account of the encounter between two different worlds. When Columbus leapt ashore to claim these lands for the Catholic rulers of Spain, the Indigenous people drew close to him and his men:

> They approached the bearded men, especially the Admiral, as though by the eminence and authority of his person and his scarlet clothing they had known he was the leader, and raised their hands to his beard in wonderment (for none of them have beards), scrutinizing the whiteness of the hands and feet of the Spaniards very carefully ... As the Admiral and the rest looked at the simplicity of the Indians, they endured this with pleasure and delight. Indeed, the Christians gazed at the Indians, no less than the Indians at them, amazed at the gentleness, innocence and trust of people whom they had never met ... They walked among them and drew close, with such nonchalance and ease, with all their shameful parts uncovered, as though the state of innocence was restored or had never been lost ... We later perceived their natural kindness, their innocence, humility, tameness, peacefulness and virtuous inclinations, excellent wit, and readiness to receive our holy faith and to be imbued with Christian religion.
>
> (Castillo and Schweitzer, 2001, p. 31)

This text is imbued not only with a sense of mutual wonder and delight, but with evidence of the misconceptions of European explorers and the difficulties which they encountered in decoding the attitudes, intentions and priorities of the Indigenous people of the New World. The misnomer "Indians," first of all, reveals that the Spaniards were convinced they had pulled off the previously unthinkable feat of reaching India by sailing west; essentially, they were unaware of where they really were. The Europeans viewed the people they encountered as existing in an Edenic state of innocence, and interpreted the courtesy and hospitality with which they were received as signifying the readiness of Indigenous groups to abandon their own belief systems and be converted to European religion. At this point, since neither group spoke the language of the other, they would have communicated through gestures, and the opportunities for potentially disastrous misunderstandings on both sides are obvious.

This idyllic state of mutual enchantment was not destined to last. Writing only a few years later, Las Casas portrays the disastrous consequences of European contact for the Indigenous people of the New World:

> As the greed of the Spaniards, as I have already said, urged them on so that they did not sow in order to have bread but rather to gather the gold which they had not sown...they ordered the men and women (who did not eat enough to work, let along to live) to labor ... One told us (as though it were something praiseworthy, a great feat) that with the Indians given to him they had plowed many fields and made mounds of earth, and that he had sent them every third day or every other day to the hills to eat whatever berries and fruits they could find there. After that he would make them work two or three days more at this task without giving them anything to eat, not a single bite ... It was thus that, starving, with nothing to eat and working so hard, these people died so quickly and in greater number than in other places ... And as the Spaniards took healthy men and women to the mines and to other labors, only the old and infirm were left in the village without anyone to look after them; they all died of anguish and disease, and raging hunger. On some occasions, as I was walking in those days around the island, I heard them cry out from inside the houses, and when I entered to see them, asking what was the matter, they answered, "Hunger, hunger."
>
> (Castillo and Schweitzer, 2001, p. 32)

Many Indigenous groups were decimated, not only because of brutal and exploitative labor practices on the part of the European invaders, but also because of diseases such as smallpox and measles which they brought along with them, against which Native Americans had no immunity. Population estimates of the Americas at the time of Contact range widely, from 8.4 million (Kroeber, 1963) to over 100 million (Dobyns, 1983); Russell Thornton (2004, p. 68) suggests 75 million as a reasonable estimate. It is impossible to ascertain exactly what mortality figures were in the years immediately after the first contact with Europeans, but what is clear is that certain groups were completely wiped out, others saw their population decline drastically, and others experienced a decline in numbers for a time but then experienced a degree of population recovery (Thornton, 2004, p. 69). It is equally clear, however, that Native Americans were enormously resilient and resourceful in resisting European attempts to eradicate or suppress their cultural and religious traditions. One of the most important ways in which this resistance took form was in the stories Indigenous people told, and tell, about themselves.

In this chapter, we begin by looking at representative Indigenous oral and scribal traditions. We then analyze the European motives for expansion in the New World, looking at the Early Modern emergence of the Atlantic world-system, and then go on to discuss Spanish imperial policy, and the Conquest of Mexico from both Spanish and Indigenous perspectives. After an examination of the extraordinary narrative of Álvar Núñez Cabeza de Vaca, the chapter ends with a discussion of the ways in which Native people adapted Spanish religious practices to their own belief systems in the wake of the violence of the Conquest, as embodied by the image of Our Lady of Guadalupe.

Indigenous Narratives

In analyzing Indigenous traditional narratives, there are several things that it is important to keep in mind. First of all, to lump all the Indigenous groups of the Americas together under the label "Indians" is rather like making crude generalizations about "Europeans" in which the very considerable differences which exist between, say, Swedes and Italians, or Germans and Spaniards, are elided or ignored. It is vital to foreground the huge cultural and linguistic diversity of Indigenous groups, ranging from the Incas with their rich artistic traditions, to the Mayas with their advanced knowledge of astronomy and mathematics, to the Ute who subsisted on their hunting and gathering activities, to the ritual complexity of Pueblo culture, to the sedentary farming activities of the Iroquois, along with many, many others. What really did exist in the Americas when the first explorers and settlers arrived was not an Arcadian Neverland of gentle passive creatures, lacking culture and living in a state of nature, nor a wilderness haunted by savage monsters, but rather an immensely varied population consisting of many widely differing cultures, with rich and vibrant traditions of their own.

Second, most of the Native American narratives that have come to us have gone through a complex process of mediation and translation. Arnold Krupat makes the valuable point that "in varying degrees, all verbal performances studied as 'Native American literature' whether oral, textualized, or written, are mixed, hybrid; none are "pure" or strictly speaking, autonomous. Native American written literature in particular is an intercultural practice" (Krupat, 1996, p. 21). It is also the case, however, that some Native critics feel that such a perspective characterizes Indigenous cultures as mongrelized, when in fact Native people perceive themselves as having maintained their culture through oral tradition (see Weaver et al., 2006). Whatever the case, it is true of any text (European as well as Native American) that it is vital to pay attention to the conditions in which it was produced and circulated. Some early European explorers and settlers recorded Native narratives as exotic curiosities or evidence of superstition; later, in the nineteenth century, "salvage" ethnographers studied them as part of what they perceived as the need to preserve so-called "primitive" cultures doomed to disappear.[1] For all these reasons, it is impossible for us to gain access to a "pure," unmediated Indigenous voice from before European contact.

With these caveats in mind, however, it is indeed possible to point out features which are common to most Indigenous traditions. One is the belief in the interrelatedness and aliveness of all things: human beings, animals, earth, oceans, sky. Another is the idea that language not only reflects but actively creates and shapes reality. Still another is the notion that the self only has meaning as part of a community. In most Native American traditions, the sacred and the secular are intricately interwoven, and maintaining balance is vital for the survival of specific communities in specific landscapes.[2] Finally, in Indigenous thought human beings are seen, not as masters of nature, but as an integral part of a complex and infinitely beautiful ecosystem.

---

[1] For an excellent discussion of these issues see Murray (2005).
[2] See Joy Porter's useful essay, "Historical and Cultural Contexts" (Porter, 2005).

It is a commonplace to state that Native American narrative traditions are entirely oral in nature. In the case of the Mayas, however, this was not entirely the case. Before the arrival of the Spaniards, Mayan culture possessed codices or folding books, made from the inner bark of fig trees. In them, professional scribes or *ah ts'ib* recorded dynastic struggles, battles, trade routes, prophecies, songs, and information about astronomy, agriculture, and religious ritual. These codices were read in double columns from top to bottom and left to right. Mayan writing was a combination of logograms (signs standing for parts of words or whole words) and signs relating to meaning and pronunciation. In the texts of many of the early Spanish explorers and missionaries, we repeatedly find evidence of the existence of these texts. A priest called Avedaño, on seeing a ceremonial column and mask, remarked: "I came to recognize it since I had already read about it in their old papers, and had seen it in the *Anates* they use, which are books of barks of trees, polished and covered by lime, in which they painted figures and characters to say the future events they had foretold" (quoted in Arias-Larreta, 1967, p. 136). Alonso de Zorita stated in 1540 that he had seen many books of this sort in Guatemala, "which recorded their history for more than eight hundred years back, and which were interpreted for me by very ancient Indians" (Zorita, 1963, pp. 271–2).

The arrival of the Spaniards was, however, catastrophic for Maya culture despite the fascination which Indigenous traditions held for many of the early missionaries. Present-day readers and scholars often find it hard to believe that extensive knowledge of another culture could fail to create a sense of respect for that same culture. Sadly, however, knowledge and respect often do not go hand in hand. For example, Diego de Landa, a Dominican priest, recorded in very considerable detail many of the histories and traditions of the Mayas, and indeed is one of the key sources of information about pre-Columbian Mayan culture. And yet he was convinced that the content of these manuscripts described heathen deities and worldviews which it was his obligation as a Christian missionary to eradicate once and for all (Arias-Larretta, 1967, p. 136). In a 1526 *auto–da-fé* he burned no fewer than 27 Mayan codices, in an act which has been compared to the burning of the Library of Alexandria. Only four codices have survived until the present day.

Among the Mayas, and also in the great Inca empire to the South, there was a rich tradition of performance. In his **Comentarios Reales**, the Peruvian Creole historian **Garcilaso de la Vega** describes tragic and comic performances staged by the *amautas*, the Inca priestly caste:

The *Amautas* did not lack ability, inasmuch as they were philosophers, to compose comedies and tragedies, which they performed before their rulers and members of the Court during the solemn feasts and ceremonies. The performers were not peasants but Incas and people of noble lineage, sons of chiefs, and captains, and generals; because the plot of the tragedies were about relevant matters, and were always about military deeds, triumphs, and accomplishments, and the heroic acts and greatness of the late kings and other heroic warriors. The plots of the comedies were about farmers, agriculture, and household affairs. They never dealt with low or vile subjects, but rather with serious and honest matters, with the observations and wit permitted in such a place. Those who acted particularly well were given jewels and tokens of great esteem.

(Vega, 1943, p. 121, my translation)

Further to the north, Native Americans in what is now known as North America had a rich variety of stories through which they made sense of the world and of their place in it. One important category was that of origin stories. For instance, the **Popol Vuh**, the sacred text in which we encounter an account of the origins of the Mayas, was probably destroyed by the Conquistadores in the flames of Utatlán, but an anonymous Quiché transcribed what he could recall. In it, we encounter a description of the sky as an empty silent void over the sea, immobile and darkness and called the Heart of Heaven or Huracán,[3] where Tepeu and Gucumatz, the Forefathers, were hidden under green and blue feathers. They come together and dream the world into being:

"Earth" they said, and instantly it was made. Like the mist, like a cloud, like a cloud of dust was the creation, when the mountains appeared from the water, and instantly the mountains grew. Only by a miracle, only by magic art were the mountains and valleys formed; and instantly the groves of cypresses and pine put forth shoots together on the surface of the earth.

(quoted from *Popul Vuh: The Sacred Book of the Quiché Maya*, in Castillo and Schweitzer, 2001, pp. 19–20)

Other groups, however, saw Creation differently. Among the Indigenous people of what is now the US Northeast as well as in Eastern Canada, there exist numerous variants of the **Earthdiver** story. In common with traditional stories from all over the world, they speak of a primeval flood. In

---

[3] This is also the origin of the word "hurricane."

some versions, the protagonists are beings living in the sky, and in others water birds or other creatures living on the surface of the water. Ultimately longing for a stable base of land, several of the animals dive to the depths in search of earth, but they drown in the attempt. Finally, one of the animals (sometimes Muskrat, sometimes Beaver or Loon) or one of the Sky people makes a final desperate attempt and comes up exhausted but alive with a bit of soil. This clod of earth is used to create the world.[4] In some accounts, the world is created on the back of a giant turtle. What this story reveals is the Indigenous vision of the world as an ecosystem of infinite power and beauty cocreated by humans and animals living in harmony.

However, for the Hopi, the Pueblo, and many other groups in what is now the US Southwest, Creation was described as emergence from an underworld, with Earth viewed as a womb from which people emerge gradually, as in childbirth. Some versions of these accounts describe the Underworld as a place of dissatisfaction and social upheaval which provides the impetus for emergence. Others paint a picture of comforting authority and harmony. The Ácoma version describes two female human beings existing in the dark, who are given language and seeds by the deity Sus'sistinako along with images of all the animals which are to exist in the upper world. Finally, a tree lets in a little light, enabling them to create a badger who makes a hole big enough to let them out. On emerging into the light, they sing the creation song, bringing into being living things and creating the surrounding landscape. Later, the eldest sister is impregnated by a steaming mist and gives birth to twin boys. One of the boys is adopted by the younger sister, who later marries him, and it is this couple who proceeds to produce children who will become the Ácoma people (see Tyler, 1964, pp. 103–8).[5]

Another type of Indigenous story is the **Trickster** tale. The Trickster figure is also encountered among the ancient Greeks, Africans, and many other groups across the world. The Trickster is a liminal being who pushes at and subverts boundaries; the usual Western binaries of human/animal, hero/buffoon, male/female have no meaning in the Trickster's world. Laguna critic Paula Gunn Allen describes three different types of Trickster figure: the Heroic Transformer, who is usually depicted as a slayer of

---

[4] See Reichard (1921) for an outline of the main features of Earthdiver tales. Paula Gunn Allen's excellent *Studies in American Indian Literature* (1993a) provides extensive bibliographical references for various types of Native American oral literatures. A useful account of Earthdiver myths can also be found in Dundes (1962).

[5] For an account of Hopi traditional stories, see Nequatewa (1994).

monsters, an aggressive hero, or creator of order, who achieves power by action; the Cunning Transformer, usually a human or animal figure who attempts to gain power by outwitting his opponents in gambling or games or through marriage or sexual encounters; and the Overreacher, a figure who attempts more than he can achieve and consequently suffers humiliation or injury, though he lives to tell the tale (Allen, 1993b, p. 50). Often Trickster figures combine features of these types; heroes can be both courageous and sly, and even the bravest among them can make fools of themselves and others (see Carroll, 1984). Common to all of these types is the idea that one can only survive in a chaotic and often adverse universe by the use of subversive intelligence and the cathartic power of laughter.

One of the most commonly encountered Trickster figures is that of **Coyote**. Richard Gray, in his definitive *History of American Literature*, observes that Coyote in all his diverse incarnations is characterized by spontaneity, skill at disguise, and a talent for shape-shifting or metamorphosis (Gray, 2004, pp. 12–13). Coyote, like most of us, is a mixture of astuteness and buffoonery, noble aspirations and low lechery, the sacred and the profane, high courage and comical grandiloquence.

Some Coyote tales attempt to explain natural phenomena. For instance, in one account it is said that the Bluebird originally was a pale dun color, but that its feathers were transformed to blue by bathing in the blue water of a nearby lake four times over four days. Coyote spies on Bluebird, and is envious of its beautiful blue color. Bluebird teaches Coyote an incantation, and he leaps into the lake four times as instructed. On the fifth day, Coyote emerges bright blue, and he struts around wondering if anyone has noticed how blue he is. He then begins to run, looking back at his shadow to see if it too is blue, only to collide with a stump and fall onto the dusty ground. For this reason, all coyotes are the color of earth. A Coyote story from the Northwest accounts for the eruption of a nearby volcano. Coyote's own village has no fish, so he visits the nearby Shasta people, who receive him with hospitality and allow him to take all the fish he could catch and carry. Predictably, Coyote is greedy, and loads himself down so heavily that he gets tired. When he lies down to sleep, a horde of voracious insects descends upon the salmon, leaving only fish bones in their wake. He returns to the village, and the Shasta again allow him to load up with fish, but again he falls asleep and loses his cargo to the insects. The Shasta allow him to fish for a third time, but hide in the bushes when he departs. Coyote meets Turtle on the way, and greets him with scorn; he is so intent on the conversation that he is unaware of the return of the insects, which devour the fish once more. Finally, Coyote and the Shasta depart in pursuit of the insects, but Turtle, who is slow and steady, tracks them to Mount Shasta, where the insects have vanished into a hole in the summit. There, Coyote suggests that the people start a fire to smoke them out, but this is unsuccessful because the smoke escapes through holes in the side of the mountain. Finally, when Coyote and the people manage to close all the holes, a rumbling sound is heard. An enormous explosion ensues, spewing out delicious cooked salmon. Coyote, the Shasta and the Turtle sit down to a banquet of fish. And thus began the eruptions on Mount Shasta.

Some Coyote stories tell of the difficulties encountered by Indigenous people in dealing with the duplicity and hostility of whites and in defining their own identity. One tells of two coyotes crossing a farmer's field; they do not know each other. When the farmer shouts that there is a coyote in the field, the first coyote turns back to the second to warn him to run. When they flee toward the trees, the farmer espies the second and shouts that there is another one. When they reach the trees, the coyotes introduce themselves. The first coyote says that he is called Wanderer, and that he too is a coyote. The second coyote looks askance at his companion, and tells him that he is called Sleek, but is not a coyote like his friend. After arguing the point, Wanderer tells Sleek that he will demonstrate what he means. He runs across the field, and the farmer shouts again that there is a coyote. Sleek then streaks across the field, and the farmer shouts that there goes another one. Complacent, Wanderer tells Sleek that the farmer has called them both coyotes. Sleek demurs, retorting that the farmer called Wanderer a coyote but that he is Another One. This story illustrates the fact that that the coyotes (and presumably the Indigenous people of the Americas) are in danger of allowing the farmer (the white invaders) to tell them who they are.

European Expansion

However, European perceptions of the Indigenous peoples of the Americas, as indeed we have seen at the beginning of this chapter, were not always reliable and were often downright wrong. From the moment in which Columbus and his expedition made landfall in the Caribbean, European explorers and *conquistadores* saw America through the prism of narratives describing travel, not to the West, but to the East. Examples of such narratives include Marco Polo's *Book of Marvels* with its tales of islands rich in gold, or Mandeville's apocryphal voyages, or Spanish chivalric romances such as *Amadís de Gaula* which tell of monsters, enchanted islands, and strange creatures. Columbus, who was a remarkably obstinate man with a rigid medieval worldview, held until his death the unshakeable conviction that he had discovered, not a New World, but the easternmost borders of Asia. His exploits had been preceded by those of Portuguese navigators, particularly Prince Henry the Navigator, whose explorations of the African coast were prompted by a complex mixture of motivations: the desire for access to precious metals in the African interior along with the Crusading urge to encounter the Christian kingdom of the mythical Prester John, with whom he hoped to regain Jerusalem (see Pagden, 2003, pp. 50–4). The motives underlying Columbus's own quest for a sea route to India, financed by Spain's Catholic monarchs Ferdinand and Isabella, were a curious blend of Christian ideological zeal and a sharp eye for the commercial bottom line.

The Atlantic world-system

Given, then, the obsession of the European monarchies with the immense wealth of Asia, what impelled them in the years after Columbus's voyage to undertake expeditions to the New World? Certainly a major factor was the need for raw materials. Immanuel Wallerstein (2004) describes the emergence in the Early Modern period of the capitalist world-system, predicated on an international division of power that determined relationships between different regions as well as the types of labor conditions within each region. Wallerstein proposes four different regional categories: core, semiperiphery, periphery, and external, which describe each region's relative position within the world economy. Core regions, which are characterized by strong central governments, complex bureaucracies, and large armies, are those which gain most economic benefit from the core–periphery structure. Peripheral areas, however, are controlled politically and militarily by other regions, export raw materials to core regions, and rely on coercive labor practices. Examples of this in the Early Modern period might include certain areas of the Americas where Indigenous elites were decimated during the Conquest; coercive labor practices introduced by the Spanish and Portuguese colonizers included the neofeudal *encomienda* system and the importation of African slaves. Traditionally, core regions absorb much of the capital surplus generated by the peripheral areas. Between core and periphery, there exists an intermediate category of semiperipheries, buffer zones which are usually either core regions in decline or peripheries struggling for advancement in the world economy. External regions are those who maintain their own economic systems outside the world economy. According to Wallerstein (2004), semiperipheries are characterized by tensions between the central government and local landowning classes and are exploited by the core but are themselves predicated on exploitative labor practices and political inequalities among their citizens. Recent scholarship, however, suggests that rather than looking to the conventional "gold, glory and gospel" accounts or narratives focusing on world-systems, it makes sense to conceptualize the colonization of the Americas as resulting from two different phenomena: a first phase spearheaded by military adventurers in the first half of the sixteenth century (the conquest of Indigenous nations and the subsequent efforts at evangelization), followed by a second phase characterized by what Philip Curtin (1998) has designated the "plantation complex,"[6] as we shall see in Chapter 2.

Historian Carole Shammas has demonstrated that the lion's share of European migration to the Americas prior to 1550 can be linked to the expeditions of military adventurers. In the Early Modern period, and coinciding with the growing power of European nation-states, one of the most popular literary genres was the chivalric novel, marvelously satirized in Cervantes' immortal *Don Quixote*; these accounts of adventures in faraway lands address not only issues of ideology but also of personal glory. For Shammas, this phase of Atlantic migration arose more as the consequence of political and religious developments in Europe and the Near East than as a response to commercial imperatives. The failure of papal crusades to reconquer Jerusalem and the fall of Istanbul to the forces of the Ottoman Empire in the fifteenth century threatened the *raison d'être* of the Christian warrior class in Europe. In Spain, the forces of Ferdinand and Isabella completed the Reconquest of the Iberian peninsula in 1492 and expelled those Muslims and Jews who refused to convert to Christianity, leaving many of their troops (drawn from the lesser Christian gentry of the Extremadura region and the Andalusian port towns) at loose ends. The opportunity for adventure in the New World thus must have had considerable appeal for these soldiers of fortune.[7]

---

[6] For a lucid overview of these issues, see Shammas (2006).

[7] Shammas (2006, p. 29) comments that up to 1550, around 60,000 Spanish, 15,000 Portuguese, and 41,000 Africans emigrated to the New World. African emigration (usually involuntary, since most were taken as slaves), however, grew fourfold from 1550 to 1600.

The Conquest of Mexico

One such was the redoubtable **Hernán Cortés**. Born in the village of Medellín, he sailed to the island of Hispaniola with Nicolás de Ovando, and was then chosen by Diego Velázquez to build a colony in Mexico. Velázquez, who subsequently became a bitter enemy of Cortés, was convinced that the latter would exceed his orders and subsequently attempted to stop the expedition. By the time he did so, however, Cortés and his fleet were on their way to Mexico. Landing at Veracruz, in a gesture that illustrates his courage and utter ruthlessness, Cortés burned his boats so that retreat for him and his men would be impossible. In November 1519 the Spaniards marched on Tenochtitlán, the capital, where they were graciously welcomed by the Aztec emperor **Montezuma**. Subsequently, Montezuma was taken prisoner, and Tenochtitlán was laid waste by the Spanish forces.

One eyewitness to these events was **Bernal Díaz del Castillo**, a soldier who fought alongside Cortés. Although Díaz characterizes himself as lacking in eloquence, his text reveals him as a keen observer with an eye for the telling detail, and his evocation of the principal characters in this real-life drama (and historical tragedy) is remarkably vivid. In his *History of the Conquest of New Spain*, he speaks of the important part played in events by **Doña Marina** (also known as **La Malinche**), the Native mistress of Cortés, whose role as translator and cultural intermediary was crucial to his success in the Conquest of Mexico. Cortés himself emerges as a brilliant tactician and as a driven and ambitious man of considerable physical courage, utterly lacking in scruples and determined to achieve his goals. Montezuma, the Aztec emperor, is portrayed as a ruler with considerable presence and dignity, treated with enormous respect by his courtiers but not, sadly, by the thuggish Spanish soldiers who eventually became his jailors; in one passage, Bernal Díaz describes Montezuma's extreme annoyance when his guards "commit a nuisance" (i.e., break wind) in his presence. Díaz also describes in vivid detail the beauty and prosperity of the imperial city of Tenochtitlán, which he and his fellow soldiers are about to destroy. He speaks of Montezuma's palaces and of his retinue:

> There were dancers and stilt-walkers, and some who seemed to leap flying through the air, and men like jesters to make him laugh. There was a whole district full of these people who had no other occupation.

He had as many workmen as he needed, too, stone cutters, masons, and carpenters, to maintain his houses in good repair ... We must not forget the gardens with their many varieties of flowers and sweet-scented trees planted in orderly fashion, and their ponds and tanks of fresh water where the water flowed in at one end and out at the other, and the baths he [Montezuma] had there, and the variety of small birds that nested in the branches, and the medicinal and useful herbs that grew there in the gardens. They were a wonderful sight, and required many gardeners to take care of them. Everything was built of stone and plastered; baths and walks and closets and rooms like summer houses where they danced and sang. There was so much to see in these gardens, as there was everywhere else, that we could not tire of contemplating his great power and the large number of craftsmen employed in the many skills they practiced.

(Díaz, 2001, pp. 47–8)

What seems extraordinary to the present-day reader is that, despite being able to appreciate the beauty of the doomed city, the Spanish forces did not hesitate to destroy it and slaughter its inhabitants. Many more died from smallpox, a European disease brought by the invaders against which they had no defenses. After the Spanish victory, Bernal Díaz paints a haunting picture of the devastated capital:

We could not walk without treading on the bodies and heads of dead Indians ... the dry land and the lagoon and the stockades were piled high with the bodies of the dead. The stench was so strong that no one could endure it, and for that reason each of us captains returned to his camp after Guatemoc's capture; even Cortés was ill from the smells which assailed his nostrils during those days in Tlatelolco ... When Cortés went into the city, he encountered the houses full of dead Indians, and some poor Mexicans in them who were unable to move away. Their excrement was the sort of filth that scrawny pigs pass which have been fed only on grass. The whole city looked as if it had been ploughed up.

(Díaz, 2001, p. 61)

It is difficult to remain unmoved at a similar description from an Indigenous perspective, recorded by the Spanish friar **Bernardino de Sahagún:**

Worms are swarming in the streets and plazas, and the walls are splattered with gore. The water has turned red, as if it were dyed, and when we drink it, it has the taste of brine ... we have pounded our hands in despair against the adobe walls, for our inheritance, our city, is lost and dead.

(Castillo and Schweitzer, 2001, p. 69)

The aftermath of the conquest

In the decade following the Conquest of Tenochtitlán, Spanish exploration of the lands to the north of Mexico continued. **Alvar Núñez Cabeza de Vaca** provides us with the earliest description of the peoples and landscapes of what is now the United States in his *Relación*, published in Spain in 1542. Cabeza de Vaca[8] was one of the heads of the Narváez expedition, which set out in 1527 to explore the lands surrounding the Gulf of Mexico. The expedition seems to have been jinxed from the start: Narváez, its leader, was singularly incompetent, and many of his troops deserted en route. After this, two of his six ships were sunk in a hurricane, and the survivors suffered from hunger and ill-treatment among the Indians of the Florida coast among whom they eventually sought refuge. Finally, some escaped on rafts, which after many trials and vicissitudes were washed up on what is now known as Galveston Island. Ultimately, the only men who survived were three Spaniards (Cabeza de Vaca, Andrés Dorantes, and Alonso del Castillo) and Dorantes's slave Estevanico, an Arabic-speaking African from the Portuguese enclave of Azemmour. The four men were in desperate straits; they were cold and naked, and had lost all they possessed. They were helped, however, by the local Indians, who wept in sympathy with their plight; Cabeza de Vaca comments (rather ungratefully if truth be told), "It was strange to see these men, wild and untaught, howling like brutes over our misfortunes." Later, the Indians built a series of fires on the road to their village and bore the Europeans from fire to fire, pausing briefly at each to allow them to get warm and giving them fish and roots to eat. After this, Cabeza de Vaca spent several years wandering from the Texas coast and going as far as New Mexico, gaining a certain renown among the Indians as a healer. Initially, he told his captors that he and his companions had no idea of how to heal when they requested him to do so, but when they withheld food he decided to obey:

[8] Rolena Adorno has demonstrated that the account of the origin of this surname (namely that an ancestor who had fought against the Moors had used a cow's skull to mark a strategic mountain pass) is apocryphal. For detailed contextual material, see the Introduction to her definitive edition, *The Narrative of Cabeza de Vaca* (Adorno and Pautz, 2003).

Their custom is, on finding themselves sick, to send for a physician, and after he has applied the cure, they give him not only all they have, but seek among their relatives for more to give. The practitioner scarifies over the seat of pain, and then sucks about the wound. They make cauteries with fire, a remedy among them in high repute, which I have tried on myself and found benefit from it. They afterwards blow on the spot, and having finished, the patient considers that he is relieved ... Our method was to bless the sick, breathing upon them, and recite a Pater-noster and an Ave-Maria, praying with all earnestness to God our Lord that he would give health and influence them to make some good return. In his clemency he willed that all those for whom we supplicated should tell the others that they were sound and in health, directly after we made the sign of the blessed cross over them. For this the Indians treated us kindly; they deprived themselves of food that they might give to us, and presented us with skins and some trifles.

Cabeza de Vaca, *Narrative*, in Castillo and Schweitzer, 2001, pp. 38–9)

After this, and given the apparent success of his healing techniques, Cabeza de Vaca gained quite a following among the Indians. Some months later, however, he and his group encountered a group of Spanish slavers, who arrested him and enslaved more than six hundred of his Native followers. Taken to Mexico City, he returned to Spain in 1537, where he hoped to protest against the cruel treatment suffered by the Indians. Later he returned to the New World, this time to Río de la Plata in South America, but there he was removed from office and sent back to Spain in chains. His *Narrative* is a remarkable document, which provides not only important information about the customs and beliefs of the Indigenous groups he encountered in the course of his wanderings, but about his own complex relationship with the people he encountered.

As we have seen, the coming of the Europeans often brought disease, suffering, and extreme hardship to the Native peoples of the Americas. It would be misleading, however, to characterize the Indigenous people of the New World as mere passive victims of European perfidy and brutality. Often they were able to manipulate the invaders, for instance by encouraging the latter to build churches in sites where the Indians had buried statues of their gods, so that when they knelt to pray they were in reality worshiping their own deities. In many cases, they discovered common features in their own beliefs and those of the Europeans.

A case in point is the cult of **Our Lady of Guadalupe**. In traditional accounts, a young peasant boy called Juan Diego is walking from his village into Mexico City on the morning of December 9, 1531. On the hill of Tepeyac, he sees a shimmering vision of the Virgin, an adolescent girl surrounded by light. Speaking to him in Nahuatl, she asks him to build a church in her honor on the site; she tells him to gather some flowers, although it is winter and no flowers had ever bloomed there. Juan Diego finds some Castilian roses and gathers them into his cloak. He then speaks to the Spanish bishop Father Juan de Zumárraga, who asks him to prove his allegations with a miraculous sign. As he opens his cloak to offer the roses to the Bishop, there appears on the fabric of the cloak a miraculous imprint of the Virgin.

This story illustrates in graphic fashion the ways in which the two very different cultures and religions interacted and influenced each other. The turquoise color of the Virgin's mantle has been interpreted as representing the Indigenous deities Ometecuhtli and Omecihuatl;[9] for some, a cruciform image called *nahui-ollin* symbolizing the cosmos can be discerned under her robes. Others suggest that she was presented to the Indigenous people of Mexico by the missionaries as a Christian version of the Indigenous deity Tonantzin. Whatever the case, Our Lady of Guadalupe, often called "the first mestiza," has become a symbol of racial and religious syncretism, and of the power of cultures to influence and transform one another.

---

[9] For a discussion of religious syncretism in Guadalupean imagery, see Harrington (1988).

Chapter 2

European Exploration and Settlement:
The Anvil and the Golden Fleece

Introduction

As the sixteenth century drew to a close, the European monarchies began in earnest to jockey for position in North America. The English, to be sure, were relative latecomers to the process of transatlantic colonization. It is true that to the north an English expedition under the leadership of the Italian **John Cabot** (Giovanni Caboto) had sailed to Newfoundland in 1497 and had discovered the great cod stocks of the Grand Bank. However, it is often forgotten that **St. Augustine**, the first permanent European settlement in what is now the United States, was established by the Spanish in 1565, nearly 40 years before Jamestown.

Transatlantic trade and migration really only took off with the growth of what Philip Curtin has described as the "plantation complex," that is, of highly capitalized agricultural undertakings producing sugar, cacao, coffee and tobacco, produced by a labor force made up successively of Indians, European indentured servants, and ultimately African slaves (see Curtin, 1998 and Shammas, 2006). In many ways, the career of **John Smith**, the maverick adventurer who played such a prominent role in ensuring the survival of the Jamestown colony, is emblematic of this shifting paradigm, of the transition from the colonizer as soldier-adventurer to the settler motivated by commercial interests. In the "Panegyrick Verses" which preface the volumes of Smith's *Generall Historie of Virginia, New England and the Summer Isles*, a poet called R. Gunnell denounces Smith's detractors and desires that his friend may

In spight of Pelias, when his hate lies cold
Returne as Jason with a fleece of gold.
Then after-ages shall record thy praise
That a New England to this Ile did raise
And when thou di'st (as all that live must die)
Thy fame live here; thou, with Eternity.[1]

The imagery of the Golden Fleece, of colonization as a heroic quest for immortal fame and national glory, is very much in the Spanish model. In this chapter, we shall examine the transition from a model of colonization as military conquest to one of settlement and economic production based on farming and settlement by family units, beginning with an overview of English colonial policy and privateers/explorers such as Sir Walter Ralegh.

Ralegh and Harriot

With Spain and England at war in the 1580s, Elizabethan soldiers of fortune took great delight in (and profit from) raiding, with the tacit blessing of their sovereign, the rich treasure fleets carrying precious metals and gems from the Caribbean to Seville. One of the most prominent privateers was the dashing **Sir Walter Ralegh**, who attempted to establish a colony called Roanoke on the barrier islands off the Atlantic coast of what is now North Carolina to serve as a base for his piratical endeavors. Like most of the privateers, Ralegh was from the West of England; John Aubrey in his *Brief Lives* describes him as a "tall, handsome and bold man, but damnable proud … he spake broad Devonshire to his dying day." Initially, as historian Karen Kupperman has pointed out, the Roanoke colony followed the Spanish model, consisting mainly of young men under the (singularly inept) military authority of Captain Ralph Lane (Kupperman, 2007, pp. 4–11). Factional strife soon broke out among its fractious inhabitants, who had managed to antagonize the Carolina tribe of Algonquians on whom they depended for food, and the colony was eventually abandoned. Ralegh, however, was nothing if not persistent, and in 1585 he established a new colony based on a very different model: that of families (under civil rather than military government), to whom he had promised tracts of land.

---

[1] R. Gunnell, poem "To that worthy and generous Gentleman, my very good friend, Captaine Smith," in Smith (1629), p. xviii.

One of the earliest accounts of early Virginia was that of **Thomas Harriot**, a remarkably intelligent man who had served as Ralegh's household tutor and who took part in the latter's second voyage. The title of Harriot's text, *A briefe and true report of the new found land of Virginia: of the commodities there found, and to be raised, as well merchantable as others* clearly reveals the author's commercial priorities. In one passage, he describes a plant cultivated by the Indians:

> There is an herbe which is sowed apart by it selfe, and is called by the inhabitants Uppowoc: in the West Indies it hath divers names, according to the severall places and countreys where it groweth and is used: the Spanyards generally call it Tabacco. The leaves thereof being dried and brought into pouder, they use to take the fume or smoake thereof, by sucking it thorow pipes made of clay, into their stomacke and head; from whence it purgeth superfluous fleame and other grosse humors, and openeth all the pores and passages of the body: by which meanes the use thereof not only preserveth the body from obstructions, but also (if any be, so that they have not bene of too long continuance) in short time breaketh them: whereby their bodies are notably preserved in health, and know not many grievous diseases, wherewithal we in England are often afflicted.
>
> (Harriot in Castillo and Schweitzer, 2001, p. 93)

Ralegh's second voyage, however, was also doomed to failure; the colony was neglected amid the febrile English preparations to repel the Spanish Armada in 1588, and when Ralegh's ships next visited Roanoke the colonists had vanished. The new model of colonization, of families farming tracts of land, was nonetheless the one which would ultimately endure, given the fact that it served many of the emerging commercial interests of the European powers.

Captain John Smith

One writer who described the transition from conquest to settlement was the Elizabethan/Jacobean adventurer John Smith. Smith's life was nothing if not eventful. Born in 1580 to a farming family in Lincolnshire, he was apprenticed at the age of 15 to a shopkeeper, but hankered after adventure. After his father's death, Smith managed to waive his indenture and volunteered to fight on behalf of the Dutch in their struggle against the Spanish crown. After a time as a privateer in the Mediterranean, he joined the Austrian army and fought against the Turks, allegedly beheading three Turks in a single battle in Romania, a deed commemorated on his coat of arms. Later, however, he was taken prisoner and sold to a Turk, who passed him on to his betrothed as a slave. According to Smith, this woman fell in love with him, but he then repaid her affections by murdering her intended and escaping, returning to England in the winter of 1604.

Smith returned at a time that was propitious for adventurers. In London, he became involved in the projects of the Virginia Company, which had received its charter from King James I as a profit-making venture to colonize Virginia. The expedition embarked for the New World in 1606, and Smith immediately gained a reputation as a troublemaker, to the extent that Captain Newport, the leader of the expedition, threatened him with execution. When, however, the list of council members was opened on shipboard, Smith's name was on it, and he was spared by Newport and sworn in to the Council of the colony. The beginnings of the Jamestown colony were not auspicious, however. The harsh winter and epidemics of fever carried off many of the colonists, and many were not remotely fit for the rigors of colonial life. Smith was put in charge of procuring foodstuffs and supplies for the colony, and it was in the course of carrying out his duties and seeking food along the Chickhominy River that he was taken captive for a period of six or seven weeks by a group of Native Virginians. The only version that we have of events is Smith's own, first in his 1608 *A True Relation of Such Occurrences and Accidents of Note, as Hath Hapned in Virginia* and his 1624 *The Generall Historie of Virginia*. By any standard, and even taking into account Smith's tendency toward exaggeration and self-aggrandizement, it is quite a tale. It is told in the third person, which enables Smith to foreground his own bravery and resourcefulness.

One of Smith's exploits which has had enormous historical resonance is his encounter with **Powhatan** and **Pocahontas**. While foraging for food with two other colonists and two Powhatan Indian guides, Smith ordered the latter to accompany him ashore so that he could explore the woods. In the forest, Smith was ambushed by a group of Indians, and used his Indian guide as a shield to ward off their arrows. Smith sustained a minor wound in the thigh, and was taken prisoner; the other two Englishmen were killed. At this point, he demanded to be taken to the Indians' leader, and when he was brought before Opechancanough, Smith showed the indigenous leader the marvels of Early Modern technology:

He demanding for their captain, they showed him Opechancanough, King of Pamunkey, to whom he gave a round ivory compass dial. Much they marvelled at the playing of the fly and needle, which they could see so plainly and yet not touch it because of the glass that covered them. But when he demonstrated by that globe-like jewel the roundness of the earth and skies, the sphere of the sun, moon and stars, and how the sun did chase the night round about the world continually, the greatness of the land and sea, the diversity of nations, variety of complexions, and how we were to them antipodes and many other such like matters, they all stood as amazed with admiration.

(Smith, 1629, p. 200)

Here Smith portrays some of the qualities that made him such a natural survivor: ruthlessness, courage, sheer arrogance and nerve (in demanding to see the leader of the Indians when he was on the verge of being shot), and quick thinking, as demonstrated in his attempt to establish ascendancy over his captors with a demonstration of advanced technology, since glass and indeed the compass were unfamiliar to the Native peoples of the Americas. This manifestation of technological superiority is a topos we frequently encounter in texts describing colonial encounters between Europeans and Indigenous groups. There are obvious reasons for its appeal to European writers as a strategy of empowerment in situations when the balance of power is apparently not in their favor, in that it reinforces the authority not only of the narrator but of his allegedly more advanced culture. How well Smith was actually able to convey his ideas, however, is unclear, though he did have a rudimentary grasp of Algonquin.[2] But all this notwithstanding, his captors tied him to a tree and presumably were preparing to shoot him when Opechancanough held up the compass and they lay down their bows and arrows. After this, he was taken to the settlement of Oropaks, guarded by "three great savages holding him fast by each arm," with six more on each side, and was given food and drink. After this, Smith describes their dancing in a ring, "with hellish notes and screeches":

Every one (had) his quiver of arrows and at his back a club, on his arm a fox or an otter's skin or some such matter for his vambrace, their heads

---

[2]   In his *Generall Historie*, Smith provides a brief Algonquin vocabulary. Most of the words listed are related to items ("sword," "target," "land"), concepts ("friend," "enemy"), or requests for information ("I am very hungry; what shall I eate,"), all of a practical nature (Smith, 1629, pp. 82–4).

and shoulders painted red with oil ... which scarlet-like colour made an
exceeding handsome show, his bow in his hand and the skin of a bird with
her wings abroad, dried, tied on his head, and a piece of their snakes tied
to it, or some such like toy.

(Smith, 1629, p. 100)

Clearly Smith was in fear for his life, and his text is a curious mixture
of remarkably close observation of his surroundings and figurative language reflecting his own terror, particularly metaphors demonizing his
captors, with the Indians characterized as "devils" and "hellish." Smith was
then taken to a long house and given even more venison and bread.
Unsurprisingly, he tells us that he had little appetite, and was convinced
"that they would fat him to eat him." This is a trope which occurs over and
over again in early texts, and perhaps reflects not only the captive's literal
fear of being eaten, but also his or her horror on a symbolic level at being
ingested and engulfed by the culture of the Other, with the concomitant
loss of individual identity.[3] Nonetheless, Smith does mention acts of kindness from individual Indians, such as that of one elderly man he had met
on arriving in Virginia to whom he had given beads.

In the following days, Smith was taken to several other settlements.
Finally, he was brought to Powhatan's camp in Pamunkey. He describes
the ritual which took place, framing it at both beginning and end with
couplets highlighting the Indians' diabolical attributes:

where they entertained him with most strange and fearefull Coniurations;

As if neare led to hell,
Amongst the Devils to dwell.

Not long after, early in a morning a great fire was made in a long house,
and a mat spread on the one side, as on the other, on the one they caused
him to sit, and all the guard went out of the house, and presently came
skipping in a great grim fellow, all painted over with coale, mingled with
oyle; and many Snakes and Wesels skins stuffed with mosse, and all their
tayles tyed together, so as they met on the crowne of his head in a tassell;

---

[3]   The Mexican writer Carlos Siguenza y Góngora, in *Los infortunios de Alonso Ramírez*
(1690) tells of a protagonist captured by English pirates, who is convinced that they are
cannibals about to devour him.

and round about the tassell was as a Coronet of feathers, the skins hanging round about his head, backe, and shoulders, and in a manner covered his face; with a hellish voyce and a rattle in his hand. With most strange gestures and passions he began his invocation, and environed the fire with a circle of meale; which done, three more such like devils came rushing in with the like antique tricks, painted halfe blacke, halfe red: but all their eyes were painted white, and some red stroakes like Mutchato's, along their cheekes: round about him those fiends daunced a pretty while, and then came in three more as ugly as the rest; with red eyes, and white stroakes over their blacke faces, at last they all sat downe right against him; three of them on the one hand of the chiefe Priest, and three on the other. Then all with their rattles began a song, which ended, the chiefe Priest layd downe five wheat cornes: then strayning his armes and hands with such violence that he sweat, and his veynes swelled, he began a short Oration: at the conclusion they all gave a short groane; and then layd down three graines more. After that, began their song againe, and then another Oration, ever laying downe so many cornes as before, till they had twice incirculed the fire; that done, they tooke a bunch of little stickes prepared for that purpose, continuing still their devotion, and at the end of every song and Oration, they layd downe a sticke betwixt the divisions of Corne. Till night, neither he nor they did either eate or drinke, and then they feasted merrily, with the best provisions they could make. Three dayes they used this Ceremony; the meaning whereof they told him, was to know if he intended them well or no. The circle of meale signified their Country, the circles of corne the bounds of the Sea, and the stickes his Country. They imagined the world to be flat and round, like a trencher, and they in the middest. After this they brought him a bagge of gunpowder, which they carefully preserved till the next spring, to plant as they did their corne; because they would be acquainted with the nature of that seede. *Opitchapam* the Kings brother invited him to his house, where, with as many platters of bread, foule, and wild beasts, as did environ him, he bid him wellcome; but not any of them would eate a bit with him, but put up all the remainder in Baskets. At his returne to *Opechancanoughs*, all the Kings women, and their children, flocked about him for their parts, as a due by Custome, to be merry with such fragments.

But his waking mind in hydeous dreames did oft see wondrous shapes,
Of bodies strange, and huge in growth, and of stupendious makes.

(Smith, 1629, p. 100)

This passage gives us a fascinating insight into communicative strategies in early America. For Smith and for his captors, interpreting each other's meanings was literally a matter of life and death. For obvious reasons Smith was in a state of extreme apprehension, and it is possible that by representing his captors as diabolical alien creatures he is highlighting his own bravery and also rendering his narrative more marketable. He had without a doubt notable powers of observation, and this description is one of the few extant accounts of the ritual practices of the Indigenous inhabitants of early seventeenth-century Virginia, characterized by remarkable richness of detail, with the Indians explaining to him the meaning of different facets of the ceremony performed and their worldview. Smith also conveys the fact that the apprehension was not only on his side. Clearly it was to the Indians' advantage to ascertain the intentions of Smith and his fellow colonists and the meaning of their gifts; the image of the Indians planting gunpowder as though it were seeds is a fascinating one which, given the subsequent behavior of the Europeans, is uncannily prescient. In the couplets taken from a translation by Lucretius by Bishop Fotherby which frame the narrative, however, we gain an insight into the sense of alienation and estrangement that Smith was experiencing. The text as a whole is characterized by this curious oscillation between factual information gained from close observation of Smith's captors, conveyed in a dispassionate tone, and lurid imagery. This may be in part due to the fact that Smith's narrative was intended to promote settlement in Virginia (and thus convey information about conditions in the colony), but at the same time to replenish Smith's own coffers by selling well, which would account for the occasionally lurid tone of derring-do and adventure.

The narrative then goes on to describe one of the most famous – and enigmatic – episodes in American literary and cultural history. Smith is brought before Powhatan and two hundred of his courtiers:

> At his entrance before the King, all the people gave a great shout. The Queene of *Appamatuck* was appointed to bring him water to wash his hands, and another brought him a bunch of feathers, in stead of a Towell to dry them: having feasted him after their best barbarous manner they could, a long consultation was held, but the conclusion was, two great stones were brought before *Powhatan*: then as many as could layd hands on him, dragged him to them, and thereon laid his head, and being ready with their clubs, to beate out his braines, *Pocahontas* the Kings dearest daughter, when no intreaty could prevaile, got his head in her armes, and laid her owne upon his to save him from death: whereat the Emperour

Figure 2.1 Pocahontas, from *The Travels of John Smith: The Generall Historie of Virginia, New England, and the Summer Isles* (Glasgow: MacLehose, 1907), facing p. 104.

was contented he should live to make him hatchets, and her bells, beads, and copper; for they thought him as well of all occupations as themselves. For the King himselfe will make his owne robes, shooes, bowes, arrowes, pots; plant, hunt, or doe any thing so well as the rest.

(Smith, 1629, p. 101)

The meaning of this episode has been the subject of much debate in recent years. Smith himself clearly was convinced that he was about to breathe his last and that he had been saved only through the intervention of Pocahontas. Scholars such as Karen Kupperman and Frederic Gleach have suggested that she was actually acting as cultural mediator by taking part in an adoption ceremony in which Smith underwent a symbolic death and was then adopted into Powhatan's family (Gleach, 1997; Kupperman, 2007, pp. 222–30). Smith himself mentions that two days after the ceremony Powhatan had said that if Smith brought him two cannons and a grindstone from Jamestown he would give him a territory of his own and "for ever esteeme him as his sonne Nantaquoud." Conceivably Powhatan's intention at the end was to have the English settle within his territory as his subordinates. This clearly was not what Smith himself understood, as subsequent events would demonstrate.

John Smith was, nonetheless, one of the first colonizers to realize the limitations of a system of colonization based on the heroic deeds of aristocrats and soldiers of fortune. Earlier in this chapter, we mentioned the "Panegyrick Verses" which frame his text and the imagery they invoke of Jason and the quest for the Golden Fleece. Alongside these metaphors of colonization as a heroic quest for individual glory, however, there lie other images of colonization as predicated on hard work and consistent endeavor. Punning on Smith's surname, an anonymous poet called S. M. compares him to Vulcan, the god of blacksmiths:

> He was the Smith that hammered famines foyle
> And on Powhatan's Emperour had his will
> [...]
> He Vulcan like did forge a true Plantation,
> And chain'd their Kings, to his immortall glory;
> Restoring peace and plenty to the Nation,
> Regaining honour to this worthy story.
>
> (Smith, 1629, p. xxvii)

Tobacco Monoculture

The crop which enabled Smith and his counterparts to build their "true Plantation" was tobacco. Some years earlier Sir Walter Ralegh had brought tobacco back to England, and it is said that he smoked a consolatory pipe shortly before going to his untimely end on the scaffold (Brogan, 1999, pp. 26–7). Elizabeth's successor **James I** loathed the weed and said so in no uncertain terms. In his **"Counter-Blaste to Tobacco,"** published in 1604, he denounced smoking as "a custome lothsome to the eye, hatefull to the Nose, harmefull to the braine, dangerous to the Lungs, and in the blacke stinking fume thereof, neerest resembling the horrible Stigian smoke of the pit that is bottomlesse." Nonetheless, James was quick to realize that the ready cash arising from import duties that commodities such as tobacco, sugar, coffee and tea would bring into the royal coffers was not to be scorned.

John Rolfe, the husband of Pocahontas, was the first colonist to cultivate tobacco and the first to ship it to England. Soon his fellow colonists realized the economic potential of this "lothsome" custom, and they took up the challenge of growing tobacco with alarming enthusiasm. Hugh Brogan (1999, p. 29) comments that at one juncture, even the streets of Jamestown were sown with tobacco, and that the fact that the crop exhausted the soil in seven years impelled the colonists to search for new lands. Overproduction created a vicious cycle: prices fell, prompting Virginians to cultivate still more tobacco and thus causing prices to plummet even further.

Indentured Servants and Slavery

Revel and Equiano

The solution encountered was to reduce labor costs, first with indentured servants and then by importing slaves. In seventeenth-century England, over three hundred different crimes were punishable by death. However, and given the need of the colonies for labor, younger criminals were often punished by transportation to America as indentured servants. The lot of convicts transported to the American colonies was not easy. One early chapbook depicting the travails of a convicted felon called **James Revel** is in all likelihood an apocryphal attempt on the part of the author to take advantage of the vogue for transatlantic adventures.[4] Whatever the case, the story of Revel, a young man brought up by virtuous parents in London near Temple Bar, is a gripping cautionary tale of youthful misadventure told in rhyming couplets. The young Revel falls into bad company with disastrous results, and is sentenced to transportation to the colonies:

> And after sailing seven Weeks and more
> We at Virginia were put on shore.
> Where, to refresh us, we were wash'd and cleaned
> That to our buyers we might the better seem.

---

[4] John Jennings has concluded that the account of Revel's misadventures provides a realistic picture of the life of a transported felon. See Jennings (1948).

He describes how the convicts are inspected by their prospective masters:

> Some ask'd our trades, and others ask'd our names
> Some view'd our limbs, and other's turn'd us round
> Examining like Horses, if we're sound [...]
> Some felt our hands and view'd our legs and feet
> And made us walk, to see we were compleat;
> Some viewed our teeth, to see if they were good,
> Or fit to chew our hard and homely food.

Once Revel is chosen by a "grim old man," he is put to work in the tobacco fields:

> No shoes or stockings had I for to wear,
> Nor hat, nor cap, both head and feet were bare,
> Thus dress'd into the Field I nex[t] must go,
> Among tobacco plants all day to hoe,
> At day break in the morn our work begun,
> And so held to the setting of the Sun.
> My fellow slaves were just five Transports more,
> With eighteen Negroes, which is twenty four.
>
> (James Revel, "The Unhappy Transported Felon,"
> in Castillo and Schweitzer, 2001, pp. 231–5)

The indenture system, however, proved not to be wholly satisfactory for the planters, since many indentured servants managed to flee before their term of servitude was up. Planters then increased their reliance on slave labor, which had been used extensively in the Spanish and Portuguese colonies. In the English colonies in the West Indies, sugar had become the most lucrative cash crop, and tens of thousands of Africans were brought to labor as slaves in the sugar plantations of Barbados and Jamaica. For the captured Africans, the conditions of the Middle Passage, as the trajectory from Africa to America was called, were horrific. In a narrative published at the end of the following century, **Olaudah Equiano** provides one of the few extant descriptions:

> The stench of the hold while we were on the coast was so intolerably loathsome, that it was dangerous to remain there for any time, and some of us had been permitted to stay on the deck for the fresh air; but now that the whole ship's cargo were confined together, it became absolutely pestilential. The closeness of the place, and the heat of the climate, added

to the number in the ship, which was so crowded that each had scarcely room to turn himself, almost suffocated us. This produced copious perspirations, so that the air soon became unfit for respiration, from a variety of loathsome smells, and brought on a sickness among the slaves, of which many died, thus falling victims to the improvident avarice, as I may call it, of their purchasers. This wretched situation was aggravated by the galling of the chains, now became insupportable, and the filth of the necessary tubs, into which the children often fell, and were almost suffocated. The shrieks of the women, and the groans of the dying, rendered the whole a scene of horror almost inconceivable.[5]

Despite the enormous toll in human suffering, the slave traders continued to bring large numbers of Africans to work on the plantations of the West Indies and of the British colonies in North America. The English jurist **Sir Edward Coke**, in his ***Institutes of the Laws of England***, justified the practice on the following grounds: "then it was ordained by the Constitution of Nations … that he that was taken in Battle should remain Bond to his taker for ever, and he to do with him, all that should come of him, his Will and Pleasure, as with his Beast, or any other Chattel, to give, or to sell or to kill" (Coke, 1739, p. 116, quoted in Blackburn, 1998, p. 236). Coke adds that kings had subsequently revoked the power to kill because of the disciplinary excesses of certain lords, but then suggests that a biblical precedent for bondage existed as a punishment for the disobedience of Ham, the son of Noah. Blackburn (1998) cites the comment of a contemporary clergyman that "the accursed seed of Cham [Ham] … had for a stampe of their fathers sinne, the colour of hell set upon their faces." Blackburn adds that the English perception of racial difference, particularly as regards skin color, had a sharper edge than that of the Spanish or Portuguese (1998, p. 236).

Bacon's rebellion

With the importation of large numbers of slaves, tensions rose between the more affluent planters and their poorer counterparts. Many of the smaller planters sought greener pastures by seeking lands in the interior, but there

---

[5] Equiano (2001, pp. 40–1). Vincent Carretta (2007) argues that Equiano may have fabricated his African roots to help advance the movement against the slave trade, citing baptismal records and a naval muster roll linking Equiano to South Carolina, but acknowledges that the evidence for Equiano's American origins is not conclusive.

they encountered resistance from Native American tribes such as the Susquehanna. Under the leadership of **Nathaniel Bacon**, they rose up in 1676 against the Governor **William Berkeley**, whom they accused of favoring the Indians because of the lucrative fur trade. Bacon's rebellion is often characterized as a precursor of the revolutionary movement in Britain's colonies, but it is seldom acknowledged that its leader's expressly genocidal aim was "to ruine and extirpate all Indians in Generall" (Nathaniel Bacon, "Manifesto Concerning the Present Troubles in Virginia," in Castillo and Schweitzer, 2001, p. 227). At the height of the revolt, however, Bacon died of dysentery and the rebellion was suppressed. After this, the wealthier landowners enjoyed the backing of royal authority, and the power of this class was consolidated by its control of land, labor, and political authority (see Brogan, 1999, p. 29).

French Colonization

To the north and to the west, English colonizers faced formidable rivals for empire. With the decline of Spanish power in Europe, and with the granting of religious freedom to the French Protestants known as Huguenots by Henry IV in the **Edict of Nantes** (1598), French colonizing efforts continued apace in northern North America. Henry IV also granted a charter to the *Compagnie d'Occident*, which led to further exploration and settlement. Searching for a northwest passage to Asia, the French explored the St Lawrence River; **Samuel de Champlain** founded Quebec in 1608, and subsequently an extensive network of trading posts was established. The Jesuit and Recollect orders dedicated considerable effort to the conversion of the Indians, and the *Jesuit Relations*, which recounted their adventures, became runaway best-sellers in France. French policy toward the Indians was markedly different from that of the British; rather than enslaving or exterminating them, the French sought to make military and commercial allies of them through conversion. Men such as **Robert de LaSalle** and **Louis Hennepin** explored the Mississippi Valley, providing invaluable ethnographic information about the indigenous groups they encountered. Rivalry with the English ultimately led to **King William's War** (1689–97), when Sir William Phipps seized Nova Scotia for the English and the Count de Frontenac carried out border raids on New England.

Spanish Expansion: Pérez de Villagrá and Otermín

In the Southwest, explorers such as **Juan de Oñate** established permanent settlements in what is now New Mexico. The poet-soldier **Gaspar Pérez de Villagrá** chronicled the deeds of Oñate's expedition in a neo-Virgilian verse epic titled ***Chronicle of New Mexico*** (**1610**), representing Spanish colonialism as a heroic enterprise and the massacre at Ácoma Pueblo as the justified execution of those who, like Lucifer, rose up against the forces of heaven (Pérez de Villagrá, 1992). Subsequently, the Spaniards attempted to extinguish all traces of indigenous religious translations and destroyed the ceremonial chambers known as *kivas*. In 1680, the indigenous Tewa leader Popé led a rebellion against the Spanish forces garrisoned in Santa Fe in which 21 Franciscan priests were killed, giving the Indians control of Northern New Mexico. The Governor of New Mexico, **Don Antonio de Otermín**, in a letter to his ecclesiastical superior, in an attempt to explain the embarrassing ease with which the Pueblo had overcome Spanish resistance, describes the Indians as resorting to "wickedness and treason." The destruction wreaked by the Spaniards that led to the revolt, however, was characterized as part of a divine mission to spread the gospel and eradicate paganism.

Such a mindset was not limited to the Spaniards. In the following chapter, we turn to Puritan colonization in the Anglophone Atlantic, and the powerful Puritan rhetoric describing American settlement as the establishment of a divine City upon a Hill.

Chapter 3

The City on a Hill:
Alternative Visions

Introduction

It is said that an ancient Chinese curse is "May you live in interesting times." For the English, the sixteenth and seventeenth centuries were interesting times indeed, characterized by religious turbulence, economic hardship, political instability, and civil unrest. In what follows, we provide a brief overview of religious affairs in England in the Early Modern period and the emergence of the Puritan movement, going on to discuss the factors which prompted the emigration of Puritans, first to Leyden, and later to America. We then look at Puritan personal narrative, captivity narratives, and poetry. The chapter concludes with a brief comment of the impact of Puritan ideas on American culture and political thought.

The Emergence of English Puritanism

In the wake of the civil strife of the Wars of the Roses in fifteenth-century England, dynastic continuity was vital for the Tudors. In 1525, the redoubtable Tudor monarch **Henry VIII** had begun to despair of his wife **Catherine of Aragon**'s ability to bear a male heir, and had become obsessed with **Anne Boleyn**, a charming and charismatic young woman in the Queen's entourage. In the context of the **Protestant Reformation** and its challenges to papal authority by theologians such as **Martin Luther** and **Huldrych Zwingli**, Henry then sought to annul his marriage to Catherine in order to marry Anne. However, Pope Clement VII refused to grant this. Ultimately, Henry broke off relations with Rome and declared himself head of the Anglican Church.

On Henry's death in 1553, his Catholic daughter **Mary Tudor** ascended the throne. Perhaps understandably, she held the Protestants responsible for what she saw as ill-treatment of her mother. Impelled by bitterness and by genuine religious zeal, she began a campaign against Protestants which gave her the nickname by which she is best known in history, **Bloody Mary**. This policy, plus her unpopular marriage to Philip II of Spain, ensured that she was widely detested by her subjects. When Mary died without an heir, her half-sister **Elizabeth** inherited the crown. Elizabeth reestablished the Anglican Church as the official religion, but allowed it to retain many of the trappings of Catholicism. Later, Elizabeth I's successor, **James I**, maintained her policies of (relative) religious tolerance, although he, like Elizabeth, was aware that the **Puritans** represented a growing political threat.

The winds of change, however, were making themselves felt in England, and some English Protestants had begun to question what they perceived as pernicious traces of papistry in church ritual and structure, advocating an aesthetic of simplicity and plainness in both church architecture and liturgical style. Initially, the designation "Puritan" was applied to this radical Protestant group as a term of opprobrium, and referred to the movement's desire to purify the Anglican Church of what were seen as vestigial Catholic features such as the Latin mass, incense, and ornamentation such as statuary and stained glass. The Puritans also advocated the creation of small autonomous congregations of the faithful, a move which would ultimately be fraught with political consequences both in England and later in America.

John Calvin

In intellectual terms, one of the continental thinkers who influenced English Puritan thought most directly was the French theologian Jean Chauvin, known to history as **John Calvin**. Particularly influential were Calvin's five tenets. The first tenet propounded the concept of Original Sin, according to which human beings were born to a state of complete depravity and corruption. Secondly, Calvin advocated the notion of Election, that every human being is predestined to be either saved or damned. The third tenet, Atonement, suggests that Christ's suffering on the cross gives life to those predestined for Heaven. Fourthly, grace is seen as a radical gift which can be neither earned nor refused. Finally, the converted are seen as justified and righteous.[1]

---

[1] For a lucid and thorough discussion of American Puritan thought and literature, see Elliott (1994).

Puritan writing, perhaps inevitably, is rich, complex, and woven thick with contradictions. On the one hand, the Puritans, with their mistrust of graven images and aesthetic form, felt that language was designed to convey religious truth or enhance religious belief, and that its purpose was primarily utilitarian. On the other, they realized that figurative language and stirring rhetoric (in, for example, sermons) were valuable tools to be used in propagating their ideals. Consequently, and in spite of their iconoclastic tendencies, Puritan writing is characterized by elaborate symbolic frames of reference. One of the most salient features of Puritan style, for example, is the recourse to **biblical typology**, understood in the first instance as interpreting events in the Old Testament as harbingers of occurrences in the New Testament. Later, however, Puritan notions of typology expanded into a complex symbolic system which used biblical antecedents (and justifications) for contemporary events. In this perspective, the Puritans were analogous to the Israelites, the Chosen People of God; the English ruler corresponded to Pharaoh; the crossing of the Atlantic paralleled Moses and the Israelites crossing the Red Sea; and America was the embodiment of Canaan, the Promised Land, a new premillennial Zion.

Separatism and the Pilgrims

Under **Charles I**, the persecution of Puritans increased, and some chose to emigrate; many of those who chose to leave their mother country were impelled by economic hardship as well as religious persecution. This was particularly the case with the **Separatists**, thus designated because they refused to accept the authority of the Church of England and felt that it was beyond redemption; this was viewed as an act of treason punishable by death. One Separatist group, which had been meeting clandestinely in Scrooby in Nottinghamshire, migrated to Leyden. The Protestant Netherlands were, in many ways, a logical choice. Moreover, the Dutch had been actively exploring the North American coast; under the auspices of the Dutch West India Company, they established trading posts and founded a colony called New Amsterdam on Manhattan Island under the leadership of **Peter Minuit** in 1625–6.

William Bradford

William Bradford, the orphaned son of a yeoman farmer, was among the group of Separatists who emigrated to Leyden. In Bradford's ***Of Plymouth***

Plantation, he describes the difficulties he and his countrymen encountered in the Netherlands, such as the "strange and uncouth language" of the Dutch and "the grim and grisly face of poverty." Bradford mentions as well the fact that the Separatist congregation was aging, and the younger people were in danger of succumbing to the temptations of what he viewed as the dissoluteness and corruption of their Dutch counterparts. The company finally concluded, after extensive debates, that the ideal place to carry out their designs was "those vast and unpeopled countries of America, which are fruitful and fit for habitation, being devoid of all civil inhabitants, where there are only savage and brutish men, which range up and down, little otherwise than the wild beasts of the same" (Bradford, 1901, p. 78). It is notable that they viewed America as an empty landscape, and its indigenous inhabitants as an obstacle to their grand design, mere nomadic vermin to be eradicated. Finally Bradford's group acquired a ship called the Speedwell and set sail for the New World. This ship, however, proved unseaworthy, and on reaching London the Puritans were transferred to another ship, the **Mayflower.**

The crossing was a difficult one, beset by storms. Bradford describes the sentiments of the Pilgrims (as they later came to be known) on reaching Cape Cod:

> And for the season it was winter, and they that know the winter of that country know them to be sharp and violent and subject to cruel and fierce storms, dangerous to travel to known places, much more to search an unknown coast. Besides what could they see but a hideous and desolate wilderness, full of wild beasts and wild men – and what multitudes there might be of them they knew not ... For summer being done, all things stand upon them with a weatherbeaten face, and the whole country, full of woods and thickets, represented a wild and savage hue.
>
> (Bradford, 1901, p. 95)

One can imagine that the Pilgrims, having left behind their country and their relatives, must have been daunted by what they saw as a dark hostile wilderness populated by unseen enemies. During the first winter, more than half of the company died of scurvy, starvation, and fevers. However, their perception of America as a vacant landscape proved to be wrong; other Europeans had previously explored the coast, bringing with them a smallpox epidemic that decimated indigenous populations and taking many Native Americans back to Europe as slaves. One such was **Squanto,** a Patuxet Indian taken as a slave to England; he had been held prisoner by the Pokanokets, a tribe who viewed the Puritans as potential allies against their enemies the Narragansetts. Without Squanto's help, it is unlikely that the Pilgrims would have survived; he had learned English during his involuntary sojourn in England, and served as an interpreter, helping the Pilgrims trade with Native American groups for food and furs. Squanto has been enshrined in American history as a protagonist of the first Thanksgiving and a linchpin of the myth of harmonious relations between Indians and Europeans. As Emory Elliott has conclusively demonstrated, however, the reality of Squanto's relationship to the Pilgrims was far more complex (Elliott, 1994, p. 91).

Massachusetts Bay

Not all Puritans believed, like Bradford and his Pilgrims, that the Church of England was beyond redemption. Some felt that the Church should be cleansed of its remaining vestiges of Catholicism and reformed from within. The settlement established by the Pilgrims in Plymouth was, because of its radical Separatist views, deprived of valuable support from the mother country. Other Puritans, however, saw the storm clouds gathering in England with the absolutist policies of Charles I and his main political advisor, the Archbishop of Canterbury **William Laud**. Economic conditions were worsening, with deepening poverty and punitive taxation. Thus in March 1629 a group of Puritan merchants, later called the **Company of Massachusetts Bay**, obtained a charter from the Council of New England allowing them to settle in America.

John Winthrop

John Winthrop, descended from landed gentry, was chosen to be Governor of the Massachusetts Bay Colony, and in March 1630 the group set sail from Southampton for America. On board the fleet's flagship *Arbella*, Winthrop presented a lay sermon titled **"A Modell of Christian Charity"** in which he set forth his vision for the colony. While acknowledging that according to divine will "some must be rich some poore, some highe and eminent in power and dignitie, others meane and in subjeccion," he envisions a community bound together by love and collective interest. He speaks of the Puritan endeavor in America as a special errand to make

God's purposes manifest, not in the Hereafter, but on Earth. If the Puritans are able to sustain this vision of a model Christian community, he says,

> The Lord will be our God and delight to dwell among us, as his owne people and will command a blessing upon us in all our ways, soe that wee shall see much more of his wisdome power goodnes and truth than formerly wee have beene acquainted with, wee shall finde that God of Israell is among us, when tenn of us shall be able to resist a thousand of our enemies, when hee shall make us a prayse and glory, that men shall say of succeeding plantacions: the lord make it like that of New England: for wee must Consider that wee shall be as a Citty upon a Hill, the eies of all people are upon us; soe that if wee shall deale falsely with our god in this worke wee have undertaken and soe cause him to withdrawe his present help from us, wee shall be made a story and a by-word though the world.
>
> (Castillo and Schweitzer, 2001, pp. 244–50)

This text is important for many reasons. In it, the Puritans are characterized as the exemplary Chosen People of God. The image of the luminous **City on a Hill**, of America as the ideal Christian community with the duty to set an example to all nations is an extraordinarily powerful one which has resonated down the centuries, for better or worse. It is implied that God is working through human history, and that the success of Puritan endeavors in America will be a sign of divine favor.

This notion that the will of God can be discerned in historical events led many Puritans to look for signs of divine guidance and sanction in even the most commonplace everyday occurrences. **Winthrop's *Journal***, which he kept over a period of 19 years, provides some wonderful examples of this. The entry for July 5, 1632, speaks of a combat between a mouse and a snake in view of several witnesses. The mouse killed the snake, which led the pastor of Boston, a Mr. Wilson, to interpret this event as symbolizing a combat between Satan (the snake) and the mouse ("a poor contemptible people, which God had brought hither"); the victory of the mouse is viewed as foreshadowing the ultimate victory of what Winthrop (1790) describes as "a marvelous goodly church" (Castillo and Schweitzer, 2001, p. 250). References to rodents could, however, also be used to signify the decadence of Anglicanism. On December 15, 1640, Winthrop noted:

> Mr. Winthrop the younger, one of the magistrates, having many books in a chamber where there was corn of divers sorts, had among them one

wherein the Greek testament, the psalms and the common prayer, were bound together. He found the common prayer eaten with mice, every leaf of it, and not any of the two other touched, nor any other of his books, though there were above a thousand.

(Winthrop, 1790, p. 214)

For Winthrop and his contemporaries, the fact that the Anglican Book of Common Prayer had been devoured by mice and the remaining books left intact was a compelling sign that the Puritans, with their emphasis on Scripture, were on the path to salvation.

Voices of Dissent

Roger Williams

There were, however, dissenting voices among the Puritans. Among them was that of **Roger Williams**. Williams was an extraordinarily complex man, a brilliant linguist with deeply held Puritan convictions. Almost immediately after reaching the New World, he was thrust into controversy because of his refusal to compromise his deeply held Separatist convictions, refusing a ministry on arriving in Boston in 1631 because the local congregation had not explicitly proclaimed their separation from the Church of England. After a brief sojourn in Salem, Williams went on to Plymouth, where he managed to alienate his fellow Separatists by publishing in 1632 a treatise questioning the colonists' right to annex Native lands without appropriate monetary compensation. In certain quarters, this was viewed as treason, and Williams was forced by the authorities to retract his opinions. Even more problematically, he then refused to swear an oath of allegiance to the British crown, alleging that Church and State should be separate, and that oaths properly belonged to the spiritual realm. The Salem church nonetheless invited him in 1634 to become its minister, but both Salem and Williams were admonished by the General Court in Boston. Finally, Williams was asked to leave the area, and a ship was sent with instructions to arrest him, but he escaped and took refuge with the Narragansetts, where he established a small settlement on land which he ultimately purchased from the Natives. He named his settlement **Providence**.[2]

[2]   See John Teunissen and Evelyn J. Hinz's excellent Introduction to Williams (1973), pp. 13–22.

In order to ensure Providence's survival it thus became crucial for Williams to secure a parliamentary charter. In 1643 he set sail for England in order to lobby influential individuals to favor the cause of his settlement. During the long sea voyage, he wrote his *Key to the Language of America*, truly a transatlantic text in every sense of the word. Williams describes it thus:

> I drew the *Materialls* in a rude lump at Sea, as a private *helpe* to my own memory, that I might not by my present absence *lightly lose* what I had so *dearely bought* in some few yeares *hardship*, and charges among the *Barbarians*; yet being reminded by some, what pitie it were to bury those *Materialls* in my *Grave* at land or Sea; and withal, remembering how oft I have been importun'd by worthy *friends*, of all sorts, to afford them some helps in this way.
>
> (Williams, 1973, p. 83)

Here Williams casts himself as the altruistic, unassuming author, who has thrown together his material in a "rude lump" during his voyage so that it might serve him as an *aide-memoire* to keep him from forgetting the Narragansett language that (as he states in terms permeated with the discourse of economic exchange) he had "so dearely bought" in exchange for his "hardship and charges" among the Indians. He presents himself as holding a monopoly on linguistic knowledge of Narragansett with the allegation that if he were to be shipwrecked, "these Materialls" (his linguistic and cultural capital) would drown along with him. In a tactic which would be used by later Puritan writers, he attempts to avoid charges of pride and self-advancement by protesting that he is only compiling the Key at the urging of "worthy Friends."

When Williams's *Key* was printed in London in 1643 it ensured him not only instant notoriety but also consolidated his standing as an expert on Native culture.[3] The metaphor of the Key had multiple resonances for Puritan readers of his day. Ivy Schweitzer (1991, p. 192) comments that a number of works invoking "Keys" to Holy Scripture existed in the seventeenth-century Anglophone world, such as *A Key of Knowledge for the Opening of the Secret Mysteries of St. Johns Mysticall Revelation* (1617), written by Williams's father-in-law Richard Barnard; and, perhaps most

---

[3] According to Edwin Gaustad, Cromwell is said to have solicited Williams's advice on Native affairs. Williams was also in contact with influential Puritans such as Henry Vane and John Milton. See Gaustad (1991), p. 137.

significantly, ***The Keys to the Kingdom of Heaven***, published in London in 1644 by **John Cotton**, Williams's arch opponent in the New England debate over freedom of conscience. Williams's *Key* is a complex text which speaks to diverse audiences and works on many levels. In his Preface he dedicates the text to a transatlantic audience of "my Deare and Welbeloved Friends and Countrey-men, in old and new England." He opens his book with the following declaration:

> I present you with a *Key*; I have not heard of the like, yet framed, since it pleased God to bring that mighty *Continent* of *America* to light ... This *Key*, respects the *Native Language* of it, and happily may unlocke some *Rarities* concerning the *Natives* themselves, not yet discovered ... I resolved (by the assistance of the Most High) to cast those *Materialls* into this *Key*, *pleasant* and *profitable* for *All*, but specially for my *friends* residing in those parts: A little *Key* may open a *Box*, where lies a bunch of Keyes.
>
> (Williams, 1973, p. 83)

Williams portrays himself as one who holds the key (the interpretative power) to unlock the virtually inexhaustible meanings of America (Castillo, 2005). Moreover, the key offering access to Native language opens up and multiplies possibilities not only of Indian conversion but of lucrative Indian trade (Murray, 1997).

Initially, Williams had intended to write a dictionary or grammar, and had considered using the dialogue form, but maintains that he chose not to do so for reasons of brevity,[4] adding that he has framed each chapter as an implicit dialogue. The arrangement of material in the *Key* is organized thematically, with the first seven chapters dealing with practical communicative situations such as "Salutation," "Eating and Entertainment," and "Sleepe and Lodging." The eighth chapter, "Of Discourse and Newes" deals with concepts of truth, falsity, and belief. The following 11 chapters deal with the natural world, the cosmos, and with human orientation to both. This is followed by a series of chapters in which the Indian as social and economic being is foregrounded: "Of their Nakednesse and Clothing," "Of Religion, the Soule, &c," "Of their Government and Justice," "Of Marriage," "Concerning their Coyne," "Of Buying and Selling," "Of their Hunting, &c," "Of their Gaming, &c," "Of their Warre, &c," "Of their Paintings," "Of their Sicknesse," and finally, "Of their Death and Buriall."

---

[4] This seems implausible, in that it is hard to conceive how presenting the material in dialogic form would have had a significant impact on the length of the text.

Each chapter has a tripartite structure, beginning with a vocabulary of words or phrases in Narragansett and their English counterpart. The vocabulary read vertically, however, unfolds as a dialogue. This is followed by observations explaining the concepts discussed, thus establishing Williams's position as authority and "keyholder." Each chapter closes with a short poem, usually consisting of three four-line stanzas in ballad meter (iambic tetrameter alternating with iambic trimeter, in an abcb rhyming scheme). The organization of the chapters is similar to that of emblems, a seventeenth-century mode characterized by a tripartite composition consisting of a symbolic engraving, a motto or epigram from the Bible or from classical texts, and an explicatory poem (see Teunissen and Hinz in Williams, 1973, pp. 61–2).

One example of this is Chapter XXII, "Of their Government and Justice." After describing what he perceives as the "monarchical" nature of Native American government by a king or sachem, Williams describes the way in which justice is dispensed by the ruler:

Pyeaùtch naûgum.	Let himself come here.
Péteatch.	Let him come.
Mishaúntowash.	Speake out.
Nanántowash.	Speake plaine.
Kunnadsíttamen wèpe.	You must inquire after this.
Wunnadsittamútta.	Let us search into it.
Neen pitch-nnadsíttamen.	I will inquire into it.
Michíssu ewò.	He is naught.
Cuttianantacompàwwem.	You are a lying fellow.
Wèpe cukkúmmoot.	You have stole.
Mat méshnawmônash.	I did not see those things.
Mat mesh nummám menash.	I did not take them.
Wèpe kunnishquêko cummiskissâwwaw.	You are fierce and quarrelsome.

(Williams, 1973, pp. 202–3)

Read horizontally, Algonquin words and phrases correspond to their English equivalent. Read vertically, however, a dialogue emerges between a Narragansett sachem and a person brought before him accused of a crime. This is followed by an observation from Williams that he has never been able to discern "an excess of scandalous sins" among the Indians like those that abound in Europe, such as drunkenness and gluttony. He adds, "although they have not so much to restraine them (both in respect of God and Lawes of men) as the *English* have, yet a man shall never heare of such crimes amongst them of robberies, murtheres, adulteries, &c. as amongst the *English*" (p. 203). The chapter closes with the following verses:

> Adulteries, Murthers, Robberies, Thefts
> Wild Indians punish these!
> And hold the Scales of Justice so,
> That no man fathering leese.
>
> When Indians hear the horrid filths,
> Of Irish, English Men,
> The horrid Oaths and Murthers late,
> Thus say these Indians then:
>
> We weare no Cloaths, have many Gods
> And yet our sinnes are lesse:
> You are Barbarians, Pagans wild
> Your Land's the Wildernesse.
>
> (Williams, 1973, p. 204)

In the third stanza, Williams ventriloquizes the allegedly barbaric Indian voice in order to praise the indigenous sense of justice and pose a direct challenge to the "civilized" status of his fellow Englishmen and the inconsistencies between their professed Christian ideology and their violent behavior. Sadly, however, not all Puritans shared Williams's openness to indigenous language and culture, and relations between Puritans and certain Indigenous groups in the Connecticut Valley eventually degenerated into armed conflict.

The Pequot War

In the Pequot War (1636–7), William Bradford describes the attack on a Pequot village by the Puritans and their Narragansett allies:

> And those that first entered found sharp resistance from the enemy who both shot at and grappled with them; others ran into their houses and brought out fire and set them on fire, which soon took in their mat; and standing close together, with the wind all was quickly on a flame, and thereby many more were burnt to death than was otherwise slain; it burnt their bowstrings and made them unserviceable; those that scraped the fire were slain with the sword, some hewed to pieces, others run through

with their rapiers, so as they were very quickly dispatched and very few escaped. It was conceived they thus destroyed about 400 at this time. It was a fearful sight to see them thus frying in the fire and the streams of blood quenching the same, and horrible the stink and scent thereof; but the victory seemed a sweet sacrifice, and they gave the praise thereof to God, who had wrought so wonderfully for them, thus to enclose their enemies in their hands and give them so speedy a victory over so proud and insulting an enemy.

(Castillo and Schweitzer, 2001, p. 258)

It is notable that the slaughter of four hundred men, women and children, with the evocation of the smell of burning flesh is viewed as a divinely sanctioned "sweet sacrifice." In a chilling account of the same events, **John Underhill** (the Captain of Militia in the Massachusetts Bay colony who led the Puritan forces), mentions that some of the younger soldiers who had never seen armed conflict were distressed on seeing the bodies of those killed in the massacre. Invoking biblical typology, Underhill provides a justification of the violence:

It may bee demanded, Why should you be so furious (as some have said) should not Christians have more mercy and compassion? But I would referre you to David's warre, when a people is growne to such a height of bloud, and sinne against God and man, and all confederates in the action, there hee hath no respect to persons, but harrowes them, and sawes them and puts them to the sword, and the most terriblest death that may bee: sometimes the Scripture declareth women and children must perish with their parents; some-time the case alters: but we will not dispute it now. We had sufficient light from the word of God for our proceedings.

(Underhill, 1638, pp. 39–40)

An arresting image engraving which accompanies Underhill's text shows a ring of musket-bearing Puritan soldiers surrounding the village; behind them is another ring consisting of their Indian allies with bows and allies. Within the village are blazing houses, Puritan soldiers firing guns and Pequots shooting arrows, and Indian corpses littering the ground.

Anne Hutchinson

Another dissenter from Puritan orthodoxy was **Anne Hutchinson**. Hutchinson had emigrated to Massachusetts Bay with her family in 1634, and (perhaps because of her activities as a midwife) became known for her kindliness and practical assistance to women in difficulties. As might be expected from someone who was a devout student of the Bible and who was known in the community for her intellectual acumen, she soon began to take part in the religious life of the colony. Initially, she invited women to informal gatherings at her home, where the sermons of the previous Sunday were discussed. These sessions were soon expanded to include men as well, and attracted an average attendance of 60 or more persons, including the influential young governor **Henry Vane**, several prominent merchants, and other powerful members of the colony. As the numbers of these gatherings increased, the nature of the topics discussed began to change: rather than simply recapitulating and discussing the sermon of the previous Sunday, Anne Hutchinson (described as "a woman of ready wit and bold spirit" by John Winthrop) criticized their content and authenticity, thus placing her on a collision course with the local theocracy.

The main differences between Hutchinson's beliefs (which her opponents denounced as antinomian heresy), and the Puritan elites of Massachusetts Bay centered essentially on the ways in which the theological concepts of the **Covenant of Grace** and of divine Election were to be applied to life in colonial America. As we have seen, the Puritan leaders were concerned with harnessing the spiritual and physical energies of the colonists in order to create an ideal society, the City on a Hill, which would be the earthly embodiment of divine perfection. In this perspective, the function of religious and civil institutions should be those of sustaining and strengthening the bonds between God and his Chosen People, the Puritans. However, in the convoluted intermingling of the sacred and the secular which was typical of Puritanism, it was in turn held that full involvement with the Church organization (and consequently with civil government) was reserved only to the Elect who were predestined to be saved. Church membership, however, did not necessarily constitute proof of Election. Given the fact that the possibility of playing a meaningful role in community matters (and thus exercising power, not only in matters related to religion but also in the political and economic spheres) was restricted to those belonging to the Elect, the issue of how exactly to determine one's Elect status assumed vital importance. The Puritans, as Amy Schrager Lang has pointed out, resolved the issue through the concept of **visible saint-hood**, in which Election was manifested by public "relation" or confession of one's one private conversion experience, whose authenticity was determined by the Puritan congregation. Salvation was also felt to be revealed by individual deeds, demonstrating the capacity of the individual to perform good works on a continuing basis. Thus, by incorporating some facets of **Arminian** doctrine (namely the importance of human will in the search for salvation) in an uneasy compromise with conventional theology on the Covenant of Grace, the Puritan patriarchs were able to channel the energies of the colonists toward what would later become the federal covenant, that is, the construction of a perfect millennial society where God's will would be made manifest through his chosen people in the promised land of America (Lang, 1987, pp. 517–20). For them, Election (and access to personal and collective power) was made manifest by good behavior, and good behavior was defined as submission to the authority of the Puritan hierarchy.

The logical contradictions in such a perspective are not difficult to discern. Anne Hutchinson incurred the wrath of the local power structure by pointing out some of its contradictions in the weekly gatherings at her home. If, she argued, it is only through the absolute gift of Grace through Christ that human beings were able to do good, inherent righteousness and the merit accruing from it existed in Christ alone and not in sinful humankind; thus the concept of visible sainthood made no sense whatsoever. If, on the other hand, grace is manifested in individual human hearts, it is only the individual human being who can determine its presence or absence.

As is evident, Hutchinson's stance posed a direct challenge to the political authority of the magistrates. The fact that it came from a woman complicated things even further. Although unmarried women and widows were allowed to own property in Massachusetts Bay, married men had supervisory control over the property and behavior of their wives. Women were not permitted to vote in civil elections, and were not allowed either to vote or ask questions in church or other assemblies, and the only circumstances in which their voices could be heard in church was to sing hymns or (in some, but not all, congregations) to request membership (Koehler, 1980, pp. 1–48). Intellectual activity was seen as potentially harmful and overly taxing for female brains. One poignant and oft-cited excerpt from Winthrop's *Journal* allows us a glimpse at prevailing Puritan attitudes regarding gender roles:

Mr. Hopkins, the governor of Hartford upon Connecticut, came to Boston, and brought his wife with him, (a godly young woman, and of special parts), who was fallen into a sad infirmity, the loss of her understanding and reason, which had been growing upon her divers years, by occasion of her giving herself wholly to reading and writing, and had written many books. Her husband, being very loving and tender, was loath to grieve her; but he saw his error when it was too late. For if she had attended her household affairs and such things as belong to women, and not gone out of her way and calling them to meddle in such things as are proper to men, whose minds are stronger, etc., she had kept her wits and might have improved them usefully and honorably in the place God had set her.

(Winthrop, 1908, p. 225)

Eventually, Anne Hutchinson was called before the General Court and was banished from the community to Aquidneck Island off the Rhode Island coast. She later suffered a miscarriage, which Winthrop described as "a monstrous birth ... twenty-seven several lumps of man's seed, without alternation or mixture of anything from the woman" (Winthrop, 1790, p. 160). After her husband's death, Hutchinson moved with part of her family to Long Island. There, in the summer of 1643, she and all but one of her family were massacred by the Indians.

Thomas Morton

Another person whom the Puritans viewed as a threat to their most deeply cherished values was **Thomas Morton**. Morton, a larger than life Anglican who told the Indians that he prayed with the help of the Book of Common Prayer, had a far more affirmative view of Native American culture and customs. In his ***New English Canaan (1637)***, a promotional tract designed to attract settlers to New England, he comments that the "Salvages" were not entirely without religion and characterizes the region as one of great natural abundance, inhabited by friendly Indians; for Morton, the only impediment to its prosperity is the activities of those he saw as religious fanatics, such as the Separatists of Plymouth and the Puritans of Massachusetts Bay.

Morton's text is divided into three parts or books. The first describes the indigenous people of New England, praising their "tractable nature and love toward the English" (Morton, 1637, p. 1). He compares their austerity and generosity to Plato's visions of the ideal community:

They love not to bee cumbered with many utensilles, and although every proprietor knows his owne, yet all things (so long as they will last) are used in common amongst them: A bisket cake given to one; that one

breakes it equally into so many parts, as there be persons in his company,
and distributes it. Platoes Commonwealth is so much practiced by these
people ... According to humane reason guided onely by the light of nature,
these people leades the more happy and freer life, being voyde of care,
which torments the mindes of so many Christians.

(Morton, 1637, p. 57)

What stands out in Morton's description of his relations with the Indians
is his search for common values: joy in earthly pleasures and seasonal
rituals, and a deep-seated perception of shared humanity. Speculation
about the origins of the Indians and a description of Native customs is
followed by another section describing the natural wealth of New England
and the abundance of game, fish, and commodities such as furs and metals
to be found there. The third book is a delicious mock-heroic satire of the
Puritans and their clashes with Morton, in which he describes the Puritans
as joyless and faintly ridiculous bigots.

The loathing was clearly mutual. At one point, Morton and his men
erect a maypole to celebrate the First of May. They frolic around it with
their Indian guests:

> Drinke and be merry, merry, merry boyes
> Let all your delight be in Hymens ioyes
> [...]
> Give to the nymphe that's free from scorne
> No Irish stuff[5] not Scotch over worne
> Lasses in beaver coats come away,
> Yee shall be welcome to us night and day.

(Morton, 1637, pp. 134–5)

The Puritan William Bradford was horrified at such antics. He accused
Morton of setting up a School of Atheism, of erecting the Maypole, "drinking and dancing around it many days together, inviting the Indian women
for their consorts, dancing and frisking together like so many fairies, or
furies rather, and worse practices" (Castillo and Schweitzer, 2001, pp.
264–5). The vehemence of Bradford's reaction reveals his horror at the
possibility of "going native," and the fear of ideological as well as physical
contamination resulting from close contact with Native Americans. In
many ways Morton's attitude toward the Indians was similar to that of the

---

[5] Cloth.

French, who felt that their economic interests were best served by relations of cordiality and friendship. Ultimately Morton was imprisoned by the Puritans in the winter of 1644–5, and died not long thereafter in Maine. His text is notable not only for its openness to Indigenous culture, but the very different perspective it offers us on key events in early New England history. More than two hundred years later, the maypole episode would form the basis for **Nathaniel Hawthorne's** short story **"The May-Pole of Merry Mount."**

Captivity Narratives

One literary genre which enjoyed considerable commercial success in the period from 1680 to 1720 was that of the captivity narrative. It is easy to understand the reasons for the popularity of these first-person accounts written by settlers, usually women, who had been taken captive by the Indians. On the one hand, they offer a glimpse at the searing violence which the captives witnessed and to which they and their families were subjected. On the other, there was always the question of whether the female captive had been subjected to sexual abuse and suffered the Fate Worse than Death, which readers found titillating. The central image of most captivity narratives is the confrontation between "savage" Native Americans and white colonists, who are portrayed as morally superior and civilized, embodying the image of Puritan society as the exemplary City on a Hill.

One of the first captivity narratives, that of **Mary Rowlandson**, was published in 1682 and went through two more editions that same year, in Cambridge, Massachusetts and London; it remained in print for many years to come (Slotkin, 1973, pp. 97–8). Rowlandson, who lived in the settlement of Lancaster, was the wife of a Puritan minister. As the *Narrative* begins, Rowlandson is vaguely disquieted by the relative prosperity in which she and her family live, and she describes herself as longing for affliction as a reaffirmation that she is one of God's chosen, as in Hebrews 12.6: "For whom the Lord loveth he chasteneth, and scourgeth every son whom he receiveth." Indeed, as Tara Fitzpatrick points out, adversity and suffering as manifested in **jeremiad** discourse were for the Puritans inextricably bound up with Elect status (Fitzpatrick, 1991). Rowlandson's tranquility, however, was not destined to last for long. Times were unsettled in the colony; the Wampanoag leader **Metacomet**, who was called **King Philip** by the settlers, had been carrying out a series of bloody raids on settlers in what would come to be known as **King Philip's War**. On February 20, 1676, Lancaster was attacked. Rowlandson describes the ensuing carnage:

> When we are in prosperity, Oh the little that we think of such dreadful sights, and to see your dear friends, and relations lie bleeding out their heartblood upon the ground. There was one who was chopped into the head with a hatchet, and stripped naked, and yet was crawling up and down. It is a solemn sigh to see so many Christians lying in their blood, some here, and some there, like a company of sheep torn by wolves, all of them stripped naked by a company of hell-hounds, roaring, singing, ranting, and insulting, as if they would have torn our very hearts out; yet the Lord by His almighty power preserved a number of us from death, for there were twenty-four of us taken alive and carried captive.
>
> (Rowlandson, 1682, p. 2)

Rowlandson and three of her children were taken prisoner. The two eldest were taken from her, and the youngest, who had been wounded in the attack, died in her arms some days later. She describes herself as "like one in a maze, and like one astonished," and was unable to shed a tear. Clearly she was in a state of shock, but her failure to weep or complain of her lot may have saved her life. She was then forced to accompany the Indians as they fled from the colonial militia, and her narrative is divided into 20 different "Removes" or stages in her journey. Finally, a ransom was paid, and Rowlandson was reunited with her husband.

Rowlandson's *Narrative* is an extraordinarily moving text. Initially (and perhaps understandably, given the violence she and her family have suffered) the Indians are presented as "ravenous beasts," "black creatures," and "bloody heathens." As her account progresses, however, they begin to emerge as individuals. One Indian gives her a Bible, which is a source of great consolation; citations of Scripture are sprinkled throughout the text, and her strong religious faith clearly provided her with crucial spiritual sustenance enabling her to make sense of her suffering and regain a sense of agency. She becomes the servant of an Indian, whom she calls her Master, and his three wives, describing one as "an old squaw" who allows her to lie in her wigwam and provides her with a mat and a rug as covering. Another wife, Wetamoo, is characterized as "a severe and proud dame." Other Indians give Rowlandson groundnuts, and she is able to barter her knitting skills for food. Finally, she is ransomed for £20 and reunited with her family. Rowlandson declares firmly that her virtue is intact: "not one of them ever offered me the least abuse of unchastity to me, in word or action." Her narrative ends with a reflection on the extreme precariousness of this world and the vanity of outward things, concluding that it is on God whom one must rely. Throughout the *Narrative*, Rowlandson emerges as a loving mother and courageous woman whose deep religious faith and personal strength enable her to give structure and meaning to extreme adversity.

Captivity narratives are, as a genre, rife with contradictions. Although they relate the first-person experience of the captive, this is often mediated by a Puritan minister who edits the narrative for didactic ends. The notion of God's covenant with the Puritans as the Chosen People implied that if a member of the community transgressed, all would be punished. At the same time, however, the voice of the (often female) narrators are fiercely personal in their relation of deeds of individual resourcefulness and courage. This tension between community and individual values was particularly apparent in the last years of the seventeenth century, when the collective energy and purpose of the descendants of the first generation of settlers seemed to be flagging. At the same time, captivity narratives helped to construct Puritan identity by defining the boundaries of the community and by emphasizing the notion that beyond those boundaries lay a hostile Other; social cohesion was thus enhanced by fear of the unknown. As well, the Puritans were torn between reaffirming their English identity (and thus their distance from what they saw as the seductive anarchy of the American wilderness and its inhabitants) while justifying to themselves their decision to emigrate.

Cotton Mather and the narrative of Hannah Dustan

At times the ministers who transcribed captivity narratives faced certain difficulties in resolving these tensions. One such was **Cotton Mather**, who related the captivity of the redoubtable **Hannah Dustan** in his *Magnalia Christi Americana (1702)*. Dustan, her newborn baby, and the child's nurse, Mary Neff, were taken prisoner in an Indian attack which took place shortly after she had given birth. Later, the baby's brains were dashed out against a tree. Hannah, Mary, and a boy called Samuel were taken north by the Indians, and as her captors slept Hannah and her companions murdered them with their own tomahawks. After this, they scalped the Indians in order to claim a cash bounty of 50 pounds from the Massachusetts General Court. Clearly, Hannah Dustan did not exemplify the virtues of submissive Puritan femininity. Cotton Mather thus casts Dustan as a victim by suggesting that her violence is an aberration prompted by divinely inspired maternal love. By doing so, he reconfigures an episode of female violence (and indeed economic initiative, with Dustan's insistence on being paid for scalps) in order to realign it with existing Puritan gender roles.

The Salem Witch Trials (1692)

One of the darkest episodes in Puritan history, and one which has haunted American literature ever since, are the Salem Witch Trials. Seventeenth-century Puritans inhabited a pre-Enlightenment world, in which the visible realm of everyday reality mingled with an invisible world inhabited by spirits (Norton, 2002, pp. 5–6). In the decade preceding the trials, the father and son Increase and Cotton Mather had published accounts of demonic possession, malign activities, spectral evidence, and dramatic visions of Satan, said to appear to the unwary as a "black rogue," an Indian, or as an animal. The events leading to the Salem Witch Trials can be summarized succinctly. According to one source, John Hale, a group of local girls began to experiment with fortune-telling, attempting to discern the future by gazing into an egg and a mirror. One of them was badly frightened by what she saw, "a Spectre in likeness of a Coffin" (Karlsen, 1999, p. 36). Soon thereafter, several of them, including **Betty Parris**, the daughter of the local pastor **Samuel Parris**, and **Abigail Williams**, his 11-year-old niece, began to exhibit strange symptoms, claiming that they were being bitten and pricked by invisible demons. At some juncture, at the instigation of a woman called Mary Sibley, Parris's Carib Indian slave **Tituba** was asked to prepare a witch cake, consisting of the girls' urine mixed with rye meal, and feed it to a dog.

Although Parris had the children examined by doctors, their condition continued to worsen. Finally, a local physician, William Griggs, concluded that the girls were "under an Evil Hand." In February 1692 the afflicted children were put under considerable pressure to name those responsible for their suffering, and they named three persons: Sarah Good, Sarah Osborne, and Tituba, the slave. In the interrogations which followed, all three were presumed guilty; indeed, the magistrates did not hesitate to use torture where a presumption of guilt existed (Karlsen, 1999, p. 13). Good and Osborne protested their innocence, but Tituba, possibly out of fear of her master, confessed that she had made the witch cake and that "her Mistress in her own Country was a Witch," but denied being a witch herself. She did, however, go on to give detailed evidence about her encounters with the Devil and the witches' gatherings she had attended in the forest, and alluded to other witches who still had not been identified (Norton, 2002, pp. 16–42; Karlsen, 1999, pp. 33–43).

At this point, the witch hunt began in earnest. Local women were denounced, and charges of witchcraft were brought; the local magistrates, **John Hathorne** and **Jonathan Corwin**, examined the accused. The accusations spiraled in number, often including relatives of those accused, including four-year-old **Dorcas Good** and farmer **John Proctor**. Over two hundred persons were accused during the entire episode; of these, three-fourths were female, and half the males were relatives of accused women (Karlsen, 1999, p. 40). Those who maintained their innocence were executed; unsurprisingly, confessions began to pour forth.

Historians have advanced numerous explanations for the outbreak, ranging from class conflict within the Salem congregation to gender issues, collective hysteria, and the traumatic effects of the First and Second Indian Wars. Probably each of these was a contributing factor: Puritan culture, as we have seen, was deeply misogynist, and many households had experienced directly or indirectly the consequences of strife with the Indians. Moreover, as the seventeenth century drew to a close, many Puritans felt that they were succumbing to the temptations of individual financial gain and losing the sense of collective purpose that had sustained the first generation of settlers. Whatever the case, this dark episode would be woven for many years after into the writing of authors from Nathaniel Hawthorne to Arthur Miller and William Carlos Williams.

Samuel Sewall

One of the Salem judges responsible for sentencing accused witches to death was **Samuel Sewall**, along with John Hathorne, the ancestor of Nathaniel Hawthorne. Sewall, however, was a man of conscience, who later confessed his feelings of guilt and error regarding his role in the Salem Witch Trials and begged the forgiveness of his congregation. Sewall was also troubled about the issue of slavery, and wrote the first antislavery tract to be published in North America, titled *The Selling of Joseph* (1700). In it, in true Puritan fashion, he invokes biblical typology to maintain that all human beings are descended from Adam and Eve and thus benefit from the radical liberty granted to humankind after the Fall. Later, however, he goes on to more practical considerations, claiming that slaves, unlike indentured servants, are not motivated to work hard for their masters. The essay concludes with a refutation of the most common objections to freeing the slaves, including the allegations that Africans are descended from Ham, the son of Noah, and because of the curse on him and his descendants (Genesis 9:20–7) are condemned to slavery, and that, though enslaved, they had been brought from a pagan country to a Christian one. The fact that Sewall's treatise is torn between biblical typology and pragmatic concern for the commercial bottom line mirrors the dilemma faced by second and third-generation Puritans in light of the waning sense of common purpose and the increasing secularization of Puritan culture.

It is in Samuel Sewall's *Journal (1672–1729)*, however, that we gain a fascinating insight into the personal lives of Puritans at the beginning of the eighteenth century. Particularly interesting is Sewall's relentless, unwittingly comical, and ultimately unsuccessful courtship of Katherine Winthrop after his wife's untimely death. He meticulously takes note of the price of the gifts he gives her and calls on her assiduously. The entry for October 12, 1720, reads as follows:

Madam Winthrop's countenance was much changed from what 'twas on Monday, look'd dark and lowering ... I got my Chair in place, had some Converse, but very Cold and indifferent to what 'twas before. Ask'd her to acquit me of Rudeness if I drew off her Glove. Enquiring the reason, I told her 'twas great odds between handling a dead Goat, and a living Lady. Got it off. I told her I had one Petition to ask of her; that was, to take off the Negative she laid on me the third of October ... In some of our Discourse, I told her I had rather go to the Stone-House[6] adjoining to her, than to come to her against her mind. Told her the reason why I came every other night was lest I should drink too deep draughts of Pleasure. She had talked of Canary,[7] her Kisses were to me better than the best Canary.

(Sewall, 1973, p. 960)

Puritan Poetry

Puritan attitudes to poetry were ambivalent, to say the very least. On the one hand, the Puritans distrusted imaginative language, with its appeal to the senses as well as to the intellect. Their iconoclastic stance against graven images implied a certain antipathy to poetic form, but they were not blind to the didactic and communicative power of poetry. This was especially important at a time when first-generation Puritans were beginning to die

---

[6] The local jail.
[7] Sweet wine from the Canary Islands.

off and the communitarian values of the first settlers had begun to give way to increased materialism. Poetry thus became a useful tool to inculcate and disseminate Puritan ideology; scriptural texts recast in ballad meter and printed alphabets facilitated memorization and communication. The *New England Primer* (of which it is estimated that five million copies were sold in the period from 1683 to 1830) taught children their letters with couplets like these:

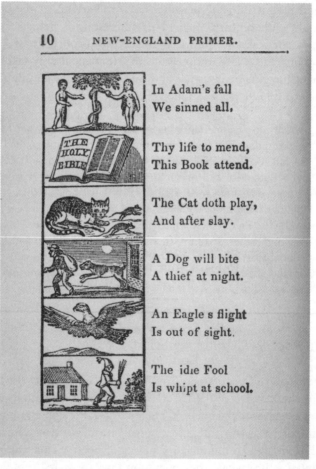

Figure 3.1   Excerpt from the *New England Primer* (Concord: Rufus Merrill, 1849), p. 10. By permission of the British Library.

This emphasis on the transitory character of human existence is also found in a poem possibly by Cotton Mather:

> I in the Burying Place may see
> Graves shorter there than I;
> From Death's Arrest no Age is Free
> Young Children too may die;
> My God, may such an awful Sight,
> Awakening be to me!
> Oh! That by early Grace I might
> For Death prepared be.

The poetic subject of the poem is a child contemplating the graves of other children. Written in the meter of popular ballads (alternating lines in iambic quadrameter and trimester), it evokes vividly for unruly students the dire consequences of being unprepared for salvation.

In the **Bay Psalm Book**, published in 1640, the Puritans also harnessed the didactic and mnemonic power of the ballad form, as in this excerpt from a version of the 23rd Psalm:

> The Lord to me a shepherd is,
> Want therefore shall not I.
> He in the folds of tender grass
> Doth cause me down to lie.
>
> (Cotton, 1640, unpaginated)

At times, the rollicking rhythm of ballad meter sits oddly with the apocalyptic content of some Puritan verse. **Michael Wigglesworth's** hell-fire and brimstone poem **The Day of Doom (1662)** describes the Last Judgment:

> For at midnight brake forth a Light
> which turn'd the night to day,
> And speedily an hideous cry
> did all the world dismay.
> Sinners awake, their hearts do ake,
> trembling their loynes surprizeth;
> Amaz'd with fear, by what they hear
>   each one of them ariseth.
>
> (Wigglesworth, 1666, p. 2)

After setting the apocalyptic scene, Wigglesworth describes with alarming relish the torments of the damned:

> They wring their hands, their caitiff hands
> and gnash their teeth for terrour;
> They cry, they roar for anguish sore,
> and gnaw their tongues for horrour.
> But get away without delay,
> Christ pitties not your cry;
> Depart to Hell, there may you yell,
> and roar Eternally.
>
> (Wigglesworth, 1666, p. 62)

Anne Bradstreet

Anne Bradstreet, like Wigglesworth a devout Puritan, also describes her longing for salvation and her extreme awareness of the precariousness of earthly life, but her poetic voice is very different from that of Wigglesworth and those of his ilk. She was born in England, and she and her husband Simon migrated to Massachusetts Bay with John Winthrop's group in 1630 on the *Arbella*. Simon Bradstreet came from a well-connected Puritan family, and ultimately became governor of the colony. The couple had eight children.

As we have seen previously, Puritan women who (like Anne Hutchinson) dared to step outside prescribed gender roles did so at great risk to their standing in the community and indeed their lives. In 1647, Bradstreet's brother-in-law John Woodbridge took a collection of her poetry to England, where it was published allegedly without her knowledge with the title of **The Tenth Muse Lately Sprung up in America**. The volume contains a preface written by Woodbridge stating that the book really had been written by a woman, known for "her gracious demeanor, her eminent parts, her pious conversation, her courteous disposition, her exact diligence in her place, and discreet managing of her family occasions." That is to say: although she had dared to write and even publish poetry, Bradstreet was a decorous Puritan housewife and not a dangerous radical who posed a threat to the Puritan community. Bradstreet's Prologue to her book begins with the following self-deprecatory statement:

> To sing of wars, of captains, and of kings,
> Of cities founded, commonwealths begun,

> For my mean pen are too superior things,
> Or how they all or each their dates have run,
> Let poets and historians set these forth,
> My obscure lines shall not so dim their worth.

She acknowledges ruefully that she will have to deal with misogyny and accusations of plagiarism:

> I am obnoxious to each carping tongue
> Who says my hand a needle better fits,
> A poet's pen all scorn I should thus wrong,
> For such despite they cast on female wits:
> If what I do prove well, it won't advance,
> They'll say it's stol'n, or else it was by chance.

The poem concludes with gentle irony:

> And oh ye high flown quills that soar the skies,
> And ever with your prey still catch your praise,
> If e'er you deign these lowly lines your eyes,
> Give thyme or parsley wreath, I ask no bays;
> This mean and unrefined ore of mine
> Will make your glist'ring gold but more to shine.
>
> (Bradstreet, 1650, p. 4)

Bradstreet's deft comparison of her own "lowly lines" to the "high flown quills" of her male counterparts (with the wonderful punning on "prey" and "praise") is an astute rhetorical tactic designed to use the discourse of domesticity in order to render her verse and indeed her person unthreatening. Her declaration that she would be content with wreaths of parsley and thyme (both humble domestic herbs used in cooking) rather than the usual bay laurels which garlanded the heads of male dignitaries reinforces the image of Bradstreet as well-behaved Puritan housewife, and gently satirizes the pomposity of her male contemporaries. The tone of subtle irony is unmistakable when Bradstreet compares her "mean and unrefined ore" to the "glist'ring gold" of her male contemporaries.

In another volume published some years later, Bradstreet offers lyrical insights into Puritan daily life. Her poems to her husband are frank expressions of love and physical longing. One, written when he was away at Ipswich, speaks of her loneliness and desire:

My chilled limbs now numbed lie forlorn
Return, return sweet Sol from Capricorn,
In this dead time, alas, what can I more
Than view those fruits which through thy heat I bore?
Which sweet contentment yield me for a space
True living pictures of their father's face.

(Bradstreet, 1678, pp. 240–1)

In an era of high infant mortality, there are poignant elegies to three dead grandchildren. One, to her granddaughter Elizabeth, who died at the age of a year and a half, evokes in its final stanza the tension between Bradstreet's own grief at the child's untimely death and her religious faith:

By nature trees do rot when they are grown,
And plums and apples thoroughly ripe do fall,
And corn and grass are in their season mown,
And time brings down what is both strong and tall.
But plants new set to be eradicate,
And buds new blown to have so short a date,
Is by His hand alone that guides nature and fate.

(Bradstreet, 1678, p. 248)

Edward Taylor

Edward Taylor, who owned a copy of Anne Bradstreet's second volume of poems, was an extraordinarily prolific poet whose work is characterized by arresting and evocative metaphors. In **"Upon Wedlock & Death of Children"** he, like Bradford, reflects on the transient quality of earthly joys, comparing the marriage bond to the original Covenant between God and humankind:

A Curious Knot God made in Paradise,
    And drew it out inamled neatly Fresh,
It was the True-Love Knot, more Sweet than spice
    And Set with all the flowers of Graces dress.
    Its Weddens Knot, that ne're can be unti'de.
    No Alexanders Sword can it divide.

This idyllic portrayal of the enduring lovers' knot enameled with floral images gives way later in the poem, however, to a darker vision describing the death of his year-old daughter Abigail:

But praying ore my branch, my branch did Sprout
And bore another manly flower, & gay
And after that another, Sweet brake out,
The which the former hand soon got away.
But oh! The tortures, vomit, Screechings, groans
And Six weeks Fever would pierce hearts like Stones.

Like Bradstreet, Taylor finds consolation only in religious faith and submission to Divine will:

Griefe o're doth flow: & nature fault would finde
Were not thy Will, my Spell Charm, Joy & Gem:
That as I said, I say, take, Lord, they're thine.
I piecemeale pas to Glory bright in them.
I joy, may I sweet Flowers for Glory breed,
Whether thou getst them green, or lets them Seed.

(Taylor, 1966, pp. 117–18)

Sarah Kemble Knight

Although she too was a Puritan, Sarah Kemble Knight offers us a very different perspective on life in New England. Knight was left a widow when she was around 30 years old. Taking on her husband's business affairs, she showed considerable commercial flair, and traveled around the rural and urban northeast. Her narrative, **The Journal of Madam Knight**, written around 1705, reveals her as a keen observer of colonial culture in all its diversity, with comments on the ruling elites, backwoodsmen, slaves, and Native Americans. Murray's narrative voice has a marvelously picaresque ring, and she describes her world with warmth, humor, and formidable intelligence.

In recent years, there has been an outpouring of scholarship on American Puritan writing and culture. It is not a field for the faint of heart; distinguished scholars such as Emory Elliott (1994, p. 183) point out that almost any statement one can make about the Puritans will create controversy. For some, the Puritans were dreamers and idealists aiming to create a better world. For others, they are the source of virtually everything that is negative about America.

The truth, perhaps, lies somewhere in between. What is undoubtedly the case is that the Puritans cast a long shadow. On the one hand, they leave a lasting legacy of literacy and of commitment to creating a better world. On the other, however, their doctrinal rigidity and their notion of America as an exceptional, God-driven nation with the obligation and indeed the right to serve as a template for every other society on earth has proved frighteningly resilient and has endured until the present day.

Chapter 4

From Colonies to Nation

Introduction

As the seventeenth century drew to a close, the Onandaga leader **Garangula** addressed a stirring oration to Antoine Lefebvre de la Barre, the Governor of New France – the regions of North America colonized by the French. Speaking on behalf of the Five Nations, he declared:

> Hear, Yonnondio, take care for the future, that so great a number of soldiers as appear here do not choke the Tree of Peace planted in so small a fort. It will be a great loss, if after it had so easily taken root, you should stop its growth and prevent its covering your country and ours with its branches.
>
> (Castillo and Schweitzer, 2001, p. 353. See Calloway, 1994)

Regrettably, the Tree of Peace proved to be a fragile plant in Early America. With a marked increase in the pace of European settlement and the consequent uprooting of Native American groups, eighteenth-century North America underwent vast changes. Some of these transformations occurred as a result of events in Europe. In 1713, the **Treaty of Utrecht** marked the end of the **War of the Spanish Succession**, with France ceding Nova Scotia and Newfoundland to the English; the Spanish lost their European possessions (the Duchy of Milan, Sardinia, Naples, Gibraltar, and Menorca) and thus turned their attention to their holdings in the American Southwest, sending religious orders to establish missions and proselytize among the indigenous groups of the area. Because of religious and political turmoil in Europe, immigration to America flourished, with Scots-Irish, Germans, Dutch, French Huguenots and others flooding into the Atlantic colonies to establish plantations, small farms, and businesses.

Living standards rose markedly as a result. Writing in 1666, Maryland poet
George Alsop speaks of the growing importance of trade:

> Trafique is Earth's great *Atlas*, that supports
> The pay of Armies, and the height of Courts,
> And makes Mechanicks live, that else would die
> Meer starving Martyrs to their penury;
> None but the Merchant of this thing can boast,
> He, like the Bee, comes loaden from each Coast,
> And too all Kingdoms, as within a Hive,
> Stows up those Riches that doth make them thrive.
> Be thrifty, *Mary-Land*, keep what thou hast in store
> And each years Trafique to thy self get more.
>
> (Castillo and Schweitzer, 2001, pp. 217–18)

Alsop characterizes "trafique" or trade as the classical figure of Atlas
bearing on his shoulders the financial viability of armies and courts and
the survival of "mechanicks" or craftsmen and laborers, and goes on to
compare the industrious tradesmen of Maryland to bees storing honey.
This georgic imagery of an inhabited, commercial landscape, with its exhortation to thrift and economic effort, presages the increasing impact of
mercantilist theory and of secularization on America's Atlantic colonies.

Newton and Locke. Jonathan Edwards and the Great Awakening

Enlightenment thinkers such as **Sir Isaac Newton** and **John Locke** were
particularly influential in eighteenth-century America. Newton, in his
Principia Mathematica (1687), had described the universe as designed
according to rational principles and governed by rational laws, which, once
set in motion by its Creator (seen as an abstract First Cause), no longer
required divine intervention. From this perspective, once human beings
could understand these natural laws and principles through the use of
reason, they could use them to improve self and others. For Locke, human
beings were neither damned at birth nor predestined for salvation, but
rather were blank slates upon which lived experience and sensory perceptions inscribed knowledge and a sense of self. In America, the theologian
Jonathan Edwards applied the ideas of Lockean empiricism and Newtonian
science to describe Nature as God's own book, in whose beauty and order

Grace was revealed, a concept which would reappear in the work of nineteenth-century writers such as Emerson. His vivid sermons were part of an evangelical religious revival called the **Great Awakening** that swept the English colonies in the 1730s and 1740s.

Quakerism

Another influential religious movement was Quakerism. Pennsylvania, named for its founder **William Penn**, was originally intended as a state to be run on Quaker principles. As Hugh Brogan points out, the **Society of Friends** were treated for the most part with relative tolerance in England, and they had established links with similar groups in Germany, where promotional pamphlets were printed and distributed in the Rhineland. By 1775 there were approximately 100,000 persons of German origin in Pennsylvania, mostly small farmers. The city of Philadelphia flourished as a major trading center where farm produce could be brought to market (see Brogan, 1999, pp. 93–7).

From their very beginnings, Quaker communities were egalitarian in nature in regard to social class, skin color, and gender. This occasionally created problems for their members, since they took Luther's concept of the "priesthood of all believers" to its ultimate conclusion, arguing that each human being possessed an Inner Light or spark of the divine. Thus some Quakers contended that inequalities such as existing gender norms or indeed the institution of slavery were a product of the Fall, but could be healed by those who lived in the Light. Unsurprisingly, Quakers were persecuted by the New England Puritans, and many were persecuted, tortured, or exiled.

Elizabeth Ashbridge and John Woolman

One such was **Elizabeth Ashbridge**. She was born to an Anglican family, but after eloping at the age of 14 and becoming a widow shortly thereafter, she was repudiated by her family. After this, she went to Ireland in search of spiritual enlightenment, and some years later emigrated to America as an indentured servant. Her autobiographical journal *Some Account of the Fore Part of the Life of Elizabeth Ashbridge* (1755) recounts her conversion to Quakerism and the courage and determination with which she resisted abuse at the hands of her non-Quaker husband until his death.

Another Quaker, **John Woolman**, was prosperous in business, but eventually gave up trade altogether in order to dedicate himself to issues related to his faith. In 1754, he wrote an antislavery treatise titled *Some Considerations on the Keeping of Negroes*. Woolman begins by stating that all nations are of one blood, but that some have been more favored than others. He then declares that to consider mankind otherwise than brothers, or to allege that divine favor is directed at one nation and not to others, is simply wrong, adding that if our ancestors and we had been subjected to constant servitude or had been deprived of reading and of religious instruction we would probably be in a state similar to that of slaves (Woolman, 1754). For the present-day reader, Woolman's tone is ethnocentric, with its assumption of the superiority of Western culture. And yet in its time it was exceptional as well as courageous, not only in its compassionate recognition of the common humanity of slaves and slave-holders, but in its willingness to acknowledge the harmful effects of slavery on slaveowners as well as the slaves they exploited.

The Growth of Slavery

What is indubitable is that the number of slaves increased dramatically. Before 1790, the number of slaves imported to the 13 colonies or states on the Eastern seaboard is estimated at between 250,000 and 300,000. When tobacco monoculture became unprofitable in Virginia and points south, other crops such as rice, sugar cane, and cotton were introduced, which required an increase in the (slave) labor force. Conditions were grim. Few slaves could read and write, but one of the few who could managed to send a letter in 1723 to the Bishop of London:

> here follows our Sevarity and Sorrowfull Sarvice we are hard used on Every account in the first place wee are in Ignorance of our Salvation and in the next place wee are kept out of the Church and matrimony is denied us and to be plain they doo Look no more upon us then if we ware dogs which I hope when these Strange Lines comes to your Lord Ships hands will be looket into ... wee dare not subscribe any man's name to this for feare of our masters for if they know wee have sent home to your honour wee Should goo neare to Swing upon the galas tree.
>
> (Ingersoll, 1994)

William Byrd of Westover

The world of slaveowners was, of course, very different. The texts of **William Byrd** of Westover provide a fascinating insight into the mentality of the Virginia slave owning elites. Byrd inherited a vast plantation from his father, and was sent to school in England at the age of seven, remaining there for 24 years. In England he joined the Royal Society and mingled with men of letters. Returning to Virginia upon his father's death, he lived the life of a gentleman landowner in the family mansion at Westover, with a large library at his disposal. In 1728 he participated in the survey of the border between Virginia and North Carolina, and later recounted his exploits in *The History of the Dividing Line (1728–1736)*. In it, he satirizes the contrasts between Virginia and North Carolina, between white and Native Americans, men and women. Even more interesting (though reading it does provoke feelings of voyeuristic guilt in the reader) is his *Secret History*, written in code and only published in 1929, for it is here that Byrd's character, his attitude as a slaveowner, and his tempestuous relationship with his unpleasant and sadistic wife emerge most clearly. The entry for July 15, 1710, for example, states:

> I rose at 5 o'clock and read two chapters in Hebrew and some Greek in Thucydides. I said my prayers and ate milk and pears for breakfast. About 7 o'clock the negro boy that ran away was brought home. My wife against my will called little Jenny to be burned with a hot iron, for which I quarrelled with her.
>
> (Byrd, 1941, p. 481)

What stands out for the present-day reader is the apparent insouciance with which Byrd relates acts of cruelty toward slaves. In another entry, he states: "My wife caused Prue to be whipped violently notwithstanding I desired not, which provoked me to have Anaka whipped likewise who had deserved it much more, on which my wife flew into such a passion that she hoped she would be revenged of me."

Later, however, all was forgiven: "In the afternoon I wrote two more accounts till the evening and then took a walk in the garden. I said my prayers and was reconciled with my wife and gave her a flourish in token of it (Byrd, 1941, p. 533).

Benjamin Franklin

One of the most fascinating and complex characters to be encountered in eighteenth-century America is **Benjamin Franklin**. He was born in Boston in 1706 and was apprenticed when he was 12 years old to his brother James, a printer, in Boston. There he learned his trade and indulged in a proclivity for intellectual polemic that would remain with him throughout his life. The brothers quarreled, and Franklin ran away, first to New York and then to Philadelphia, where, after a somewhat rocky beginning, he prospered financially, and established himself both as an intellectual presence and a political figure; his experiments with electricity attracted attention on both sides of the Atlantic. As a result of his growing prominence, he was appointed agent for Pennsylvania in England. In a climate of growing dissatisfaction with British rule, he then began to act as agent for other colonies and to articulate their complaints against the mother country. Perhaps his most important contributions to American history were his activities as American minister to France during the Revolutionary War, as a negotiator for the Peace Treaty with Great Britain, and as a framer of the American Constitution.

On reading Benjamin Franklin's texts, one comes away with the impression that he was an intelligent and elusive man who was extraordinarily adept at constructing a myriad of masks and selves tailored to the audiences he was addressing, both in person and on the printed page. He was, in every sense, a man made of words. As a young indentured printer, he devoured books, reading until late at night, and composing the odd ballad. His real forte, however, was prose, and in his *Autobiography* (1793) he acknowledges, "Prose Writing has been of great Use to me in the Course of my Life, and was a principal Means of my Advancement" (Franklin, 1910, p. 14). At the age of only 16, he began his literary career under the pseudonym **Silence Dogood**, writing a series of essays for his brother's *New England Courant*. His gender-bending adoption of the persona of Silence Dogood, a garrulous and intrusive widow, enabled him to satirize certain aspects of Boston life. Much to the young Franklin's glee, his brother and friends believed the essays to be written by one of the most intelligent young men in the city. Later, in *Poor Richard's Almanac* (1733–38), he adopted the identity of **Richard Saunders**, a henpecked astronomer compelled by poverty to compose almanacs containing advice, witty sayings, moral admonitions, and ribald observations. The almanacs became hugely successful, enabling Franklin to hone his style and develop the tone of homespun, self-deprecatory wit that would be the hallmark of his prose style.

In his *Autobiography*, Franklin constructs himself as protagonist and literary character, relating his life from the perspective of a tolerant, worldly wise elderly narrator. The first section speaks of the author's youth in Boston, his picaresque adventures when he escapes from his indenture with his brother and flees first to New York and then to Philadelphia, and the lessons learned as he attempts to establish his economic and intellectual independence, in contrast to other less successful characters. The second section describes his attempts at self-improvement, and gently satirizes his own youthful presumption. The *Autobiography* concludes with a final section that describes Franklin's rise to economic success, his attainments as a scientist, and his political and philanthropic activities.

Franklin as historical personage and as writer arouses strong reactions. He has been characterized as a Renaissance man, a polymath, a charmingly cosmopolitan companion and brilliant negotiator, the creator of the myth of the American as self-made man. Others have evoked a less charming side to the man and his ideas. **Max Weber**, in an oft-cited essay titled **"The Spirit of Capitalism,"** describes Franklin as the embodiment of Western capitalism, a man for whom economic acquisition is the ultimate purpose and ethic in life (Weber, 1979, pp. 14–19). **D. H. Lawrence** (1977, p. 19) describes Franklin as a "snuff-coloured little man," a utilitarian philistine for whom the acquisition of wealth is the be-all and end-all: "Why the soul of man is a vast forest, and all Benjamin intended was a neat back garden. And we've all got to fit into his kitchen garden scheme of things. Hail Columbia!" (p. 16).

Whatever the case, it is undoubtedly true that Franklin made a strong mark on his era and on his country. The Franklinian notion of the self-made individual who relies only on his own efforts and virtues to achieve economic independence has resonated throughout American literature, from Emerson to Whitman to F. Scott Fitzgerald.

Hector St. John de Crèvecoeur and the Melting Pot

Another individual who for many symbolizes the endless promise of an American existence is **Hector St. John de Crèvecoeur**. Born in Caen to an affluent family of Norman gentry, he spent some time in England visiting

distant relatives in Salisbury, and would remain an Anglophile for the rest
of his life. In 1755, he embarked for New France as a soldier. France's position in North America was strong; in the previous century, *voyageurs* such
as La Salle and Hennepin had laid claim to extensive territories in the Great
Lakes area and in the upper Mississippi Valley. In the decade prior to
Crèvecoeur's arrival in New France, tensions along the frontier between
France and England's American possessions had steadily increased; both
groups wished to expand their territories in order to increase trade of all
sorts, particularly in furs, and in 1754 what would come to be known in
North America as the **French and Indian War** broke out. Crèvecoeur was
wounded in the battle in which the French general Montcalm lost Canada
for France, and after the war ended he headed south to the British colonies.
There, as a cartographer and surveyor, he quickly found employment, and
took part in 1767 in a party which explored the Appalachians, parts of the
Ohio River Valley, and the upper Mississippi. In 1769 he married a well-
to-do young woman called Mehitable Tippet, bought a farm in New York
(and not Pennsylvania, as his narrative would later suggest) and settled
down to the live of a gentleman farmer and man of letters.

The ensuing years were clearly the happiest in Crèvecoeur's life. By dint
of hard work, his farm and family prospered, and three children were born.
At the same time, he was able to devote himself to intellectual pursuits and
writing. Crèvecoeur's epistolary meditations on what it means to be an
American, and the conflicts and dilemmas of American identity, would
later be one of the texts that has most directly constructed perceptions of
America throughout the world.

Crèvecoeur's Letter III (1782) is titled **"What is an American?"** He
begins by speculating about the thoughts and feelings of an "enlightened
Englishman" on arriving on the continent. This putative Englishman, he
argues, would feel pride at the accomplishments of his countrymen, who
had taken refuge in American "when convulsed by factions, afflicted by a
variety of miseries and wants, restless and impatient" (Crèvecoeur, 1793,
pp. 46–7). There, says Crèvecoeur, they have carried their national genius
which can flourish unimpeded. He contrasts life in America with the
extremes of wealth and poverty existing in Europe, and declares that even
the most basic log cabin is a "dry and comfortable habitation." He characterizes American society as secular and American religion as undemand-
ing and tolerant. He is fascinated by the diversity of national origins to be
found among American's inhabitants:

What, then, is the American, this new man? He is either an European or the descendent of an European; hence that strange mixture of blood which you will find in no other country ... He is an American, who, leaving behind him his ancient prejudices and manners, receives new ones from the new mode of life he has embraced, the new government he obeys, and the new rank he holds. Here individuals of all nations are melted into a new race of men, whose labours and posterity are the western pilgrims who are carrying along with them that great mass of arts, sciences, vigour, and industry which began long since in the East; they will finish the great circle.

(Crèvecoeur, 1793, p. 50)

This discourse of America as a vast melting pot into which all (Northern European) ethnicities are blended into an amorphous and uniform mass, shedding their old languages and identities in order to be reborn as the new American man, has proved remarkably powerful and resilient. It is also problematic on many levels. Crèvecoeur's definition of Americanness excludes large swathes of North America's population: women, African slaves, and Native Americans. For him, the ideal American is a male European transplanted into an environment where he can grow and prosper unhindered by rigid European political, economic, and social structures. He adds that the colonies on the Eastern seaboard (those that are closest geographically to Europe) are the most "civilized" and advanced; those nearest the sea are bold and enterprising, those dwelling in the middle colonies are living in an Arcadian, egalitarian idyll; and those furthest from Europe, on the frontier, are "no better than carnivorous animals of a superior rank" (Crèvecoeur, 1793, p. 64). Thus, in a marvelous example of Eurocentric reasoning, the closer to Europe one is, the more American.

Crèvecoeur speaks of an archetypal immigrant, who on getting off the boat is hired and immediately put to work and accepted as "a member of the family." This person spends two or three years acquiring practical knowledge about agriculture, and once he has done so buys land; allegedly his good name will procure him the necessary credit to purchase two hundred acres of land. By dint of hard work,

From nothing to start into being; from a servant to the rank of a master; from being the slave of some despotic prince, to become a free man, invested with lands to which every municipal blessing is annexed! What a change indeed! It is in consequence of that change that he becomes an American.

(Crèvecoeur, 1793, p. 83)

Obviously, reality was not quite so rose-tinted for all immigrants. Crèvecoeur, however, was a decent man, and on a visit to Charleston he was confronted in all too graphic form with the horrors of plantation slavery. His Letter IX begins with a description of the opulence of Charles Town or Charleston, South Carolina, and the carefree existence of the planter caste. He then describes the contrast of this state of affairs with the economic exploitation of the toil of slaves and the destruction of slave families, with whom he finds a common humanity. As the essay draws to a close, we learn that Crèvecoeur's melancholy reflections were prompted by an incident when he was walking through the woods to a dinner engagement with a planter. In the woods, he comes upon swarms of birds hovering above a slave who is confined in a cage hanging from a tree:

> horrid to think, and painful to repeat, I perceived a Negro, suspended in the cage and left there to expire! I shudder when I recollect that the birds had already picked out his eyes; his cheek-bones were bare; his arms covered with a multitude of wounds. From the edges of the hollow sockets and from the lacerations with which he was disfigured, the blood slowly dropped and tinged the ground beneath.

> (Crèvecoeur, 1793, p. 102)

Crèvecoeur gives the dying man water, and laments that he has no bullets in his gun to put an end to the slave's agony. Later, he learns from his hosts that the man's crime was to have killed the overseer on the plantation.

Crèvecoeur lived at a time when tensions between England and its American colonies were growing steadily more acute, and his Arcadian idyll would soon be torn apart. After a period of imprisonment in New York, suspected of spying, he returned to London, then to France. He himself had taken part, on the side of France, in the **French and Indian War (1754–63)**, as the American theatre of the **Seven Years' War** was known. This conflict, provoked by the uprising of the Ottawa leader **Pontiac**, was later the subject of a play by **Robert Rogers**, the first on an "American" subject written by an author born in America; it was published in 1766, but after receiving excoriating reviews was never actually performed (see Castillo, 2005, p. 223).

Mercantilism. The Brewing Storm

The French and Indian War proved to be financially onerous for the British Crown, and it was determined, given the fact that British subjects already bore a considerable tax burden, that revenue for colonial defense would have to be raised from the colonies themselves. The mercantile system was thus transformed from one of supporting and regulating trade to one of revenue generation. This subsequently proved to be a recipe for political mayhem, since the colonies were not directly represented in Parliament.

On reading texts from this period, one is struck by the constant reference to familial metaphors. Jack Greene has described the divergence in the ways this metaphor was understood in Britain and in the colonies. For the British, the colonies were viewed as (often wayward) children, dependent, subordinate, and generally incapable of discerning their own best interests. For the colonists, however, the Mother Country's role was to be that of a protective, nurturing parent, who would not undermine their own self-esteem and capacity to act effectively as individuals, would not interfere with activities meant to redound in their own best interest, would respect the validity of local self-governing institutions, and finally would manifest respect for the rights of Englishmen (which the colonists considered themselves to be) for the preservation of life and property. The divergences between theory and fact (what the authorities believed colonies should be, and what the colonies believed about themselves), and between conceptions of what the colonial relationship should actually consist of, and the collapse of mutual expectations, would ultimately drive Britain and America apart. Moreover, given the enormous distances which separated England from its American colonies, enforcing compliance with imperial edicts was often problematic. Greene points out that by 1750, the colonies had attained certain conditions necessary for self-government, namely the emergence of coherent local elites; the development of local sites of acknowledged and functional authority, capable of resolving internal conflicts; competence in spheres such as commerce, education, and print culture; and crucially, the increased size and wealth of the colonies in terms of population, productive land, and skills (Greene, 1973).

In England, as the result of the political turmoil of the previous century with the execution of **Charles I (1649)**, the **Interregnum (1653–59)** under **Cromwell**, and the **Restoration (1660)** of **Charles II**, in which debates about the absolute power of monarchy and the rights of Parliament had

torn the country apart, a certain set of assumptions had emerged. Power
and luxury were viewed as forces of corruption and natural enemies of
freedom and civic virtue, and only an arrangement by which different
components of the political system held each other in check could somehow
halt degeneracy and tyranny. John Locke's theory of the **Social Contract**,
according to which the legitimacy of governments was derived from the
consent of the governed, was also vastly influential. Any political developments which appeared to be at odds with the basic interests of British
constitutional law were viewed as emerging from a conspiracy of corrupt
men in power to threaten liberty for selfish personal reasons. These ideas
had an enormous impact in eighteenth-century Britain's political debates,
but their impact among Britain's American colonists, removed as they were
from the centers of imperial power and lacking the capacity to influence
decisions which had direct impact on their daily lives, was nothing short
of extraordinary.

Previously, trade with England's American colonies had been regulated
by the **Navigation Acts**, according to which all European commodities
bound for America were to be shipped through England or Wales. Certain
commodities (such as sugar, tobacco, and rice) were unloaded and taxed
before continuing on to other countries, a system which not only implied
a longer shipping time but also increased costs for the colonists. One such
law, passed in 1733, was the **Molasses Act**, according to which the trade of
sugar from the French West Indies to the American colonies was heavily
taxed, forcing the colonists to buy more expensive sugar from the British
West Indies. Smuggling, as a result, was rife. In 1762, when King George
III vetoed a law passed by the colonial legislature, the Virginia firebrand
Patrick Henry stated: "a King, by disallowing Acts of this salutary nature,
from being the father of his people, degenerated into a Tyrant and forfeits
all right to his subjects' obedience." The **Sugar Act** in 1764 and the **Stamp
Act** of 1765 caused riots and prompted the colonists to produce a
"Declaration of Rights and Grievances." Although the Stamp Act was later
repealed, the **Townshend Acts** passed by Parliament in 1767, with its taxes
on trade, provoked outrage, and the colonists retaliated with boycotts of
taxed goods such as sugar, paint, and linen. In 1770 an angry Boston mob
was fired upon by a British military detachment, killing five people. This
event, which became known as the **Boston Massacre**, brought people in
from the countryside to take up arms. After this, Parliament revoked the
Townshend taxes on all commodities except tea. In response, a group of
Patriots (as they had come to be called), disguised as Indians, went aboard

British ships in the winter of 1773 and dumped their cargo of tea into Boston Harbor in what came to be called the **Boston Tea Party**. In order to show that further insubordination would not be tolerated, the imperial authorities decided to punish Massachusetts by closing the port of Boston. In response to this, the **First Continental Congress**, a meeting of representatives from the various colonies, took place in Philadelphia in 1774. Parliament responded with the **Coercive Acts** which restricted colonial trade to Britain and Ireland. What came to be known as "the shot heard round the world"[1] rang out in April 1775 when Massachusetts minutemen met a British detachment on its way to capture a cache of arms at Concord, and the American **War of Independence** had well and truly begun.

Thomas Paine

One of the writers who contributed most directly to the transformation of the colonists from British subjects to revolutionary citizens was **Thomas Paine**. He emigrated to America from England in 1774, with a letter of introduction from Benjamin Franklin in his pocket. He did so at a time when print culture was flourishing in the British Atlantic world of which America was a part. As Edward Larkin has demonstrated, magazines were a relatively new form of publication which included essays on a variety of subjects, and had been invented by London printer Edward Cave in the 1730s. Franklin's letter of introduction enabled Paine to be hired as editor of one such publication, the *Pennsylvania Magazine* (see Larkin, 2004, pp. 11–14). Another format which encouraged the circulation of ideas was the political pamphlet. It was this format that Paine used in 1776 to publish his *Common Sense*, which perhaps more than any other text prepared public opinion in the colonies to accept the notion of a separation from Great Britain.

In order to encourage colonists who still considered themselves as British subjects to countenance the idea of separation, Paine uses the familial discourse so dear to colonial writers. He does so very skillfully by means of a developmental narrative, asserting that as the colonies have attained maturity, the "protection" of the Mother Country is obsolete. He adds, moreover,

> We may as well assert, that because a child has thrived upon milk, that it is never to have meat, or that the first twenty years of our lives is

---

[1] From Ralph Waldo Emerson's "Concord Hymn."

to become a precedent for the next twenty. [...] We have boasted the protection of Great Britain, without considering, that her motive was *interest* not *attachment*; that she did not protect us from our enemies on our account, but from her enemies on her own account, from those who had no quarrel with us on any other account, and who will always be our enemies on the same account. Let Britain waive her pretensions to the continent, or the continent throw off the dependence, and we should be at peace with France and Spain were they at war with Britain [...] But Britain is the parent country, say some. Then the more shame upon her conduct.

(Castillo and Schweitzer, 2001, p. 518)

In short, America had come of age. The impact of Paine's pamphlet, which was circulated widely throughout the colonies, was incalculable. George Washington commented in a letter to a friend that the sound reasoning in *Common Sense* would persuade most readers of "the Propriety of a Seperation," later adding in a subsequent message "by private Letters which I have lately received from Virginia, I find common sense is working a powerful change there in the Minds of many Men" (quoted in Larkin, 2004, p. 7).

Thomas Jefferson and the Declaration of Independence

After these events, and given the groundswell of public opinion, the Continental Congress organized a committee to draw up the **Declaration of Independence**, which was written by **Thomas Jefferson** and proclaimed on July 4, 1776. Jefferson, in many ways, embodies the virtues and personal contradictions of the Revolutionary generation. He was born in 1743 in Albemarle County, Virginia. His father was a planter and surveyor, from whom he inherited more than 5,000 acres of land, and his mother was a Randolph, one of the First Families of Virginia. He studied at the College of William and Mary, in Williamsburg, with William Small, a Scotsman who introduced him to the views of Enlightenment thinkers such as John Locke, Francis Bacon, and Sir Isaac Newton, and then went on to read law. As we have seen, it was a time of great revolutionary ferment, and Jefferson took part in the Virginia House of Burgesses and in the Continental Congress, but his most valuable role was not as a speaker of the eloquent stripe of Patrick Henry but rather as a writer and brilliant rhetorician.

The Declaration is by any standard an extraordinary document. The tone throughout is carefully calculated to present separation from Britain as a rational, carefully thought-out move which has only been taken as a result of extreme provocation. After a brief preamble, the Declaration states:

> We hold these truths to be self-evident: that all men are created equal; that they are endowed by their creator with certain inalienable rights; that among these are life, liberty, & the pursuit of happiness; that to secure these rights, governments are instituted among men, deriving their just powers from the consent of the governed; that whenever any form of government becomes destructive of these ends, it is the right of the people to alter or abolish it, & to institute new government, laying its foundation on such principles, & organizing its powers in such form, as to them shall seem most likely to effect their safety & happiness.
>
> (Castillo & Schweitzer, 2001, p. 525)

These ringing words have echoed down the years. And yet African slaves and Native Americans are excluded, as are women. Howard Zinn has commented that the point of observing that certain groups are outside the human rights proclaimed in the Declaration is not to lay an unfair burden on the past or to impose present-day mindsets on history, but rather to try to understand how the document functioned to mobilize certain groups of Americans and ignore others (Zinn, 2003, p. 73). Indeed, Jefferson had included a phrase (later removed) accusing King George III of transporting slaves from Africa and thwarting attempts to outlaw or restrain the slave trade. However, Jefferson himself owned large numbers of slaves all his life. One phrase which *was* included, however, accused the King of inciting Indian raids: "He has excited domestic insurrections amongst us, and has endeavoured to bring on the inhabitants of our frontiers, the merciless Indian Savages, whose known rule of warfare is an undistinguished destruction of all ages, sexes and conditions." As for women, as Zinn points out, the phrase "all men are created equal" was probably not designed to exclude women; they were simply deemed not worthy of notice.

Patriot and Tory lyrics

Both Patriots (as the Revolutionary troops were called) and Tories (British loyalists) were aware of the power of poetry and songs in mobilizing public support. One Loyalist song called **"Burrowing Yankees"** ridicules the revolutionaries as vermin to be eradicated:

> Ye Yankees who, mole-like, still throw up the earth
> And like them, to your follies are blind from your birth;
> Attempt not to hold British troops at defiance,
> True Britons, with whom you pretend an alliance.

It concludes with a sneer:

> And the time will soon come when your whole rebel race
> Will be drove from the lands, nor dare show your face;
> Here's a health to great *George*, may he fully determine,
> To root from the earth all such insolent vermin.
>
> (Moore, 1856, p. 34)

The Patriots, however, gave as good as they got. **Philip Freneau's "A Political Litany"** ends with a double-barreled blast at George III and his Prime Minister Lord North:

> From the caitiff, Lord *North*, who would bind us in chains,
> From a royal king Log, with this tooth-full of brains,
> Who dreams, and is certain (when taking a nap)
> He has conquered our lands, as they lay on a map.

> From a kingdom that bullies, and hectors, and swears,
> We send up to heaven our wishes and prayers
> That we, disunited, may freemen be still,
> And Britain go on—to be damned if she will.
>
> (Castillo & Schweitzer, 2001, pp. 568–9)

The War of Independence. The Articles of Confederation

The War of Independence lasted until 1781, when the British general **Charles Cornwallis** surrendered to the Continental Army under **George Washington**. Undoubtedly, the support of the French was crucial in ensuring the victory of the colonial troops, as was the military astuteness and resourcefulness of George Washington, who succeeded in molding groups of local militia into a cohesive fighting force. The **Treaty of Paris**, signed in 1783, signaled the formal end of the War. In it, the 13 English colonies were recognized as sovereign states.

How to best govern them was something else again. Initially, the fledgling Republic functioned as a loose confederation of sovereign states, under the **Articles of Confederation** framed by the delegates to the **Second Continental Congress (1775)**. This document reflected the Revolutionary generation's distrust of centralized government and its potential for tyranny. According to the Articles of Confederation, the states retained sovereignty over all aspects of government not specifically stipulated to the national government; among the latter were the capacity to wage war and conduct diplomatic negotiations. Such an arrangement was unwieldy, for many reasons: crucially, the central government did not have the capacity to levy taxes, and was obliged to obtain funding from the states, which was cumbersome in terms both of practical logistics and political sensibilities. Concerns also existed about asymmetries of power (and representation) between larger, more populous states whose economies were based on commerce and emerging industries, and less populous states where agricultural interests predominated.

The framing of the Constitution

Widespread dissatisfaction with the Articles of Confederation led delegates to meet in Annapolis in 1786 to discuss changes to the Articles that might improve conditions for trade. They took the decision to organize a conference in 1787 to amend the Articles, but subsequently it was determined that they would draft a Constitution. What emerged was a document proposing a tripartite system of government, with executive, legislative, and judicial branches; a system of checks and balances was designed to keep any one branch from becoming excessively powerful. The Constitution reflects the different constituencies of its framers. One issue, for example, was whether states should have equal representation in the legislative branch of government regardless of their population. The solution, called the **Great Compromise**, created a bicameral legislature, with a House of Representatives based on representation proportional to population and a Senate in which all states are equally represented.

This in turn raised the problem of whether slaves should be counted as human beings for effects of taxation and for calculating the number of Representatives to which a state was entitled. Predictably, the Southern delegates argued that five slaves should be counted as three-fifths of a human being for purposes of taxation, but as equal to whites for calculating representation. The bizarre arrangement that was reached came to be known as the **Three-Fifths Compromise**, in which five slaves counted as three persons for purposes both of taxation and representation. Slavery raised problems in other areas as well. One provision of the Constitution forbade congressional interference in the slave trade until 1808; another provided for the return of fugitive slaves. The drafting of the Constitution was completed in September 1787.

Federalists and Anti-Federalists

The Constitutional debates had highlighted some of the fault lines in the Early Republic. Its supporters, called **Federalists**, were for the most part those with interests that went beyond the local, particularly merchants with interstate interests and the urban workers who depended on them. For the Federalists, state governments were excessively subject to popular control and too easily swayed by the masses who did not respect the interests of property, thus threatening the stability of the nascent Republic. The **Anti-Federalists**, on the other hand, were deeply mistrustful of centralized, geographically distant power, feeling that local government would better defend the interests of citizens.

When the final text of the Constitution was sent to the states for ratification, there was a spate of Anti-Federalist articles in the popular press. One of the leading Federalists, **Alexander Hamilton**, addressed the objections voiced by the Anti-Federalists in a series of essays called the **Federalist Papers (1787–88)** in an attempt to mobilize public opinion. Although the lion's share were written by Hamilton, other papers were authored by James Madison and John Jay. The Federalist Papers offer a fascinating window into the worldview of some of the Founding Fathers and the nature of their concerns. In **Federalist Number 6**, for example, Hamilton takes a dark Hobbesian view of human nature, arguing that popular assemblies are "frequently subject to the impulses of rage, resentment, jealousy, avarice, and other irregular and violent propensities" and advocating a strong national government as a bulwark against factionalism and civil strife. In **Federalist No. 10**, Madison comments that power is most effectively wielded by a "chosen body of citizens, whose wisdom may best discern the true interest of their country, and whose patriotism and love of justice, will be least likely to sacrifice it to temporary or partial considerations." What emerges from these documents is a vision of government as something best left to economic and social elites, whose superior vision enables them to keep the horrors of mob rule at bay.

Subsequently, the Constitution was ratified by the states. Later, a series of amendments known as the **Bill of Rights** (based in part on the 1689 English Bill of Rights) were added. Noteworthy among these amendments are those enshrining freedom of religion, speech, assembly, and petition; the right to bear arms; the right to trial by jury; the rights of those accused of crimes; and the prohibition of cruel and unusual punishments.

In a few short years, the inhabitants of the 13 colonies had severed their ties with Britain. The transition from British subject to American citizen was not, however, without its difficulties, as we will see in the following chapter.

Chapter 5

The Struggle for Identity in Post-Revolutionary America

Introduction

The Declaration of Independence, with its ringing assertion that all men had the right to life, liberty, and the pursuit of happiness, had sown the winds in ways which its author Thomas Jefferson had perhaps not quite intended. The whirlwinds were not long in making themselves felt. The **French Revolution**, with its appeal to liberty, equality, fraternity, and basic human rights, swept away the Bourbon monarchy, with the heads of Louis XVI and Marie Antoinette falling to the guillotine in 1793. The ensuing Terror, under Robespierre and the Jacobins, claimed the lives of tens of thousands of French citizens accused of counterrevolutionary activities. Ultimately, a degree of stability was achieved under the Directory (1795–99), but when the Directors encountered opposition from royalists on the one hand and Jacobins on the other, the army stepped in to impose order, leading to the rise to power of Napoleon Bonaparte. In its initial phases, however, the French Revolution was genuinely revolutionary, unlike the American Revolution in which power remained for the most part in the hands of the property-owning elites. America's leaders thus faced the challenge, as we have seen in the previous chapter, of on the one hand meeting the expectations which had been raised by their stirring rhetoric, and on the other of ensuring that these expectations did not pose a serious challenge to their own hegemony. At the same time, they felt themselves to be under the obligation to prove their distance from Europe, while affirming the superiority of America and all things American.

This chapter focuses on three intellectual controversies in the Early Republic: the debate in which European and American intellectuals advocated or challenged notions of American inferiority to Europe; the issue of female equality; and the legal, political, and literary status of African-Americans and Native Americans. It concludes with a brief analysis of Gothic novelist Charles Brockden Brown.

Thomas Jefferson and the Debate of the New World

In the years following the American Revolution **Thomas Jefferson** took a very active part in the intellectual debates of his era. One of the most important of these was what came to be called the Debate of the New World, in which certain Enlightenment thinkers made sweeping allegations about the alleged inferiority of the human and animal species of the New World. Mary Louise Pratt (1992) explores the ways in which European science and its projects of hierarchical global classifications of species were used to naturalize European narratives of presence and authority. This classificatory enterprise did not limit itself to animal and plant species but to human ones as well, and often the nature of the New World was seen as somehow lesser or inferior. The Italian scholar Antonello Gerbi, in his definitive treatise *The Dispute of the New World*, analyzes this discourse of American inferiority in relation to Europe and traces it to the writings of the French naturalist the Comte de Buffon. According to Gerbi, Buffon was the first to articulate a generalized theory of American inferiority, in his descriptions of the alleged smallness and immaturity of American animals, the sexual frigidity of the indigenous peoples, and the cold and damp of the American climate. Other Enlightenment thinkers such as Hume, Voltaire, and the Abbé Raynal contributed to the debate. But it was indubitably the publication in Berlin in 1768 of **Cornelius de Pauw**'s *Recherches Philosophiques sur les Américains, ou Mémoires intéressantes pour server à l'histoire de l'espèce humain* that unleashed a violent polemic about the alleged inferiority not only of the plants and animals but also of the human beings of the New World (Gerbi, 1973, pp. 52–79).

De Pauw never set foot in the New World, but this did not prevent him from making sweeping assertions about New World nature. For him, both humans and animals had degenerated in the Americas, and were clearly smaller and weaker than their Old World counterparts. Many, he says, lack tails, dogs cannot bark, and the reproductive capacities of camels have, to use de Pauw's own term, become "deranged." He maintains that only animals such as spiders, snakes, and beasts of prey had become larger and had multiplied in the Americas; he adds, moreover, with disconcerting exactitude, that most other species were smaller by exactly one-sixth. The human beings of the New World were seen in even more negative terms, as inferior and degenerate. He characterized, for example, the monumental stone constructions of the Inca empire in Cuzco as "a heap of little huts" (Pauw, 1768, p. 185).

This polemic regarding the alleged inferiority of all things American broke out with equal vigor in the Anglophone Atlantic intellectual milieu of which Thomas Jefferson was very much a part. The Scottish Enlightenment historian **William Robertson**'s *History of America* (1777) draws heavily on the ideas of Buffon and de Pauw. For Robertson, American jaguars and pumas were "inactive and timid animals," and the indigenous peoples of America as well as the descendents of European settlers, were also denigrated. He describes New World natives as "feeble" and "indolent." But the first-generation descendants of European settlers, called Creoles, are attacked by Robertson as well, and are described as beings with "broken minds" due to the "enervating influence of a sultry climate" (Gerbi, 1973, pp. 158–60).

Thomas Jefferson, who read widely and who was familiar with the major intellectual debates of his day, was aware of the allegations of de Pauw and Robertson regarding the inferiority of the New World, and had very little time for either. Of de Pauw, he states: "Paw, the beginner of this charge, was a compiler from the works of others; and of the most unlucky description, for he seems to have read the writings of travellers, only to collect and republish their lies. It is really remarkable, that in three volumes 12mo of small print, it is scarcely possible to find one truth" (Jefferson, 1999, p. 267). His comments on Robertson are even more negative: "As to Robertson, he never was in America, he relates nothing on his own knowledge, he is a compiler only of the relations of others and a mere translator of the opinions of Monsieur de Buffon." The Comte de Buffon, however, is clearly the only natural philosopher for whom Jefferson had a modicum of respect, although he disagreed openly with many of his ideas.

Anglophone writers in the New World were vehement in their defense of New World nature. The **Hartford Wits (David Humphreys, Joel Barlow, John Trumbull, and Lemuel Hopkins)** describe in **"The Anarchiad"** (1786–787) a visit to something called "the Region of Preexistent Spirits" where they encounter the ghosts of thinkers who are about to appear on earth to denigrate the New World. The Abbé Raynal, de Pauw, the Comte de Buffon, and Robertson are parodied in heroic couplets as stay-at-home travelers who nonetheless make sweeping comparisons between European and New World nature without having a clue as to what they are talking about:

These shades shall late in Europe's clime arise
And scan new worlds with philosophic eyes:
Immured at home, in rambling fancy brave,
Explore all lands beyond th'Atlantic wave;
Or laws for unknown realms invent new codes,
Write natural histories for their antipodes;
Tell how th'enfeebled powers of life decay,
Where falling suns defraud the western day;
Paint the dank, steril globe, accurst by fate
Created, lost, or stolen from ocean late;
See vegetations, man, and bird, and beast,
Just by the distance squares in size decreased;
See mountain pines to dwarfish reeds descend
Aspiring oaks in pigmy shrub oaks end:
The heaven-topp'd Andes sink a humble hill –
Sea-like Potomac run a tinkling rill –
Huge mammoths dwindle to a mouse's size –
Columbian turkeys turn European flies; –
Exotic birds, and foreign beasts, grow small,
And man, the lordliest, shrink to least of all;
While each vain whim their loaded skulls conceive,
Whole realms shall reverence, and all fools believe.

(Humphreys et al., 1861, pp. 74–5)

In this climate, when in 1780 the Secretary to the French Legation in Philadelphia, François Marbois, sent Thomas Jefferson a series of queries related to the land, crops, social and political institutions, religion, and economy of Jefferson's beloved home state of Virginia, it would have seemed to afford him an ideal opportunity to refute those who sought to diminish the New World. He did so not in poetry but rather in the measured expository prose which would later become **Notes on the State of Virginia**. For Jefferson, Virginia was a representative section of North America, and in extolling the qualities of Virginia's flora and fauna he felt himself to be defending the entire continent against the slanders of European thinkers. The manuscript was sent to Marbois in 1781, and an English edition was published in 1787 in London.

The *Notes* are organized as responses to the 22 queries sent by Marbois (which Jefferson expands to 23) with topics ranging from Virginia's landscape and natural features, social and demographic characteristics, and ending with questions related to its economy. Jefferson sets out some of Buffon's ideas regarding the alleged superiority of Old World species: namely that those that are common to both the Old World and the New are smaller in the New, that indigenous species of the New World are smaller in size, that those domesticated in both have degenerated in America, and that New World species are fewer in number. According to Jefferson, the underlying issue is that Buffon believes that "the heats of America are less; that more waters are spread over its surface by nature, and fewer of these drained by the hand of man. In other words, that heat is friendly, and moisture adverse, to the production and development of large quadrupeds" (Jefferson, 1999, p. 44). He goes on to refute these ideas, stating that there is no reliable evidence regarding the temperatures of the Western Hemisphere; but that even if such evidence were available, there are no grounds to maintain that moisture limits the growth of species. He then offers extensive listing of the weights of animals found in both Europe and America, of those native to Europe or American only, and those which have been domesticated in both. In all cases, the American species are said to be greater in size.

Jefferson's arguments, up to this point, are couched in rational tones (in marked contrast to those of de Pauw and Robertson), and are buttressed by appeals to empirically verifiable experience. But in the end for Jefferson, as for his adversaries in Europe, sheer size was the paramount consideration. To drive home his point, Jefferson then tosses in the case of the American mammoth. To counter suggestions that bringing in an extinct species in support of his case might be a bit problematic, he adds:

> The bones of the Mammoth which have been found in America, are as large as those found in the old world. It may be asked, why I insert the Mammoth, as if it still existed? I ask in return, why I should omit it, as if it did not exist? Such is the oeconomy of nature, that no instance can be produced of her having permitted any one race of her animals to become extinct, of her having formed any link in her great work so weak as to be broken.
>
> (Jefferson, 1999, p. 47)

The bones to which Jefferson refers are those found in the great fossil repository of Big Bone Lick, discovered in Kentucky in the mid-eighteenth century. A collection of bones from this site were sent to London in 1766, and described with others by the English scientist Dr William Hunter in a paper published in 1768. The discovery of unidentified fossils caused very considerable interest among European scientists such as Hunter and Peter Collinson, the London merchant-naturalist. They had concluded that the tusks and molars found belonged to elephants and hippopotami. Jefferson, however, disagreed with their conclusion, stating:

> Whenever these grinders are found there also we find the tusks and the skeleton ... It will not be said that the hippopotamus and elephant came always to the same spot, the former to deposit his grinders, and the latter his tusks and skeleton ... We must agree, then, that these remains belong to each other, that they are of one and the same animal.
>
> (Jefferson, 1999, p. 45)

He thus concluded that both tusks and grinders belonged to an unknown species resembling the elephant, which he called a mastodon or mammoth.

Buffon's derogatory comments on American nature extended to the indigenous peoples of the Americas, whom he described as impotent, lacking in affection for their families, and possessing minute genitals. Jefferson vehemently defended all Americans against these charges. Regarding Indians, he remarks,

> I am able to say, in contradiction to this representation, that he is neither more defective in ardour, nor more impotent with his female, than the white reduced to the same diet and exercise: that he is brave, when an enterprise depends on bravery ... that his friendships are faithful to the utmost extremity; that his sensibility is keen, even the warriors weeping most bitterly on the loss of their children, though in general they endeavour to appear superior to human events; that his vivacity and activity of mind is equal to ours in the same situation. ...
>
> (Jefferson, 1999, p. 63)

He then goes on to defend the Americas against the Abbé Raynal's charges that the Western Hemisphere had not produced great men, whether in literature, the arts, science, or war, by citing the examples of George Washington, Benjamin Franklin, and the astronomer David Rittenhouse. He ends Query VI with a fusillade against the British:

> The spirit in which she wages war is the only sample before our eyes, and that does not seem the legitimate offspring either of science or of

civilization. The sun of her glory is fast descending to the horizon. Her philosophy has crossed the channel, her freedom the Atlantic, and herself seems passing to that awful dissolution, whose issue is not given human foresight to scan.

(Jefferson, 1999, pp. 70–1)

Jefferson's *Notes on the State of Virginia* embody many of the quandaries of national allegiance and personal identity which Americans faced at the time of the Revolution and the early American republic. Jefferson had the greatest admiration for the thinkers of the Scottish and European Enlightenments, and his intellectual frames of reference were clearly European in nature. At the same time, however, as an American Creole (the definition of Creole, in this instance, being a person of European descent born in the New World), and as a postcolonial subject, he clearly viewed these attacks on New World nature and on the power and virility of the human beings of the Americas as direct affronts to himself and his fellow citizens. Regrettably, the vigor with which Jefferson defends the natives of the New World does not extend to slaves and their descendants; although he was capable of mounting a spirited challenge to certain currents in Enlightenment natural science, he was unable to see the injustice of certain Enlightenment ideas on race and racial taxonomies. Regarding Americans of African descent, he states:

Deep rooted prejudices entertained by the whites; ten thousand recollections, by the blacks, of the injuries they have sustained; new provocations; the real distinctions which nature has made; and many other circumstances, will divide us into parties, and produce convulsions which will probably never end but in the extermination of the one or the other race.

(Jefferson, 1999, p. 145)

In the subsequent decades, Jefferson's dark forebodings of sectional conflict would prove grimly accurate, as events would demonstrate.

Royall Tyler

In other writing emerging in the early years of the American republic, one encounters over and over again the concern with what exactly it meant to be an American citizen rather than a British colonial subject. A prime example of this is **Royall Tyler**'s play ***The Contrast***. Tyler had fought with the Continental Army in the War of Independence, and in 1787 he was involved in suppressing Shays's Rebellion, an uprising of farmers seeking to assert land rights. Tyler had gained a degree in law from Harvard University before the Revolution, but his first love was always literature. He is best known for his novel *The Algerine Captive* (**1797**) and his play *The Contrast*, which opened in New York in April 1787.

Allegedly inspired by Sheridan's *The School for Scandal*, *The Contrast* highlights the difference between American simplicity and rectitude and European decadence. In the Prologue, Tyler states his wish to focus on American themes and locales:

> Our Author pictures not from foreign climes
> The fashions or the follies of the times;
> But has confin'd the subject of his work
> To the gay scenes – the circles of New York.

He continues,

> On native themes his Muse displays her pow'rs;
> If ours the faults, the virtues too are ours.
> Why should our thoughts to distant countries roam
> When each refinement may be found at home?
>
> (Tyler, 1887, p. xxxviii)

The protagonist, Colonel Manly, is (as his surname implies) the embodiment of republican masculinity and rectitude, in contrast with the effete Billy Dimple, an Anglophile fop with a penchant for seducing innocent young ladies. Dimple flirts outrageously with two flighty young women, Manly's sister Charlotte and her friend Letitia, although he is engaged to yet another, the grave and virtuous Maria, who has agreed to marry him out of deference to her father's wishes. Manly, who had fought with Washington's Continental Army, is in love with Maria. The perfidious Dimple loses his money and jilts Maria in order to marry Letitia, a wealthy heiress, although he perseveres in his attempts to seduce Charlotte. When Maria's father learns of her suitor's treachery, he gives his blessings to Manly's courtship of his daughter. Dimple gets his just deserts when Letitia breaks their engagement on learning of his pursuit of Charlotte. He exits with a priggish sneer: "Ladies and gentlemen, I take my leave; and you will please to observe in the case of my deportment the contrast between a gentleman who has read Chesterfield and received the polish of Europe and an un-polished, untravelled American" (Tyler, 1887, p. 104). But the last word is left to the impossibly virtuous Manly as the curtain falls: "I have learned that probity, virtue, honour, though they should not have received the polish of Europe, will secure to an honest American the good graces of his fair countrywomen, and I hope, the applause of THE PUBLIC" (p. 107).

Women Writers in the Early Republic

Abigail Adams

The fair countrywomen to whom Manly alludes, however, were excluded from direct political participation in the Early Republic. One highly intelligent and articulate woman, Abigail Adams, wrote on the eve of the Revolution to her husband John, who later would become America's second president:

> I have sometimes been ready to think that the passion for Liberty cannot be Equally Strong in the Breasts of those who have been accustomed to deprive their fellow Creatures of theirs ... I long to hear that you have declared an independancy – and by the way in the new Code of Laws which I suppose it will be necessary for you to make I desire you would Remember the Ladies, and be more generous and favourable to them than your ancestors. Do not put such unlimited power into the hands of the Husbands. Remember all Men would be tyrants if they could. If particular care and attention is not paid to the Ladies we are determined to foment a Rebelion, and will not hold ourselves bound by any Laws in which we have no voice or Representation.
>
> (Castillo and Schweitzer, 2001, p. 486)

In her historic appeal to "remember the ladies," Abigail Adams deftly deploys revolutionary rhetoric – the appeal against tyranny and the injustice of the notion that citizens are bound by laws which they have had no hand in framing – to good effect. Predictably, however, her husband dismissed her concerns:

> As to your extraordinary Code of Laws, I cannot but laugh. We have been told that our Struggle has loosened the bands of Government everywhere. That Children and Apprentices were disobedient – that schools

and Colledges were grown turbulent – that Indians slighted their Guardians and Negroes grew insolent to their Masters. But your Letter was the first Intimation that another Tribe more numerous and powerfull than all the rest were grown discontented ... Depend upon it, We know better than to repeal our Masculine systems. Altho they are in full Force, you know they are little more than Theory. We dare not exert our Power in its full Latitude. We are obliged to go fair, and softly, and in Practice you know We are the subjects. We have only the Name of Masters, and rather than give up this, which would completely subject Us to the Despotism of the Peticoat, I hope General Washington, and all our brave Heroes would fight.

(Castillo and Schweitzer, 2001, p. 487)

Although John Adams's tone is teasing and even affectionate, a certain uneasiness underlies his patronizing words. Clearly he had realized that putting the genie of social and gender equality back into the bottle would not be a simple task. Elsewhere in his correspondence it would seem that (contrary to what one might gather from the excerpt quoted above) he took his wife's ideas seriously, but was aware of their potentially radical impact.

Judith Sargent Murray

Another female advocate of equality for women in the Early Republic was **Judith Sargent Murray**, an influential playwright and essayist. Murray's best-known text is "**On the Equality of the Sexes**," published in the *Massachusetts Magazine* in 1790 (two years before **Mary Wollstonecraft**'s *A Vindication of the Rights of Woman*) and signed "Constantia." In it, she questions the notion that women are less able intellectually than men. Murray argues that intellectual powers can be divided into four types (imagination, reason, memory, and judgment); that women are equal to men in imagination and memory, and that only differences in education are responsible for alleged deficiencies in reason and judgment. She contends passionately that the souls of woman are equal to those of men, and are equally enlivened by the breath of God. To those who might suggest that women should settle for the joys of the hearth, she asks pointedly whether it is reasonable that an intelligent being, destined for heavenly joys contemplating the Divine, is only allowed to think of matters such as making pudding and sewing seams.

Women and the novel in the Early Republic

One genre which seemed to lend itself particularly well to the discussion of issues related to women and their status in the Early Republic was the novel. Cathy Davidson, in *Revolution and the Word* (1986) has argued brilliantly that novels afforded women access not only to education but also to a larger literary and intellectual milieu in which social and political issues of the time were debated. To be sure, the novel was initially viewed with misgivings as a corrupt and potentially subversive form. Rhys Isaac, referring to Virginia, has described the transition from a hierarchical society in which the social and economic elites served as arbiters of religion and legislation for a relatively less educated but literate population to a society in which the authority of leaders was increasingly put into question:

> The Great Awakenings, and the popular dissent they provoked, effectively wrested the Bible and its interpretation from the custody of the learned; the republican principle of popular sovereignty subverted the conception of higher authority embodied in the wisdom of learned justices; newspapers and pamphlets (increasingly promulgating divisive ideologies, and more and more frequently involving the vulgar in affairs formerly the preserve of the learned) combined with the newly invented book product of the 1750s, the sentimental novel, to turn the flow of print into a flood.
>
> (Isaac, 1988, pp. 248–9)

This questioning of authority certainly disconcerted America's literary establishment, as one can see in the often lurid and hysterical terms in which the novel as a genre was critiqued. Novels were viewed as subverting female virtue and promoting depravity of all sorts. As Davidson (1986, pp. 44–5) convincingly demonstrates, what was at stake was legitimacy: who exactly constituted the legitimate audience of literature and who were the legitimate heirs of the Revolution? Thus, she adds, female sexuality was fetishized and nationalized, and private, personal experience was rendered public, political, and thus subject to censorship and control.

The novel of seduction. Susanna Haswell Rowson and Hannah Webster Foster

One phenomenally successful female author was **Susanna Haswell Rowson**, whose novel **Charlotte Temple**, published in 1794, went through more than 200 editions, with an estimated readership of up to half a million. Rowson was a genuinely transatlantic author. She was born in Portsmouth (England), but her mother died shortly thereafter, and she was left in the care of relatives while her father went to Massachusetts. When she was four years old, her father sent for her, and she grew up in America. Her father's pro-English sympathies, however, made their position complicated, and eventually they were detained and taken as the result of a prisoner exchange to London. There she worked as a governess and began to write and publish her work. She married William Rowson, and the two decided to go onto the stage, touring in Britain and in the United States. Ultimately they settled in Boston, where Rowson established a school for young ladies.

As is the case with most novels of the genre, the Preface to *Charlotte Temple* states not only that the text which follows is a cautionary tale designed to prevent credulous young women from perdition at the hands of a seducer, but also that it is based in reality. The story is that of its eponymous heroine, Charlotte Temple, a schoolgirl who is led astray by an army officer called Montraville, with the aid of one of Charlotte's teachers, the perfidious Mademoiselle La Rue. (Interestingly in the context of European politics at the time, both villains have Francophone surnames.) After wrestling with her conscience, Charlotte elopes with Montraville to America, but there she is abandoned by her seducer, gives birth to a daughter, and dies in the most abject poverty. Although she has placed her trust in her suitor, she is betrayed by him: despite the social and political upheavals of the American Republic, it is ultimately the men who call the shots.

Another novel that describes seduction and abandonment is **Hannah Webster Foster**'s *The Coquette*, published in 1794. In it, Foster uses the epistolary form popular with many eighteenth-century novelists to relate the story, based on fact, of a distant cousin. In a series of letters between Eliza Wharton, the protagonist; her grave and virtuous friend Lucy Freeman; Peter Sanford, the rake who is Eliza's unreliable suitor; and others, yet another tale of a young woman led astray by male perfidy unfolds. And yet there is more to *The Coquette* than meets the eye. Eliza is a feisty young woman who is unwilling to settle for the boring elderly suitors arranged by her parents. She chafes against the restrictions of conventional marriage, and longs for a companionate relationship. Sanford ultimately marries an heiress, but nonetheless manages to seduce Eliza. She later becomes pregnant, and like Charlotte Temple dies in childbirth. The evil Sanford is fittingly punished: he spends his wife's inheritance and goes bankrupt, tormented by guilt over the death of Eliza, "the darling of my soul." In the pages of *The Coquette*, we find an intriguing and often subversive repertoire of attitudes toward female sexuality, education, and the institution of marriage at the end of the eighteenth century in America.

African-American Writing in the Early Republic

The words of the Declaration of Independence resonated not only with women but with other disenfranchised groups such as African slaves. In St Domingue, **Toussaint L'Ouverture** used the rhetoric of the French Revolution to advocate an end to slavery, and led a successful revolt against the slaves' white masters. This was, of course, the worst nightmare of slaveowners in the United States, who feared that their own slaves might follow Toussaint's example.

Prince Hall

One African-American activist, **Prince Hall**, who had organized a network of African-American Masonic lodges in Boston, evoked the revolt in Santo Domingo in a Charge to the African Lodge delivered in 1797. Denouncing the slave trade, he declares in ringing tones:

> Among these numerous sons and daughters of distress, I shall begin with our friends and brethren; and first let us see them dragg'd from their native country by the iron hand of tyranny and oppression, from their dear friends and connections, with weeping eyes and aching hearts, to a strange land and strange people, whose tender mercies are cruel; and there to bear the iron yoke of slavery and cruelty til death as a friend shall relieve them ... These same sort of traders may in a short time, in the like manner, bewail the loss of the African traffick, to their shame and confusion: and if I mistake not, it now begins to dawn in some of the West-India islands.
>
> (Castillo and Schweitzer, 2001, p. 510)

Jupiter Hammon

Other African-American writers, however, advocated accommodation to existing power structures. For many, conversion to Christianity allowed them access to a public voice which otherwise would almost certainly have been silenced.

One such was **Jupiter Hammon**, who was born a slave to a family in New York. Hammon's prose and verse reveal some of the dilemmas faced by writers of color. In his sermons, there is a clear awareness of the political and ethical autonomy of African-Americans when he takes the moral high ground and calls for his fellow blacks to become an example of virtue to the nation as a whole. To the present-day reader, however, Hammon can come across as servile, with his constant acknowledgments of his status as a servant to several generations of the Lloyd family. And yet it is important to keep in mind that he was dependent on them not only for his livelihood but also for the publication of his work. This framing of African-American writing by a legitimizing invocation of white authority and sanction to publish would continue until Emancipation in 1863.

Phillis Wheatley

Phillis Wheatley provides an even more complex example of how difficult it was to navigate the shoals of ethnic and racialized identities in the Early Republic. As a child she was kidnapped by slavers from her home in Gambia and taken to America on board the ship *Phillis*, for which she was named. On arriving in Boston, she was purchased by John and Susannah Wheatley. In the Wheatley household, she was treated humanely and taught initially to read and write, and then was allowed to study Latin, history, geography, religion, and English literature. In her poetry, we encounter allusions to her African origins along with neoclassical and biblical references, reflecting both her economic status as slave and her acculturated Christianized American identity.

The emergence of Wheatley's poetry into the public realm posed a frontal challenge to the rigid racial and gendered divisions of Early America (Erkkila, 1993, p. 229). In a poem to the Earl of Dartmouth, Wheatley compares British tyranny in America to the suffering she had personally experienced as a child:

> I, young in life, by seeming cruel fate
> Was snatch'd from Afric's fancy'd happy seat:
> What pangs excruciating must molest
> What sorrows labour in my parent's breast?
> Steel'd was the soul and by no misery mov'd
> That from a father seiz'd his babe belov'd:

> Such, such my case. And can I then but pray
> Others may never feel tyrannic sway?
>
> (Castillo and Schweitzer, 2001, p. 588)

Here, with quiet dignity, Wheatley invokes the powerful image of a family torn apart by the tyranny of slavery. The word "Steel'd" describes not only the lack of compassion of the slavers who were her captors, but also evokes the steel fetters with which slaves were chained.

In a later poem, "On Being Brought from Africa to America," she begins by stating that in Africa, her "pagan" land, she had not known salvation. But then she turns this rhetoric on its head with an elegant denunciation of racism and a radical assertion of equality:

> Some view our sable race with scornful eye,
> "Their colour is a diabolic dye."
> Remember, *Christians*, *Negros*, black as *Cain*,
> May be refin'd, and join th'angelic train.
>
> (Wheatley, 1838, p. 48)

In her own time, Wheatley experienced racism directly in her adopted country. Although her poems were published in London under the patronage of the Countess of Huntingdon, and a second volume went through at least four printings in England, her work did not sell well in Boston and was not well received by critics. Thomas Jefferson, who owned many slaves, scoffed, "Religion indeed has produced a Phyllis Whately [sic]; but it could not produce a poet. The compositions published under her name are below the dignity of criticism" (Jefferson, 1999, p. 147). The vehemence of Jefferson's words is comprehensible when one realizes that Wheatley (and other African-American writers) were the living refutation of the existing racialized hierarchies that underpinned the slave-owning system of which Jefferson himself was a part. Wheatley died in poverty and obscurity.

Lemuel Haynes

Another African-American writer whose work is imbued with the discourse of Christian redemption and Revolutionary rhetoric was **Lemuel Haynes**. Haynes fought with the Continental Army in the American Revolution, and later became a minister. In **"Liberty Further Extended:**

Or Free Thoughts on the Illegality of Slave-keeping" (c. 1778), he argues passionately for abolition, asking angrily:

> Shall a mans Couler Be the Decisive Criterion, whereby to Judg of his natural right? Or Because a man is not of the same couler with his Neighbour, shall he Be Deprived of those things that Distinguisheth him from the Beasts of the Field? ... I would ask, whence is it that an Englishman is so far Distinguished from an Affrican in point of Natural privilege? Did he receive it in his origenal constitution? Or By Some Subsequent grant? Or Does He Bost of some higher Descent that gives him this pre-heminence? For my part I can find no such revelation. It is a Lamantable consequence of the fall, that mankind, have an insatiable thirst after Superorety one over another.
>
> (Castillo and Schweitzer, 2001, p. 575)

Native Americans. Samson Occom

Native Americans were also forced to struggle with the gap between egalitarian rhetoric and on-the-ground reality in the early United States. One of the earliest autobiographies by a Native American is that of **Samson Occom**, who belonged to the Mohegan tribe, a group whose numbers had been drastically reduced as a result of epidemics and the wars of the seventeenth century. In his *Short Narrative of My Life* (1768), Occom describes his childhood, his conversion to Christianity, his activities teaching Indian children to read and write, and his anger at the discrimination he experienced as a missionary when he earned in 12 years what a white missionary earned in one. His best known text, however, was a sermon preached in 1772 on the occasion of the execution of Moses Paul, a fellow Indian. Paul, after being thrown out of a local tavern for drunkenness, murdered the next person to leave – unluckily for Paul, a prominent citizen called Moses Cook. On being condemned to death by hanging, he wrote to Samson Occom to ask him to give the sermon that would immediately precede his execution.

Executions, and execution sermons, usually drew a large crowd, and this afforded Occom a rare opportunity to address a large and ethnically diverse audience consisting of Moses Paul himself, the Church authorities, white citizens, and Indians. Obviously, however, it was a complicated remit given the racial politics involved, and he was obliged to appeal to very diverse constituencies. The sermon, based on Romans 6:23 ("For the wages of sin is death, but the gift of God is eternal life through Jesus Christ our Lord") begins with a hellfire and brimstone meditation on the nature of sin and physical and spiritual death. But then he comments that death and sin are the great equalizers of humanity: "let them be who they will, great or small, honourable or ignoble, rich or poor, bond or free. Negroes, Indians, English, or of what nation soever; all that die in their sins must go to hell together." He invokes the redemptive power of divine love and grace, and turns to address the condemned man directly, calling him "my poor unhappy brother Moses," and saying: "You are the bone of my bone, flesh of my flesh. You are an Indian, a despised creature, but you have despised yourself; yea you have despised God more." Occom holds out to Moses Paul the hope of salvation through repentance and turns to address the audience. After describing the destructive consequences of alcohol, he adds, "here I cannot but observe, we find in sacred writ, a [woe] denounced against men who put their bottles to their neighbours mouth to make them drunk, that they may see their nakedness: And no doubt there are such devilish men now in our days, as there were in the days of old."[1] Here Occom is offering a not-so-veiled critique of traders who would sell whisky to Indians in order to get the better of them in trade. The sermon ends with a ringing exhortation to sobriety and to the renunciation of sin. Later, the text of the sermon was published to widespread acclaim. Occom himself, however, died in poverty.

Gothic Fiction: Charles Brockden Brown

As the eighteenth century drew to a close, and in the context of the turmoil sweeping across Europe, writers on both sides of the Atlantic began to question the validity of Enlightenment rationality. The European gothic, with its evocation of sinister castles, crumbling ruins, and ancestral curses, embodied the fears of cultures rocked by the winds of historical change. In the United States **Charles Brockden Brown** was the leading exponent of Gothic fiction, a literary mode which was singularly appropriate to evoke the suppressed fears of a nation which itself had emerged as the result of a revolution, and in which social structures and gender roles were

---

[1] The sermon is reproduced in full at http://www.learner.org/amerpass/archive/9000s/9024.pdf.

experiencing far-reaching changes. In two essays titled **"Walstein's School of History"** and **"The Difference between History and Romance,"** Brown sets forth his views on the writing of fiction, suggesting that novels blend fiction and historical events in order to place the characters in moments of historical stress or rupture.

Brown had grown up as a Quaker in Pennsylvania, and for this reason had been exposed from an early age to notions of female equality, with women often taking an active role in Meeting; in his feminist dialogue *Alcuin* (1798) he uses the ideas of Romantic radicals William Godwin and Mary Wollstonecraft to advocate women's rights. In *Wieland* (also published in 1798), allegedly based on a multiple murder in upstate New York, Brown describes how the novel's eponymous protagonist is driven insane by religious obsession and by the machinations of an evil ventriloquist who persuades him he is hearing divine voices, leading him to kill his wife and children.

Arthur Mervyn (1799) reveals fears of the rapid urbanization which the United States was experiencing, in the story of a young man from the country and his misadventures; the novel is notable for its description of the 1793 yellow fever epidemic. *Edgar Huntley: or Memoirs of a Sleep-Walker*, also published in 1799, is one of the first novels to address the theme of settler–Indian violence on the frontier, and describes one Quaker man's sleepwalking into confrontation with the dreaded indigenous Other. This topos of violence in the American wilderness would, as we shall see in the following chapter, become a compelling motif in American nineteenth-century writing.

Chapter 6

American Expansion and the Transcendentalists

But form to lend, pulsed life create,
What unlike forms must meet and mate.

("Art," Herman Melville)

Introduction

The couplet by Herman Melville quoted above is an apt description not only of the act of poetic creation, but also of the cauldron of divergent "races," ethnicities, and ideologies in the early United States. In the first decades of the nineteenth century, the republic of small farmers envisioned by Jefferson was rapidly changing into an industrialized nation, with cities linked by road, rail, and navigable lakes and rivers. In the years from 1760 to 1820, the population of the 13 colonies (later the 13 states) went from 1,500,000 to 9,500,000. In 1803, the young republic purchased the Louisiana territory, dramatically increasing the size of the nation. The nature of its economy was also undergoing a rapid transformation. This accelerated change also made itself felt in the area of politics. Power was drifting away from the elites of Virginia and the Northeast; although the vote was still restricted to adult white males, the electorate had expanded far beyond the landed gentry and wealthy merchants.

This was demonstrated in the election of 1828, when the rough-hewn General **Andrew Jackson** was elected to the Presidency. Old Hickory, as he was known, won by a substantial margin, and on the day of his inauguration a boisterous crowd of his supporters invaded the White House to celebrate his victory and were only induced to leave when vats of (presumably alcoholic) punch were placed outside on the lawns. One prominent politician, **Daniel Webster**, was bemused by the hubbub created by the aura of Jacksonian celebrity, remarking, "I have never seen such a crowd here before," adding, "Persons have come from five hundred miles to see General Jackson" (quoted in Brogan, 1999, p. 273). The Jacksonian years saw the consolidation of the spoils system, a politics of patronage in which each election heralded the dismissal of all office holders of the defeated party and a wave of appointments based on political affiliations with the victors. Hugh Brogan (1999, p. 269) points out pithily, "it was no use pretending that American politics in the nineteenth century was clean. It was as thoroughly, recklessly, unscrupulously, and joyously corrupt as the politics of wicked old eighteenth-century Britain (from which many of its practices were inherited.)" The complex and contradictory character of American writing in the nineteenth century thus reflects this turbulent atmosphere of political, social, and intellectual ferment.

Washington Irving

One writer who captures the *zeitgeist* of this historical moment of trans-formation from colony to nation is **Washington Irving**. In his short story **"Rip van Winkle,"** published in the collection ***The Sketch Book* (1819)**, Irving begins his narrative with a framing paragraph suggesting that the tale which follows has been found among the papers of "the late Diedrich Knickerbocker, an old gentleman of New York, who was very curious in the Dutch history of the province." Rip van Winkle is described as good-natured, lazy, and henpecked, descended from the first Dutch settlers who had accompanied Peter Stuyvesant. The village in which he lives is depicted as a sleepy place where Rip and other idlers gather in front of the village inn, under the portrait of George III. One day, fleeing from his shrewish wife, Rip van Winkle takes refuge in the Catskill Mountains with his faith-ful dog Wolf, where he hears what he thinks are peals of thunder. In a lonely glen, he encounters a group of men who remind him of figures in an old Flemish painting, playing at ninepins in a melancholy silence. He drinks their wine and falls into a profound slumber. On awaking, he finds that his well-oiled gun has somehow been transformed into a rusty old firelock, and suspects his companions of playing a practical joke upon him as he slept; his dog Wolf has vanished. Going into the village, he fears his wife's wrath, but suddenly realizes that he does not recognize a single person. He himself is unrecognizable, since his beard has grown a foot. His house is a desolate ruin, and he sees a starving dog who resembles Wolf, who snarls at him. The village itself has changed beyond recognition. The village inn has been replaced by the Union Hotel; the tree in the town square has vanished and in its place stands a pole where a flag waves, "a singular assemblage of stars and stripes." Even the image of King George III has been transformed, and in its place is the image of a man holding a sword rather than a scepter, with letters underneath proclaiming "General Washington." The villagers also seem different, far busier and more argu-mentative, brandishing words like "Bunker Hill" and "Heroes of '76," which Rip fails to understand. One of them demands to know whether Rip van Winkle is Federalist or Democrat, and when he replies that he is a loyal subject of the King, he is nearly lynched as a British sympathizer. He is saved by a woman who turns out to be his daughter, who had believed him to be dead. The story ends with the revelation that Rip van Winkle has been asleep for 20 years, and ultimately he is welcomed by his neighbors and restored to the bosom of his family. A framing paragraph at the end speaks of old legends of the Catskills, which are said to be haunted not only by the Dutch settlers but also by the spirits of Native Americans. Irving's Back to the Future tale, with its portrayal of not only temporal but social and political confusion, is a vivid evocation of a community in the grip of sweeping change, morphing from colony into nation, still haunted by the ghosts of its colonial past.

Cooper, Native Americans, and the Frontier Romance

Jacksonian "democracy" created other ghosts as well. One of the writers who portrays most vividly the story of the collision of civilizations on the American frontier is **James Fenimore Cooper**, one of the most popular nov-elists of nineteenth-century America. Written over a period of nearly three decades, Cooper's five **Leatherstocking** novels describe the complex inter-actions between settlers, Native Americans, and the American landscape.

Cooper's family had been early settlers in upstate New York and were the founders of Cooperstown, where Fenimore Cooper was taken as an infant. *The Pioneers* (1823), Cooper's first novel in the Leatherstocking series, draws on some of his childhood experiences on the rapidly dis-appearing Northeastern frontier. It has been suggested that the protagonist of the novel, the frontier hero Natty Bumppo (also known as Leatherstocking, Hawkeye, Pathfinder, and Deerslayer) was modeled on an old hunter whom Cooper had known as a child; others contend that the legendary frontier hero Daniel Boone may have served as a model for Cooper's pro-tagonist. Whatever the case, Natty Bumppo's complicated relation with nature and "civilization" epitomizes many of the contradictions of one of the most powerful American myths: that of the frontier.

Natty Bumppo, and his Native American alter ego Chingachgook, are liminal figures who embody on the one hand the terror, and on the other the enormous attraction experienced by nineteenth-century Americans when faced with what they perceived as the seductive anarchy of the American landscape. Natty has lived out the dream/nightmare of genera-tions of colonists and settlers, and has "gone Indian." He lives in close companionship with Chingachgook (or Great Serpent of the Delawares), a Native American chief who embodies Rousseauvian ideals of Noble Savagery, of uncorrupted humankind in a state of nature. Natty wears buckskin clothes and lives in the forest; he denounces what he perceives as the corruption of his paradise by successive waves of settlers, but at the same time constantly reaffirms his allegiance to "white" civilization, with constant references to his own whiteness and racialized identity. Similarly, in **Pioneers** Chingachgook lives in the no-man's-land between cultures; he has been converted to Christianity by Moravian missionaries and is known as Indian John, the last survivor of a tribe that has been decimated. But the two characters veer disconcertingly between very disparate worlds. In one episode set in a local tavern, Indian John begins after a few too many drinks to intone Native American chants which tell of slain warriors and battles. He morphs from the sad relic of a lost civilization, the Noble dying Savage, into something altogether different:

> Mohegan continued to sing, while his countenance was becoming vacant, though, coupled with his thick bushy hair, it was assuming an expression very much like brutal ferocity. His notes were gradually becoming louder, and soon rose to a height that caused a general cessa-tion in the discourse.
>
> (Cooper, 1985, p. 165)

Indian John, the Noble Savage remnant of a vanishing race, who has been tamed by ideology and historical events, is transformed for a moment into Chingachgook, the threatening Violent Savage, who represents a pow-erful threat to settlers and their "civilizing" mission. But Chingachgook/ Indian John is once again rendered impotent by rum, and collapses in a drunken stupor.

The saga of Natty and Chingachgook is overlaid by a stock romantic plot in the mode of Sir Walter Scott, complete with two star-crossed lovers. One is Elizabeth, the daughter of Judge Temple, a powerful local land-owner who embodies the advance of settlement and of laws; the other is Oliver Edwards, a mysterious young man who initially is thought to be the offspring of an Indian agent and a Native American woman. After a series of dramatic events (including the death of Chingachgook in a forest fire), Edwards is revealed to be the son of a Tory sympathizer who was Temple's close friend and who had entrusted his estates to him at the time of the Revolution; he is thus the legitimate heir to the lands which are the basis of Temple's fortune. Once it is established that Edwards has no Indian blood and has "legitimate" title to the land (at least in the eyes of the settlers who had expelled Native Americans from their land), the path is cleared for the two young lovers to wed. Edwards's admiration for Natty Bumppo and his attempts to emulate the latter's free frontier lifestyle are thus transformed from a rejection of European settler culture into a youthful peccadillo paralleling his own transformation from frontiersman/ hunter into "civilized" married man. At the end of the novel, Natty departs westward in search of the solitude of the forests of the Great Lakes.

Throughout the novel, Natty Bumppo's relationship with nature is contradictory. On the one hand, he deplores the wholesale destruction of the natural environment by the encroaching waves of settlers. Cooper describes how the entire village of Templeton pours into the fields to slaughter the enormous numbers of pigeons that darken the sky. Finally, one man brings out a cannon:

> So prodigious was the number of the birds, that the scattering fire of the guns, with the hurling of missiles, and the cries of the boys, had no other effect than to break off small flocks from the immense masses that continued to dart along the valley, as if the whole creation of the feathered tribe were pouring through that one pass. None pretended to collect the game, which lay scattered over the fields in such profusion as to cover the very ground with the fluttering victims.

Leatherstocking is appalled at the slaughter, but remains silent until he sees the cannon.

> "This comes of settling a country!" he said – "here have I known the pigeons to fly for forty long years, and, till you made your clearings, there was nobody to skear or to hurt them. I loved to see them come into the

woods, for they were company to a body; hurting nothing; being, as it was, as harmless as a garter-snake. But now it gives me sore thoughts when I hear the frighty things whizzing through the air, for I know it's only a motion to bring out all the brats in the village at them. Well! the Lord won't see the waste of his creaters for nothing, and right will be done to the pigeons, as well as others, by-and-by."

(Cooper, 1985, p. 248)

The contrast between the gleeful slaughter of the pigeons by the villagers, with their grotesquely disproportionate use of the cannon and their vision of destruction for destruction's sake, and the nostalgia of Natty Bumppo for the vanishing moment when he lived in harmony with the pristine forests is stark. And yet Natty himself is never without his gun; he delights in the intricacies of the hunt and in slaying deer, turkeys, and panthers, though his acts are characterized either as the defense of helpless humans (usually female) or as necessary to ensure his own subsistence.

The complexity of Natty's character, and his attitudes toward the American landscape, have been analyzed extensively by critics. D. H. Lawrence, in *Studies in Classic American Literature*, does not mince his words in his analysis of the figure of the Deerslayer: "But you have there the myth of the essential white America. All the other stuff, the love, the democracy, the floundering into lust, is a sort of by-play. The essential American soul is hard, isolate, stoic, and a killer" (Lawrence, 1977, p. 68).

More recently Richard Slotkin (1973) has argued compellingly that the act of regeneration though violence against American indigenous people and the American landscape is the structuring metaphor of American experience. In the figure of Natty Bumppo, Cooper has created the stereotype of the rough, rugged, curiously asexual frontiersman who expresses his love of the American landscape by blowing it and its creatures to bits.

Indian Removal

In the decade following the publication of Cooper's *Pioneers*, one melancholy example of the violence carried out against the indigenous peoples of America unfolded in the United States South, where white settlers were attempting to expand into the homelands of the Cherokee, Creek, Choctaw, Chickasaw, and Seminole nations in order to cultivate cotton. Even before attaining the Presidency, Andrew Jackson was a strong advocate for the interests of these settlers, who viewed the indigenous inhabitants of the

Figure 6.1 Appearance of the Trapper to the Emigrants, from *The Prairie. The Cooper Gallery: Pages and Pictures from the Writings of James Fenimore Cooper*, ed. Susan Fenimore Cooper (New York: James Miller, 1865), p. 144.

region as obstacles to progress. He commanded a military detachment that defeated the Creeks in 1814, forcing this group to give up approximately 22 million acres of land in Georgia and Alabama. He then invaded Florida in pursuit of the Seminoles, who had given harbor to escaped slaves. In the years from 1814 to 1824, Jackson was responsible for negotiating several treaties through which Indian groups gave up their ancestral homelands in exchange for lands in the West. Few, however, actually moved to the West, and most attempted to adapt to changing conditions with a strategy of acculturation. **Elias Boudinot**, a representative of the Cherokee Nation, describes this process in **"A Letter to the Whites"** (1826) asking pointedly,

> What is an Indian? Is he not formed of the same materials with yourself? For "of one blood God created all the nations that dwell on the face of the earth." Though it be true that he is ignorant, that he is a heathen, that he is a savage; yet he is no more than all others have been under similar circumstances. Eighteen centuries ago, what were the inhabitants of Great Britain?[1]

He goes on to describe **Sequoyah**'s invention of a Cherokee syllabary, the translation of the New Testament into Cherokee, the organization of the Cherokee government, the existence of printing presses as arguments to prove the tribe's "civilized" status. These attempts to adapt to white culture through a strategy of acculturation availed the Cherokees absolutely nothing. Conflict came to a head following the drafting of the Cherokee Constitution in 1827. The Georgia legislature declared that the establishment of a Cherokee nation was unconstitutional, and extended the criminal and civic jurisdiction of the state into Cherokee lands (estimated at around five million acres in Northwest Georgia).[2]

The white land grab continued, and in 1830 Jackson sponsored new legislation called the **Indian Removal Act**, which gave the President power to negotiate removal treaties with Indian tribes. The mendacity and outright dishonesty of the Jackson administration in characterizing the Cherokees as nomadic hunters rather than sedentary farmers who lived in villages is really quite extraordinary (Green and Purdue, 2007, pp. 57–67). The Act essentially signaled the death of the notion of tribal sovereignty

---

[1] See http://nationalhumanitiescenter.org/pds/triumphnationalism/expansion/text3/addresswhites.pdf

[2] For a lucid account of Removal, see Green and Purdue (2007, p. 57).

east of the Mississippi. Cherokee historians Michael Green and Theda Purdue state the case succinctly: "Only detribalized, 'civilized' individual Indians could remain in the East, where they would be subject to the laws of the states in which they lived, even if those laws denied them basic civil liberties" (p. 61). In the winter of 1838, bayonet-pointing troops forced the Cherokees into stockades without giving them time to pack their belongings. In a forced march appropriately called the **Trail of Tears**, approximately 13,000 Cherokees were forced to leave their ancestral homelands and proceed on foot to Indian Territory (Oklahoma). More than a fourth died on the way of cold, disease, and hunger.

As the debate over Removal raged, **William Apess**, a mixed-race Pequot, published his essay **"A Looking-Glass for the White Man"** (1833). In it, he (like Boudinot) appeals in powerful terms to the common humanity of Indians and whites, and highlights the hypocrisy of whites who proclaim their Christian faith while oppressing Native Americans:

> If black or red skins, or any other skin of color is disgraceful to God, it appears that he has disgraced himself a great deal – for he has made fifteen colored people to one white, and placed them here upon this earth … Now let me ask you, white man, if it is a disgrace for to eat, drink and sleep with the image of God, or sit, or walk and talk with them? Or have you the folly to think that the white man, being one in fifteen or sixteen, are the only beloved images of God? Assemble all nations together in your imagination, and then let the whites be seated among them, and then let us look for the white, and I doubt not it would be hard finding them; for to the rest of the nations, they are still but a handful. Now suppose these skins were put together, and each skin had its national crimes, written upon it – which skin do you think would have the greatest?
>
> (Apess, 1992, p. 157)

Manifest Destiny

Anglo-America's hunger for land, however, continued unabated. Since there were competing claims to much of North American territory (from Native America groups, the British, and Mexicans), the United States justified its expansionist ideology in diverse ways: by invoking natural, God-given right, geographical predestination, virtuous industry, and the spread of democratic institutions (see Weinberg, 1935 and McDougall, 1997). An Illinois governor asked rhetorically in 1812: "Is one of the fairest portions of the globe to remain in a state of nature, the haunt of a few wretched savages, when it seems destined by the Creator to give support to a large population and to be the seat of civilization, of science, and of true religion?" (quoted in McDougall, 1935, p. 83). Only a year after the Cherokee Removal and the Trail of Tears, **John O'Sullivan** set forth in the *Democratic Review* the ideology of unlimited territorial expansion that would come to be known as **Manifest Destiny**:

> We are the nation of human progress, and who will, what can, set limits to our onward march? We point to the everlasting truth on the first page of our national declaration, and we proclaim to the millions of other lands, that the "gates of hell" – the powers of aristocracy and monarchy – "shall not prevail against it."
>
> The far-reaching, the boundless future will be an era of American greatness. In its magnificent domain of space and time, the nation of many nations is *destined* to *manifest* to mankind the excellence of divine principles; to establish on earth the noblest temple ever dedicated to the worship of the Most High – the Sacred and the True. Its floor shall be a hemisphere – its roof the firmament of the star-studded heavens, and its congregation an Union of many Republics, comprising hundreds of happy millions.
>
> (O'Sullivan, 1839)

O'Sullivan draws on the exceptionalist concepts of divine mission (as seen in Puritan discourse), Jeffersonian views of rational linear progress, and James Monroe's doctrine legitimizing political intervention in defense of American economic interests, in order to propound a vision of hemispheric hegemony. The doctrine of Manifest Destiny would cast a very long shadow indeed over American foreign policy in subsequent decades. Indeed, many would argue that its influence has continued in some circles until our own days.

Two years after O'Sullivan's seminal essay was published, James Fenimore Cooper published the last of the Leatherstocking tales, titled **Deerslayer**. In it, he returns to the youthful exploits of Natty Bumppo and Chingachgook in what may in part be an attempt to expiate America's collective sense of guilt over Indian Removal. This is particularly apparent in the episode in which Natty kills his first Indian. The dying man is afraid that Natty is about to scalp him, but the young Leatherstocking reaffirms his allegedly superior whiteness:

> "All inmity atween you and me's at an ind, red-skin," he said; "and
> you may set your heart at rest on the score of the scalp, or any further
> injury. My gifts are white, as I've told you; and I hope my conduct will be
> white also."

But the dying Indian forgives him. When he learns that Natty is called
Deerslayer, he implicitly condones his own death by bestowing upon his
killer the warrior name of Hawkeye:

> "Good!" he repeated, for this was an English word much used by the
> savages – "good" – young head; young *heart*, too. Old heart tough; no shed
> tear. Hear Indian when he die, and no want to lie – what he call him?"
>   "Deerslayer is the name I bear now, though the Delawares have said
> that when I get back from this war-path I shall have a more manly title,
> provided I can 'arn one."
>   "That good name for boy – poor name for warrior. He get better quick.
> No fear *there*" – the savage had strength sufficient, under the strong
> excitement he felt, to raise a hand and tap the young man on his breast
> – "eye sartain – finger lightning – aim, death – great warrior, soon. No
> Deerslayer – Hawkeye – Hawkeye – Hawkeye. Shake hand."
>
> (Cooper, 1993, p. 102)

They shake hands, and the Indian dies. In an inevitable progression,
Deerslayer is transformed into Indian Slayer. The rite of passage from
boyhood to manhood for Natty Bumppo is contingent upon his racialized
white ability to kill or eradicate whoever or whatever lies in his expansion-
ary path.

Catharine Maria Sedgwick

A different perspective on Native American–white relations can be found
in Catharine Maria Sedgwick's **Hope Leslie**, published in 1827, a year after
Cooper's **The Last of the Mohicans**. Sedgwick's novel is set during the
Pequot wars; as with Cooper, we find a portrayal of cultures in conflict,
overlaid by a conventional romantic plot with elements of the **Pocahontas**
legend. As in the early volumes of Cooper's *Leatherstocking* series, we
encounter two protagonists of different "races": Hope Leslie, who is
white, and Magawisca, a member of the Pequot tribe. But there are important differences as well. Hope Leslie and Magawisca are courageous and
daring, and a relationship of equals exists between the two women;

Magawisca's arm is severed when she intercedes with her father to save the life of a white man called Everell Fletcher, and Hope conspires at considerable risk to herself to liberate Magawisca and another Indian woman, Nelena, who have been unjustly incarcerated. When Hope's sister Faith, who had been taken captive by the Indians as a child, marries Magawisca's brother Oneco, Hope (unlike Cooper's Natty Bumppo, who was incapable of countenancing the notion of sexual union between the two races) finds the union unproblematic. Above all, the friendship between Hope and Magawisca is one of genuine sisterhood and mutual support. But at the end of the novel Sedgwick's protagonist remains constrained by sentiment and by the discourse of Manifest Destiny. Magawisca is revealed as yet another noble vanishing Indian, when she blesses the union of Everell Fletcher and Hope Leslie and disappears forever from their sight.

Transcendentalism

During a period of expansionist violence, it is perhaps unsurprising that many American writers and thinkers turned away from grim historical events toward continental philosophies of idealism. A major current of thought in Jacksonian America was **Transcendentalism**. In a way, much Transcendental thought reflects the Puritan conundrum about how the individual comes to apprehend truth and reality: whether it was revealed directly to the human heart (as in Anne Hutchinson's antinomian theology, discussed in Chapter 3), or whether it can be discerned through the sensory perception of ordinary experience. The prose produced by Transcendentalist writers reflects this ambivalence; indeed, the more literal-minded might be forgiven for reacting with despair on attempting to distill from the clouds and mist of Transcendental prose what exactly the group stood for. **Nathaniel Hawthorne** depicts this confusion admirably in his short story **"The Celestial Railroad"** (1843), in which he recasts Bunyan's *Pilgrim's Progress* as a journey on an allegorical railroad to heaven in the rapidly industrializing America of the nineteenth century:

> At the end of the valley, as John Bunyan mentions, is a cavern, where, in his days, dwelt two cruel giants, Pope and Pagan, who had strown the ground about their residence with the bones of slaughtered pilgrims. These vile old troglodytes are no longer there; but into their deserted

cave another terrible giant has thrust himself, and makes it his business to seize upon honest travellers and fatten them for his table with plentiful meals of smoke, mist, moonshine, raw potatoes, and sawdust.

Referring to the origins of Transcendental thought, Hawthorne adds,

He is a German by birth, and is called Giant Transcendentalist; but as to his form, his features, his substance, and his nature generally, it is the chief peculiarity of this huge miscreant that neither he for himself, nor anybody for him, has ever been able to describe them. As we rushed by the cavern's mouth we caught a hasty glimpse of him, looking somewhat like an ill-proportioned figure, but considerably more like a heap of fog and duskiness. He shouted after us, but in so strange a phraseology that we knew not what he meant, nor whether to be encouraged or affrighted.

(Hawthorne, 1987, p. 326)

Hawthorne's tone is satirical, but it is indeed the case that the roots of American Transcendentalism lie in Germany and in England. **Immanuel Kant**, in his *Critique of Pure Reason* (1781) restores the primacy of the human mind as more than a passive receptacle of sensory impressions, suggesting that it actively shapes our perceptions of external reality. This dimension of Kantian thought was further developed in **Samuel Taylor Coleridge**'s *Aids to Reflection*, an edition of which was published in America in 1829. In it, Coleridge distinguishes between Reason (the inner intuitive capacity which is the source of moral judgment) and Understanding, which renders sensory data intelligible and meaningful.

This distinction enabled the young dissident Unitarian ministers of New England to have their cake and eat it too: without abandoning the Enlightenment notions of rationality, scientific enquiry, and tolerance (as products of human understanding), they were able to view the religious beliefs of Unitarianism as transcendent truths emerging from Reason to the individual soul. The younger Unitarian clergy (**Ralph Waldo Emerson, Frederick Henry Hedge, George Ripley**, among others) eventually formed a group known as the **Transcendental Club**, which met at regular intervals. In 1836, a small book titled *Nature* was published anonymously, though it later transpired that Emerson was the author. In it, the revolutionary ideas emerging from Europe were given a particularly American cast.

Ralph Waldo Emerson

Reading Emerson is an interesting experience. The man definitely had an ear for the good soundbite, and his ideas have been vastly influential in American politics as well as in the subsequent literary and intellectual life of the country. Emerson's essays are often irritatingly pointillistic, consisting of (often brilliant) *aperçus* and aphorisms strung together without discernible regard to logical or narrative sequence. In *Nature*, he sets out ideas that would be developed further in his subsequent work. Influenced by the ideas of the Swedish mystic **Emanuel Swedenborg**, Emerson argues that Nature is a vast text in which each object perceived by the senses corresponds to a moral truth. Consequently, human beings can apprehend the divine by interpreting the moral truths revealed by the contemplation and interpretation of Nature and her mysteries. This was particularly relevant for American postcolonial intellectuals who are trying to carve out an identity for themselves rooted in their own American terrain; if Nature was their primary text, they were freed from what Emerson and his contemporaries perceived as the worn-out constraints of European history and institutions. Emerson nails his colors to the mast in ringing terms:

> Our age is retrospective. It builds the sepulchres of the fathers. It writes biographies, histories, and criticism. The foregoing generations beheld God and nature face to face; we, though their eyes. Why should not we also enjoy an original relation to the Universe? Why should not we have a poetry and philosophy of insight and not of tradition, and a religion by revelation to us, and not the history of theirs? Embosomed for a season in nature, whose floods of life stream around and through us, and invite us by the powers they supply, to action proportioned to nature, why should we grope among the dry bones of the past, or put the living generation into masquerade out of its faded wardrobe? ... These are new lands, new men, new thoughts. Let us demand our own works and laws and worship.
>
> (Emerson, 1983, p. 7)

Emerson's belief that every natural fact had a corresponding spiritual meaning extends to language. He sets out the terms of his argument as follows:

1   Words are signs of natural facts;
2   Particular natural facts are symbols of particular spiritual facts;
3   Nature is the symbol of spirit.

(Emerson, 1983, pp. 14–19)

As we can see, this insistence on "accurate" use of language (that is, a language that is tied as closely as possible to facts and to the great text of nature) as a path toward spiritual truth has much in common with the Puritan aesthetic of plain speech.

Emerson's subsequent writing would develop these ideas even further. His oration to the Phi Beta Kappa society in 1837, titled "**The American Scholar**" has been characterized as America's intellectual Declaration of Independence. In it, he reiterates his advocacy of originality and his denunciation of imitation and servitude to the past, stating that "We have listened too long to the courtly muses of Europe," adding that the American scholar must become "Man Thinking" rather than one who parrots the thoughts of others. In his address to the Harvard Divinity School in 1838, he created a sensation with his allegation that the graduates were going to be part of a church that had become "an injuror of man," adding that Jesus, while he was a friend of humankind, was merely one of "the true race of prophets." Predictably, his comments were received with fury in some quarters. The Harvard theologian Andrews Norton accused Emerson and his contemporaries of "a restless craving for notoriety and excitement," thundering that his ideas were derived from those of "German speculatists" and "barbarians" as well as from "that hyper-Germanized Englishman, Carlyle."

Later, in his essay "**Self-Reliance**" (1841), Emerson continued to develop the notion of individual revelation and belief in self above all else: "To believe your own thought, to believe that what is true for you in your private heart, is true for all men, that is genius. Speak your latent conviction and it shall be the universal sense … Trust thyself: every heart vibrates to that iron string" (Emerson, 1983, pp. 260–1).

There is much that is appealing in Emerson's staunch appeal to positive thinking and trust in one's own beliefs, and one can understand its attractions for a nation that was attempting to deal with its own complex attitudes toward its European heritage in order to carve out its own postcolonial cultural turf. It is equally true, however, that this exacerbated American individualism, when it is not balanced by a sense of social responsibility, has done a great deal of harm over the years. As Richard Gray has pointed out, Emerson's unwillingness to contemplate seriously the possibility of evil could have worrying consequences.[3] And yet his notion that the poetic self could actually recreate and shape the world through words has had a lasting impact on American poetry and thought down to the present day.

Margaret Fuller

Another prominent Transcendentalist was the remarkable **Margaret Fuller**. Her father provided her with a solid if taxing education from a very early age, and Fuller was able to read and translate literary and philosophical works in four languages. After her father's death, she went into teaching, and in 1838 she moved to Boston. There she thrived in the intellectual atmosphere of the day, publishing a translation of Eckermann's *Conversations with Goethe* in 1839. In the following year she became editor of the Transcendentalist review *The Dial*, and earned a living by organizing "Conversations" for women, literary salons where women were able go beyond the limitations of conventional female education and discuss topics such as ethics, Greek mythology, and poetry. These proved so popular that Fuller was finally obliged to admit men.

Fuller's most famous work is **Woman in the Nineteenth Century**, published in 1845 at the instigation of **Horace Greeley**, editor of the *New York Tribune*. The style is reminiscent of Emerson's, but Fuller applies Emerson's ideas on self-actualization and self-improvement to the issue of women's rights. In an impassioned plea on behalf of the universal right to freedom, she derides those who would support the idea that human beings should be circumscribed to a particular sphere (in the case of women, the domestic sphere, as we shall see in Chapter 8), or indeed be treated as property rather than as persons, drawing compelling analogies between the plight of enslaved Africans and that of women. For Fuller, reality was in a constant state of flow or change, with radical consequences for gendered identities. Her thoughts on the subject have a remarkably contemporary ring:

> Male and female represent the two sides of the great radical dualism. But, in fact, they are perpetually passing into one another. Fluid hardens to solid, solid rushes to fluid. There is no wholly masculine man, no purely feminine woman ... History jeers at the attempts of physiologists to bind great original laws by the forms which flow from them. They make a rule; they say from observation what can and cannot be. In vain! Nature provides exceptions to every rule. She sends women to battle, and sets

---

[3] See Gray (2004, pp. 130–4) for a lucid discussion of Emerson's thought.

Hercules spinning; she enables women to bear immense burdens, cold, and frost; she enables the man, who feels maternal love, to nourish his infant like a mother.

(Fuller, 1998, pp. 68–9)

In 1846 Fuller left for Europe as a foreign correspondent, traveling to England and to Italy. There she interviewed writers and thinkers, including **Thomas Carlyle** and **George Sand**, and was caught up in the radical currents that were sweeping through Europe. She became involved with Italian revolutionary Giovanni Ossoli, to whom she bore a child called Angelo; the fact that Ossoli was 11 years younger scandalized many of the couple's friends. She and Ossoli and their infant son embarked for America in May 1850. Tragically, their boat was wrecked in a storm only 50 yards off Fire Island and sank; only Angelo's body was found. It is said that Henry David Thoreau spent five days combing the beach and searching for their remains or for Fuller's missing manuscripts. Her friend Sophia Hawthorne, in a letter to her mother, evokes the haunting image of Fuller on the sinking ship: "I dread to speak of Margaret. Oh, was ever anything so tragical, so dreary, so unspeakably agonizing as the image of Margaret upon that wreck alone, sitting with her hands upon her knees and tempestuous waves breaking over her! But I cannot dwell upon it … I wish at least Angelino could have been saved" (quoted in Mellow, 1980, p. 329). The reaction of Sophia's husband Nathaniel was less compassionate. Alluding to Fuller's liaison (or possibly marriage) with Ossoli, Nathaniel Hawthorne interpreted it as a sign of what he termed Fuller's moral and intellectual collapse, stating brutally, "tragic as her catastrophe was, Providence was, after all, kind in putting her, and her clownish husband, and their child, on board that fated ship" (quoted in Wallace, 1990, p. 213).

Nathaniel Hawthorne

Nathaniel Hawthorne is one of the most complex and fascinating writers of nineteenth-century America. As the above quote demonstrates, his attitude toward women was problematic to say the very least. And yet over and over again in his fiction, he creates wonderfully strong and charismatic female protagonists who challenge both the Puritan authorities of his ancestors' traditions and the Transcendental reformers of his own days.

Nathaniel Hawthorne was a direct descendent of Salem magistrate John Hathorne, who had presided over the **Salem Witch Trials**, and for him

Salem's dark legacy provided an opportunity to explore the sinister shadow side of the Puritan myth of America as exemplary, God-directed nation. In **"Young Goodman Brown"** (1854), Hawthorne's eponymous Puritan protagonist leaves his wife Faith to embark upon a mysterious errand in the forest, which is described as dark, eerie, and full of unseen hostile presences of Indians. On his way, he meets many eminent local citizens apparently heading for a sinister rendezvous in the wilderness. Finally, he hears a disconcerting murmur of voices, and shouts in despair, "Faith! Faith!" At this point, one of his wife's pink ribbons flutters down from a tree, and Goodman Brown reacts in fury and disillusionment, hastening toward what appears to be a Witches' Sabbath, where Faith is about to be received into the company of transgressors. On reaching the clearing where the ceremony is taking place, he exhorts her to look to heaven and resist Satan. Suddenly the company vanishes, leaving Goodman Brown alone in the night. The following morning he returns to Salem a somber and chastised man, uncertain of whether his dark vision had been merely a dream.

This is a richly textured story. In it, Hawthorne is evoking the hypocrisy of Puritan society with his picture of a life of external propriety and restraint in Salem village alongside an escape to darker passions in the depths of the forest, as well as revealing the ways in which the American landscape and its inhabitants have been demonized by the settlers. The story is also a meditation on the fallibility of spectral evidence, that is, accounts of specters which tormented their victims used as proofs against those accused of witchcraft. In "Young Goodman Brown," it is unclear whether the protagonist has witnessed unspeakable acts, or whether his visions were nightmares emerging from the depths of his own psyche.

It is Hawthorne's novel *The Scarlet Letter*, published in 1850, that is widely considered to be his masterpiece. It emerged from a trying time in his own life. In June 1849, Hawthorne, a Democrat, had in the best tradition of the spoils system been removed by the newly victorious Whigs from his employment as a surveyor in the Salem Customs House amid charges of corruption.[4] Less than two months later, his mother died. *The Scarlet Letter* is the product of a volatile mixture of coruscating rage at the political chicanery of Hawthorne's Whig adversaries, grief at his personal bereavement, anger at his birthplace of Salem, ambivalence and guilt about his own ancestors' role in its history, and deep concern about his own ability as a writer to support his growing family.

[4] See Mellow (1980, pp. 292–7) for a clear discussion of events.

Hawthorne opens the tale with a framing sketch describing the **Salem Customs House**. He describes with savage irony the decrepit veterans who owe their posts to political patronage:

> They spent a good deal of time, also, asleep in their accustomed corners, with their chairs tilted back against the wall; awaking, however, once or twice in a forenoon, to bore one another with the several thousandth repetition of old sea-stories, and mouldy jokes, that had grown to be pass-words and countersigns among them.
>
> (Hawthorne, 1988, pp. 12–13)

Hawthorne's description of the Customs House is not only ferocious but very, very funny, with its evocation of the reptilian mediocrity of the desiccated bureaucrats who were its inhabitants as they scuttle about the decaying wharves of Salem, which had lost much of its trade to the more prosperous ports of New York and Boston. The sketch also serves another function: Hawthorne uses it to tell the reader about a strange find, a scarlet letter A, among the papers of a predecessor, Surveyor Pue. What follows is the tale of Hester Prynne, one of the most memorable female protagonists in American fiction.

The novel is set in seventeenth-century Puritan Boston. It begins as Hester is brought from the town prison with her infant daughter in her arms and with the scarlet letter "A," for "Adulteress," emblazoned on her bosom. We learn that Hester's husband had sent her ahead to the Puritan settlement, and had later failed to appear, giving rise to conjectures that he had been lost at sea. In his absence, Hester has given birth to a child, but staunchly refuses to name the father, though she is forced to stand on the town scaffold and endure the obloquy of the crowd that surrounds her. Among them is her husband, who now goes by the name of Roger Chillingworth. He establishes himself as a doctor in Boston in order to exact revenge on his unknown rival. Hester manages to earn a living from her skills as a needlewoman, and lives with her little daughter Pearl on the edge of the community, dressing Pearl in the glowing jeweled colors that she has denied herself. Initially, she is treated with scorn and distrust by her neighbors, but her austere behavior and her kindness to those in need eventually earn her the town's respect. Her marginal status affords her a certain freedom, but it is not of the sort destined to bring her joy. Living in an isolated cottage by the sea, she gives herself over to philosophical speculation. First she thinks of the circumstances of the birth of her daughter Pearl and the consequences for not only the child but for Hester herself:

> Everything was against her. The world was hostile. The child's own nature had something wrong in it, which constantly betokened that she had been born amiss, – the effluence of her mother's lawless passion, – and often impelled Hester to ask, in the bitterness of heart, whether it were for ill or good that the poor little creature had been born at all.

This leads her to speculate about the situation of women in America, and leads her to the following dark conclusion:

> Was existence worth accepting, even to the happiest among them? As concerned her own individual existence, she had long ago decided in the negative, and dismissed the point as settled. A tendency to speculation, though it may keep woman quiet, as it does man, yet makes her sad. She discerns, it may be, such a hopeless task before her. As a first step, the whole system of society is to be torn down, and built up anew. Then the very nature of the opposite sex, or its long hereditary habit, which has become like nature, is to be essentially modified, before woman can be allowed to assume what seems a fair and suitable position.
>
> (Hawthorne, 1988, p. 113)

Eventually it is revealed that Pearl's father is none other than the Puritan minister Arthur Dimmesdale, who is tormented with guilt but who is unable to bring himself to publicly acknowledge his responsibilities to Pearl and to Hester. Hester's husband Chillingworth, who is possessed of a keen intelligence, manages to insinuate himself into Dimmesdale's ménage, and uses the opportunity to play upon the latter's sense of shame, causing him to become physically ill with repressed guilt. Hester, who had promised her husband not to reveal his identity, is alarmed at Dimmesdale's deterioration. The two meet in the forest, and Hester removes the Scarlet Letter. The lovers decide to flee. Their daughter Pearl, however, is distressed at seeing her mother without the letter, and so Hester dons it again in order not to raise suspicions among the Puritan community while she arranges passage on a ship to Europe. Disaster strikes when Chillingworth divines their intention and arranges to board with them. Dimmesdale mounts the scaffold to give the Election Sermon, and shortly thereafter he finally acknowledges Hester and Pearl – too late, because he dies shortly after. Hester and Pearl vanish and are said to travel in Europe, but ultimately Hester returns to take up the Scarlet Letter once more.

Figure 6.2 Hester, Dimmesdale, and Pearl on the scaffold, with Chillingwell below, from Nathaniel Hawthorne, *The Scarlet Letter* (New York: Grolier Club Edition, 1908), p 199.

Much critical ink has been spilled over the symbolism of the letter "A" in *The Scarlet Letter*. Besides its ostensible function of denouncing and shaming adultery, as Hester rises in the community's esteem it comes to take on more positive connotations, such as "Able" or even "Angel." One might conjecture that it means "Antinomian," given the parallels between the character of Hester Prynne and Anne Hutchinson, a brave and intelligent woman who challenged the Puritan establishment (as we have seen in Chapter 3), and who was subjected to slurs against her character and crude insinuations about the nature of her relationship to her pastor John Cotton and ultimately sent into exile. Or perhaps it may stand for America and the disjunction between the lofty rhetoric upon which the Puritan community was founded and the sordid commercial realities of its every-day existence as manifested in the Salem Customs House. In any event, it is perplexing that Hawthorne has created a female character who is beautiful, strong, and brave, only to exile her to a joyless, desexualized existence on the fringes of a community for whom she is an outcast.

Hawthorne's 1851 novel *The House of the Seven Gables* is set in his own nineteenth-century milieu. In the Preface, he offers his views on the nature of the relationship between the literary text and the real, describing the genres of the novel (presumed, he claims, to aim a minute fidelity to ordinary experience), and the romance, said to portray the truth of a human heart under circumstances of the writer's own choice or creation. Hawthorne alleges that *The House of Seven Gables* is a romance, not a novel, but this seems a trifle disingenuous, given the vividness with which it evokes the ghosts of New England's past. It is the story of Hepzibah and Clifford Pyncheon, two etiolated remnants of Salem's theocratic elites. Clifford and Hepzibah are ghostly, faintly absurd presences, who find it hard to exist in a world of cent-shops and railroads; Hepzibah laments the fact that she has to go into trade to earn a living, while Clifford has just come home after a period of incarceration for the alleged murder of his uncle. Another phantasm haunting the tale is that of the first Judge Pyncheon, cursed by the accused witch Sarah Good, who told the Salem judges that God would give them blood to drink. The curse is fulfilled when Pyncheon dies, possibly of apoplexy, in his own armchair in the family mansion, the House of the Seven Gables, built on land which had been the subject of a dispute with a neighbor, Matthew Maule, executed for witchcraft. The motif is repeated when his descendent Judge Jaffrey Pyncheon seeks to dispossess Hepzibah and Clifford in order to seize their land and to search for a mysterious document legitimizing a claim to a vast tract of Indian land in the West. In the end, the evil Jaffrey dies of apoplexy while sitting in his ancestor's chair; Hepzibah and Clifford are brought back to a semblance of life by the domestic ministrations of Phoebe Pyncheon, their cousin. Phoebe falls in love with the daguerreotypist Holgrave, who abandons his radicalism for a life of bourgeois domesticity. The tale is written in comic Gothic mode, and yet there are undercurrents of darkness: the reference to stolen Indian lands, and, once again, to witchcraft (ancestral curses, usurped lands, mesmerism) and the reference to the judge's dark corpse, rotting at the very heart of the mansion. This novel, published at a time when America was expanding Westward and was undergoing a process of rapid industrialization, reveals not only Hawthorne's uneasiness about his family's witch-hunting past, but also his disquietude about the rot at the heart of the direction America had taken in mid-nineteenth century, when (as we have seen earlier) John O'Sullivan had proclaimed that it was America's Manifest Destiny to occupy what he saw as the vacant lands to the West.

The Blithedale Romance (1852) is the last in the great trilogy of Hawthorne's mature period. In it, he describes a utopian community, Blithedale, founded on the ideals of the French Utopian philosopher **Charles Fourier** and not unlike **Brook Farm** (the agricultural commune where Hawthorne had briefly lived). Blithedale is ultimately torn apart by the erotic and political tensions between its four main characters: Hollingsworth, the philanthropist obsessed with his project for the reformation of criminals; Priscilla, a fragile young seamstress; Coverdale, the unreliable, voyeuristic narrator of the tale; and Zenobia, another of Hawthorne's exotic Dark Ladies, a feminist said to be modeled on Margaret Fuller. Ultimately, the agrarian idyll is destroyed when Zenobia, whose love for Hollingsworth is not reciprocated, drowns herself. Bizarrely, Henry James called *The Blithedale Romance* "the lightest, the brightest, the liveliest" of Hawthorne's major fictions. It is hard to comprehend what is light, bright, and lively about Hawthorne's account of the discovery of Zenobia's body by Hollingsworth, Coverdale, and the farmer Silas Foster:

> Were I to describe the perfect horror of the spectacle, the reader might justly reckon it to me for a sin and shame. For more than twelve long years I have borne it in my memory, and could now reproduce it as freshly as if it were still before my eyes, Of all modes of death, methinks it is the ugliest. Her wet garments swathed limbs of terrible inflexibility. She was the marble image of a death-agony. Her arms had grown rigid in the act of struggling, and were bent before her with clenched hands; her knees, too, were bent, and – thank God for it! – in the attitude of prayer. Ah, that rigidity! It is impossible to bear the terror of it. It seemed, – I must needs impart so much of my own miserable idea, – it seemed as if her body must keep the same position in the coffin, and that her skeleton would keep it in the grave; and that when Zenobia rose at the day of judgment, it would be in just the same attitude as now!
>
> (Hawthorne, 1991, p. 235)

Once again, Hawthorne has created a vibrant, strong, and highly intelligent female protagonist only to condemn her to a grim fate. Zenobia, even in death, is brought to her knees. Coverdale, the unreliable narrator, expresses the prissy hope that this denotes Christian repentance on her part. At the same time, however, he is haunted by the sight of Zenobia's clenched hands, and the possibility that she is expressing defiance even as she is dying.

It is possible that Hawthorne's ambivalent attitude toward strong women is derived from his anxieties about his own financial situation, particularly when viewed in comparison with the phenomenal publishing success of his female contemporaries. In a letter to William Ticknor, his publisher, Hawthorne commented peevishly: "there is the germ of a new romance in my mind, which will be all the better for ripening slowly. Besides, America is now wholly given over to a d—d mob of scribbling women, and I should have no chance of success while the public taste is occupied with their trash" (quoted in Mott, 1947, p. 122).

Henry David Thoreau

Henry David Thoreau, Emerson's and Hawthorne's close friend, was perhaps the writer who most closely translated Emerson's Transcendentalist ideals into personal lived experience, withdrawing for two years to the seclusion of **Walden Pond**, where he built a small house. Thoreau describes the reasons underlying his decision:

> I went to the woods because I wish to live deliberately, to front only the essential facts of life, and see if I could not learn what I had to teach, and not, when I came to die, discover that I had not lived. I did not wish to live what was not life, living is so dear; nor did I wish to practise resignation, unless it was quite necessary. I wanted to live deep and suck out all the marrow of life, to live so sturdily and Spartan-like as to put to rout all that was not life, to cut a broad swath and shave close; to drive life into a corner and reduce it to its lowest terms, and if it proved to be mean, why then to get the whole and genuine meanness to the world; or if it were sublime, to know it by experience. ...
>
> (Thoreau, 1966, p. 61)

In his sojourn at Walden Pond, living an austere pared-down existence in close proximity to nature, Thoreau spent his time observing the beauties of the landscape, reflecting on the destruction of the natural environment resulting from the grasping mercantile values of nineteenth-century America and putting into practice Emerson's notion that by studying nature one can apprehend the divine. His is a poet's vision:

Walden is a perfect forest mirror, set round with stones as precious to my eye as if fewer or rarer. Nothing so fair, so pure, and at the same time so large, lies on the surface of the earth. Sky water. It needs no fence. Nations come and go without defiling it. It is a mirror which no stone can crack, whose quicksilver will never wear off, whose gilding Nature constantly repairs; no storms, no dust, can dim its surface ever fresh; – a mirror in which all impurity presented to it sinks, swept and dusted by the sun's hazy brush – this the light dust-cloth, – which retains no breath that is breathed on it, but sends its own to float as clouds high above its surface, and be reflected in its bosom still.

(Thoreau, 1966, p. 127)

The inviolate specular purity and serene beauty of Walden lie in contrast, for Thoreau, to the brash commercialism of American society and its obsession with material progress. He was increasingly troubled by the issues of slavery and America's imperial westward expansion. In his 1849 essay **"Resistance to Civil Government"** (widely known as "Civil Disobedience"), Thoreau muses about the extent to which a citizen is compelled to obey a government whose policies he or she considers unjust. He feels that under a government which has promulgated the **Fugitive Slave Law** or carried out an expansionist war with Mexico or oppressed Native Americans, the true place for a just individual is a prison. To those who think that allowing themselves to be incarcerated would lessen the impact of their protest, he retorts that not only truth is stronger than error, but also that the direct experience of injustice would cause them to combat it far more effectively. He concludes:

A minority is powerless while it conforms to the majority; it is not even a minority then; but it is irresistible when it clogs by its whole weight. If the alternative is to keep all just men in prison, or give up war and slavery, the State will not hesitate which to choose. If a thousand men were not to pay their tax bills this year, that would not be a violent and bloody measure, as it would be to pay them, and enable the State to commit violence and shed innocent blood.

(Thoreau, 1966, p. 235)

For Thoreau, this was not empty rhetoric. He was prompted to write "Resistance to Civil Government" after a night spent in Concord jail, when he was imprisoned for not paying his poll tax because he disagreed with US government policy on the Mexican War and on slavery. Ultimately, he was freed because his poll tax was paid by a neighbor. Thoreau's radical ideas would ultimately have a direct impact on political thought and historical action, such as Mahatma Gandhi's movement for Indian independence and Martin Luther King's tactics of passive resistance in the Civil Rights movement in the United States. It is important to note, though, that Thoreau's dissent is eminently individual in nature. Rather than engaging with existing structures and transforming them from within, he opts to withdraw or drop out. Underlying Thoreau's thought is a strong belief in the boundaries between individual rights and morality and the authority of the state. Later, however, he would come to realize the limits of passive resistance in overcoming social injustice.

Chapter 7

The Originals:
Edgar Allan Poe, Herman Melville, Emily Dickinson, and Walt Whitman

Introduction

A dilemma faced by many literary historians of nineteenth-century America is where to place certain writers. **Herman Melville** was a close friend of Nathaniel Hawthorne, and is often grouped among the Transcendentalists or, in the work of F. O. Mattheissen (1941), as part of the American Renaissance. **Edgar Allan Poe** was a master of the short story genre, a poet of note, and an active (and often rebarbative and ferociously negative) literary critic whose work, with its generic and thematic range, resists facile categorization. **Emily Dickinson** and **Walt Whitman** are often paired in discussions of nineteenth-century poetry, but a more unlikely pair of bedfellows would be hard to imagine; the two are frequently described as late-blooming Transcendentalists, but much of their work fits uneasily within this categorization. This is not to say, of course, that Poe, Melville, Dickinson, and Whitman lived and worked in creative isolation, or that their work does not share some features with that of their contemporaries. Nonetheless, I have opted here to discuss these four writers as "originals," as writers whose work is so strongly stamped by their own individual vision that it denies facile classification.

Edgar Allan Poe

Edgar Allan Poe was the child of two itinerant actors; his father abandoned the family, and his mother died when Poe was only two years old. He was then taken in by John Allan, a wealthy Virginia tradesman, and his wife Frances. The family lived in London for several years, but then returned to

Richmond. After completing school, Poe attended the University of Virginia, but he ran up significant gambling debts and fell out with his foster father over his dissolute lifestyle. He then enlisted in the Army, but subsequently left. After his foster mother's death, Poe was reconciled with John Allan, and the latter used his influence to secure Poe a place at West Point. Ultimately, however, he was expelled, causing a definitive break with Allan. Poe then moved to Baltimore and endeavored to earn a living as a writer, publishing short stories and book reviews in the *Southern Literary Messenger*; in 1836, he married his 13-year-old cousin Virginia Clemm. After his excessive drinking provoked his resignation from the *Messenger*, Poe supported his family by publishing a serialized novel, **The Narrative of Arthur Gordon Pym**, and short fiction. In 1839, he published a short story collection titled **Tales of the Grotesque and Arabesque**, but it was only six years later that he would attain literary fame with the publication of his best-known poem **"The Raven."**

Poe's work, needless to say, has been the subject of innumerable critical readings, many of which emphasize the aesthetic and formal features of his writing and attempt to dehistoricize the man and his *oeuvre*. However, one of the most interesting currents in current Poe criticism analyzes Poe's literary production in relation to race in antebellum America. **Toni Morrison**, in *Playing in the Dark: Whiteness and the Literary Imagination*, offers a compelling description of the Africanist presence in American literature. According to Morrison, Africanism can be defined as "the denotative and connotative blackness that African peoples have come to signify, as well as the entire range of views, assumptions, readings and misreadings that accompany Eurocentric learning about these people" (Morrison, 1993, pp. 6–7), thus functioning as a discourse which not only dehistoricizes and attempts to naturalize differences based on skin color, but is crucial in the construction of an American national identity based on the exclusion of subaltern groups. She adds unequivocally that no early American writer is more important to the construction of American Africanism than Poe (p. 32).

The Narrative of Arthur Gordon Pym

This is particularly apparent in Poe's only complete novel, *The Narrative of Arthur Gordon Pym* (1838). It is a dizzying mélange of genres and motifs: adventure story, travel narrative, horror (with episodes of cannibalism and mutiny), and apocalyptic vision. Its eponymous protagonist runs off to sea as a stowaway on the ship *Grampus*. After a mutiny, Pym and his friend Augustus join forces with one of the mutineers, Dirk Peters, to gain control of the ship; the other mutineers are either killed or thrown overboard, except for one, Richard Parker. As provisions grow scarce, the men draw lots to determine who will be killed and eaten in order to keep the others alive; Parker ultimately is sacrificed. The remaining men are rescued by the *Jane Guy*, a ship sailing from Liverpool toward Antarctica. There they come upon the island of Tsalal, whose inhabitants are described as "jet-black, with thick and long woolly hair" (Poe, 1994, p. 131); even their teeth are black. Their reaction to the narrator and his companions is one of mixed fascination and horror, mirroring that of the white intruders who call them "savages": "It was quite evident that they had never before seen any of the white race – from whose complexion, indeed, they appeared to recoil" (p. 132). Although the sailors are initially received with apparent cordiality, the natives ambush them; among the whites, only Pym and Peters survive. By stealing a native boat, they manage to escape, and taking an indigenous man called Nu-Nu with them, they drift southwards into a nightmarish world of warm white seas. The novel ends suddenly with the appearance of a monstrous spectral figure: "There arose in our pathway a shrouded human figure, very far larger in its proportions than any dweller among men. And the hue of the skin of the figure was of the perfect whiteness of the snow."

As Toni Morrison points out, this nightmarish vision of whiteness appears only after the death of the only black figure, Nu-Nu; moreover, the episode of cannibalism (often associated with stereotypes of African savagery) occurs among the *white* characters, *before* they encounter the black-skinned indigenous people of Antarctica. As in many other works of the period, these images of hermetic whiteness almost invariably are constructed in conjunction with "representations of black or Africanist people who are dead, impotent, or under complete control" (Morrison, 1993, p. 33). Betsy Erkkila makes the valuable observation that an exclusive focus on the shaping influence of the Africanist presence in the constitution of American national identity may be dangerous in that it leads us to exclude or occlude the other races, cultures, and nationalities that populate early American writing (Erkkila, 2001, p. 44). This caveat notwithstanding, these recent readings of Poe (contained in collections such as ***Romancing the Shadow: Poe and Race***, Kennedy and Weissberg, 2001) offer a fascinating perspective on the simultaneous fear and desire felt by Americans of European descent toward their racial "others" in antebellum American writing.

Poe's short fiction

Poe's short fiction is extraordinarily diverse and difficult to classify. He was a pioneer of the detective story, with tales such as **"The Murders in the Rue Morgue"** and **"The Purloined Letter"** and their coldly rational protagonist, C. Auguste Dupin. Many of his other stories are darkly gothic in nature, and show a disturbing ability to enter into the pathological mindset. **"The Black Cat,"** for example, explores the perverse impulse to inflict harm simply because one can. The narrator owns a black cat, described as his "favourite pet and playmate"; under the influence of liquor, he gouges the animal's eye out with a knife. His morbid obsession grows even stronger, and he hangs the unfortunate animal:

> because I knew that it had loved me, and because I felt it had given me no reason of offence; – hung it because I knew that in so doing I was committing a sin that would so jeopardize my immortal soul as to place it – if such a thing were possible – even beyond the reach of the infinite mercy of the Most Merciful and Most Terrible God.[1]

But another black cat appears in its place, and when the narrator is about to kill it with an axe, his wife intervenes; he sinks the axe into her brain, and conceals his crime by walling up her body in the cellar. When he looks for the cat in order to kill it as well, he finds that the animal has disappeared. When the police come to search the house, the narrator in a fit of bravado taunts the police by tapping the wall in the place where the body is concealed and boasting of the house's solid construction. At this point, an inhuman wail is heard, and the police tear down the wall, only to discover the second black cat, who had been walled up with the corpse of its murdered mistress.

"The Raven" and "The Philosophy of Composition"

It was, however, with the publication of his poem **"The Raven"** in 1845 that Poe attained literary celebrity. In his essay **"The Philosophy of Composition,"** he sets out his views on literary art and on the process of the poetic composition of "The Raven," which, far from being the

---

[1]   See http://etext.virginia.edu/etcbin/toccer-new2?id=PoeBlac.sgm&images=images/
modeng&data=/texts/english/modeng/parsed&tag=public&part=1&division=div1

product of a moment of intuition or inspiration, is the consequence of painstakingly rational thought. He begins with the consideration that the paramount aim of the poet is for effect, and that to obtain the maximum effect a poem should be of a length that can be read in one sitting. Poe then goes on to declare Beauty (defined as the pleasurable elevation of the Soul) rather than Truth or Passion as the proper province of poetry. He proceeds to consider the appropriate tone for his poem, which in his view is that of melancholy; to reinforce this, he decides on a refrain with the appropriate sonorous effects: "Nevermore." For Poe, the most melancholy (and thus the most poetic) of subjects is death, and – he adds – the death of a beautiful woman, told from the perspective of a bereaved lover. Thus the figure of the Raven (the bird of ill omen) is made to reply to the increasingly desperate queries of the poetic subject regarding death and the afterlife.

The poem itself is one of extraordinary musicality. Hostile critics have often dismissed Poe's poetry as mere doggerel of the tiddly-pum variety. When, however, it is read aloud, the effect is incantatory and really quite spellbinding. What one wonders, however, is whether the poet's extreme, discarnate rationality as described in "The Philosophy of Composition" is yet another of Poe's narrative masks. Whatever the case, however, his influence on French Symbolist poets such as **Charles Baudelaire** (and later, on the Modernist aesthetic) was very strong. He died in mysterious circumstances in Baltimore in 1849.

Herman Melville

One of the most fascinating and powerful writers in nineteenth-century America was **Herman Melville**, whose work drew inspiration in part from Poe's *Narrative of Arthur Gordon Pym*. Melville's life story is a curious mixture of Gothic family dramas (of madness and financial ruin), picaresque adventure novel, and exotic travel narrative. He was descended from two Revolutionary heroes; one grandfather, Thomas Melvill (the "e" was only added later), took part in the Boston Tea Party, and the other, Peter Gansevoort, belonged to a distinguished New York family of Dutch origin. When Melville was only 12 years old, his father died bankrupt. The family's dire financial straits compelled the young Melville to work at a variety of occupations. Ultimately, he went to sea, first on a voyage to Liverpool in 1839, and later on a three-year voyage to the South Seas on several whaling ships. Later, he would comment that a whale-ship was his

Yale and his Harvard. At sea he was thrust into contact with individuals of diverse social classes and racial and national origins, in a situation that was rigidly hierarchical and physically brutal, giving him a lifelong sympathy for the oppressed. In the Marquesas Islands, Melville abandoned ship with another sailor and lived what he called "an indulgent captivity" among the Typee, causing him to challenge the values that white Christian civilization held dear. On a subsequent voyage, he became involved in a mutiny and ended up in a Tahitian prison, but then escaped and shipped out for Hawaii. He returned to Boston in 1844.

Melville in the South Seas

Melville's encounters with Polynesian culture in Tahiti, the Marquesas and Hawaii are described in his first book, *Typee: A Peep at Polynesian Life*, published in 1846. It could be argued convincingly that his experiences in the South Seas transformed him into a cultural relativist, impelling him to question the alleged superiority of imperial Europe and American culture:

> How often is the term "savages" incorrectly applied! None really deserving of it were ever yet discovered by voyagers or by travelers. They have discovered heathens and barbarians whom by horrible cruelties they have exasperated into savages. It may be asserted without fear of contradictions that in all the cases of outrages committed by Polynesians, Europeans have at some time or other been the aggressors, and that the cruel and bloodthirsty disposition of some of the islanders is mainly to be ascribed to the influence of such examples ... Let the once smiling and populous Hawaiian islands, with their now diseased, starving, and dying natives, answer the question. The missionaries may seek to disguise the matter as they will, but the facts are incontrovertible; and the devoutest Christian who visits that group with an unbiased mind, must go away mournfully asking – "Are these, alas! the fruits of twenty-five years of enlightening?"
>
> (Melville, 1924, p. 31)

Later in the book he would characterize the white "civilized" man as "the most ferocious animal on the face of the earth."

The critical reaction to *Typee* was colorful, to say the very least. One anonymous reviewer thundered, "An apotheosis of barbarism! A panegyric on cannibal delights! An apostrophe to the spirit of savage felicity!" and described the book's author as "the traducer of missions."[2] Melville's American publishers forced him to alter the text of *Typee*, deleting the descriptions of the depredations of the missionaries and the gunboat imperialism the writer had encountered in the South Seas in the version that was sold in the United States; bizarrely, the unexpurgated version was sold throughout the British Empire in sets printed in the Home and Colonial Library editions of his British publisher, Murray. Despite, or perhaps because of, the critical furore, *Typee* was wildly successful. In 1847, Melville published **Omoo**, loosely based on the mutiny he had experienced and on his Tahitian escapades. Without a doubt, however, Melville's masterpiece is his novel **Moby-Dick**, published in 1851.

Moby-Dick

Melville wrote *Moby-Dick* at a time when the quest for imperial expansion was at its apex. His adventures in the South Seas, and his experiences of living among men of many different "races" and nationalities, had given him first-hand insight into the excesses of European and American colonialism. In an appendix to *Typee*, Melville describes his personal experience of gunboat diplomacy:

> The author of this volume arrived at Tahiti the very day that the iniquitous designs of the French were consummated by inducing the subordinate chiefs, during the absence of their queen, to ratify an artfully-drawn treaty, by which she was virtually deposed. Both menaces and caresses were employed on this occasion, and the 32-pounders which peeped out of the port-holes of the frigate were the principal arguments adduced to quiet the scruples of the more conscientious islanders.
>
> (Melville, 1924, p. 337)

He goes on to comment that the occupation of the Sandwich Islands (Hawaii) by England had been widely misrepresented in the United States. Melville's mistrust of official narratives may have been a factor that led him to turn to popular accounts of a malevolent albino whale which had allegedly attacked ships in the Pacific.[3]

---

[2] Anonymous, "Typee: The Traducer of Missions," *Christian Parlor Magazine 3* (July 1846), pp. 74–83.

[3] For example, J. N. Reynolds, "Mocha Dick," in the *New York Knickerbocker* (May 1839) and Owen Chase, *Narrative of the Most Extraordinary and Distressing Shipwreck of the Whale-Ship Essex, of Nantucket, Which Was Attacked and Finally Destroyed by a Large Spermaceti-Whale in the Pacific Ocean* (New York: W. B. Gilley, 1821).

Most of us are familiar with the plot of *Moby-Dick*. It is the story of the mad pursuit of a malign, gigantic white whale of huge strength and resourcefulness by Ahab, a crazed Nantucket whaling captain who has lost his leg in a previous encounter with the leviathan. His obsessive quest for vengeance is related by the enigmatic narrator Ishmael, a member of the crew of Ahab's ill-fated ship *Pequod*. Ishmael is a curiously detached witness to Ahab's relentless pursuit of Moby-Dick; he is perhaps the only member of the crew of the *Pequod* who is not completely caught up in Ahab's mad race to self-destruction. Melville's Ishmael describes the crew of the *Pequod* as they race toward their doom:

> Such a crew, so officered, seemed specially picked and packed by some infernal fatality to help him [Ahab] to his monomaniac revenge. How it was that they so aboundingly responded to the old man's ire – by what evil magic their souls were possessed, that at times his hate seemed almost theirs; the White Whale as much their insufferable foe as his; how all this came to be – what the White Whale was to them, or how to their unconscious understandings, also, in some dim, unsuspected way, he might have seemed the gliding great demon of the seas of life – all this to explain, would be to dive deeper than Ishmael can go.
>
> (Melville, 2002a, p. 158)

The cadences here are Shakespearean, but Ishmael's reticence in explicating the individual motives of his fellow crewmen in the pursuit of the "gliding great demon of the seas of life" strikes the reader as curiously evasive. The obvious explanation for their enthusiastic adherence to Ahab's mad quest is material gain, symbolized by the golden doubloon he has nailed to the mast and promised to the first man who sights Moby-Dick's spout. But even the promise of wealth is hardly adequate to justify their commitment to a pursuit that will so clearly end in their own destruction.

In many ways, the *Pequod* and its crew embody Melville's nineteenth-century imperial universe (in which the quest for lucre is paramount) and America's own rapid transformation from colony to republic to nascent empire. The crew members emerge with clarity: Starbuck, the first mate, with his moral preoccupations; Stubb, the unflappable, easygoing second mate; and third mate Flask, who revels in the destruction of whales. Another mysterious crew member is the ghostly stowaway Fedallah, almost an Orientalist doppelganger of Ahab:

> that hair-turbaned Fedallah remained a muffled mystery to the last. When he came in a mannerly world like this, by what sort of

unaccountable tie he soon evinced himself to be linked with Ahab's pecu-
liar fortunes; nay, so far as to have some sort of a half-hinted influence;
Heaven knows, but it might have been even authority over him; all this
none knew. But one cannot sustain an indifferent air concerning Fedallah.
He was such a creature as civilized, domestic people in the temperate
zone see only in their dreams.

(Melville, 2002a, p. 191)

Even more intriguing are the three harpooners, each embodying a group
that has been caught up for good or evil in the fulfillment of America's
Manifest Destiny: Daggoo the African, described as a "coal-black negro
savage, with a lion-like tread"; Tashtego, "an unmixed Indian from Gay
Head"; and Queequeg, the tattooed South Sea islander who shares Ishmael's
bed in Nantucket and becomes his "bosom friend." The subject of Queequeg
and Ishmael's relationship has been the focus of much critical scrutiny of
late; it is homosocial in nature, and very clearly homoerotic as well. Ishmael
offers the following insight into the second night they spend together:

How it is I know not; but there is no place like a bed for confidential dis-
closures between friends. Man and wife, they say, there open the very
bottom of their souls to each other; and some old couples often lie and
chat over old times till nearly morning. Thus, in our hearts' honeymoon,
lay I and Queequeg – a cosy, loving pair.

(Melville, 2002a, p. 57)

At one point in the tale, as the hunt for Moby-Dick progresses, Queequeg
falls gravely ill of a fever, and the ship's carpenter is instructed to build a
coffin to Queequeg's specifications. Unexpectedly, however, he recovers,
and converts his coffin into a sea chest, covering it with hieroglyphic
marks similar to his own tattoos. Later the carpenter transforms it into a
lifebuoy.

Finally, the *Pequod* engages in a titanic three-day struggle with Moby-
Dick. The stricken leviathan rams the *Pequod*, and the ship begins to sink.
As the doomed sailors begin to vanish beneath the waves, Ahab cries out
that the ship is a second hearse, and that "its wood could only be American!"
He goes down with his ship, defiant to the last. In the Epilogue, we learn
that the only survivor (and witness) of the catastrophe is Ishmael. Saved
by holding on to Queequeg's coffin/lifebuoy, he is picked up by a passing
ship after floating for a day and a night.

As one might expect, not mere gallons but rather jeroboams of critical ink have been expended on interpreting Melville's *Moby-Dick*. It would be nugatory if not downright impossible to offer here an exhaustive description of its reception, initially hostile or lukewarm, and progressively more engaged and enthusiastic as the twentieth century progressed, to the point that the novel is now enshrined as one of the very highest points of American literary achievement. In a sense, *Moby-Dick* has suffered the Procrustean fate of being stretched to fit an extraordinary range of critical agendas, some more persuasive than others. By the same token, however, the number and variety of responses to Melville's novel over the years demonstrate conclusively the validity of the book's claim to canonical status, given its capacity to engage and speak to the concerns of a wide range of scholars and general readers.

Melville's short fiction

Moby-Dick was not a commercial success, and Melville increasingly turned to strategies of subterfuge in order to convey his views on issues such as slavery and the growth of American industrial capitalism. One such strategy was the use of fatuous, self-satisfied narrators to convey Melville's sense of the willful blindness of America's elites when faced with unpalatable truths about the exploitation of slaves and salaried workers which underpinned their complacent prosperity.

In **"Bartleby the Scrivener,"** published in 1853, Melville uses the narratorial voice of a smug Wall Street lawyer who is proud of the fact that he never pleads cases before a jury but rather "does a snug business among rich men's bonds and mortgages and title-deeds" (Melville, 2002b, p. 4). He delights in dropping names of clients such as John Jacob Astor, "a name which, I admit, I love to repeat, for it hath a rounded and orbicular sound to it, and rings like unto bullion" (p. 4). The narrator, however, is flummoxed by the attitude of one of his employees, a copyist or scrivener called Bartleby. Initially, Bartleby works industriously, copying documents day and night. There comes a moment, however, when upon being asked to fulfill a task, he replies, "I would prefer not to." Initially, his employer is unwilling to confront him, commenting that he is reluctant to do so because he cannot find a trace of anger or impertinence in Bartleby's manner. Matters drift along, with Bartleby continuing to state that he prefers not to carry out his tasks; the narrator comments that, "Nothing so aggravates a person as a passive resistance" (p. 13). Finally, one Sunday on his way to church, the narrator discovers that Bartleby has been sleeping in the office. He attempts to find out more information about the scrivener, but Bartleby continues with his gentle refusal to comply. The narrator is not a cruel man, and he is haunted by the pale figure of Bartleby. Ultimately, however, he decides to dismiss him, but Bartleby refuses to go. Finally, his employer resolves to move the premises to another location; when he is told by the authorities that he is responsible for the strange man occupying the law offices, he retorts that Bartleby is a former employee for whom he is not accountable. But Bartleby remains obdurate in his refusal to leave. The exasperated narrator offers to find him employment elsewhere, but he refuses. Bartleby is removed to the Tombs (a Manhattan prison) as a vagrant, and stops eating and speaking. Finally, he dies. The story ends with the haunting revelation that Bartleby's previous employment had been in the Dead Letter Office in Washington.

This is an unsettling story. Bartleby is in many ways the embodiment of the limitations of Thoreau's ideas on civil disobedience and passive resistance. Bartleby resists the dehumanizing conditions of his employment, but his resistance is purely on an individual level. Tellingly, his employer is presented not as a villain but as a man who is basically well-intentioned; what is being critiqued here is a rigidly hierarchical economic system which condemns people to long hours of dehumanized, repetitive labor whose fruits are enjoyed by the likes of Bartleby's boss. Bartleby's exacerbated individualism leads him to dissent by dropping out, first from the activities related to his work, then from food and human contact, and ultimately from life. His dissent, because it is carried out in isolation, is ultimately ineffective.

Another of Melville's obtuse narrators can be encountered in the unforgettable story **"Benito Cereno."** Its narrator, the sea captain Amasa Delano, comes across the ship *San Dominick* off the coast of Chile, and due to its erratic movements concludes that it is in distress. He and his men board the ship to offer aid, and encounter its captain, the Spaniard Benito Cereno, surrounded by Negro slaves, "among other valuable freight" (Melville, 2002c, p. 36). Delano is mystified on finding Cereno in a state of considerable agitation, and notes strange signs of chaos and indiscipline on board. He is reassured, however, by what he sees as the devotion of Cereno's servant Babo, standing at his side "like a shepherd's dog" (p. 39), apparently gazing upon his master with affection. Captain Delano, like the narrator of "Bartleby the Scrivener," is presented as a benign, oblivious character. Again, Melville deploys a canine metaphor to describe Delano's patronizing attitudes:

> At home, he had often taken rare satisfaction in sitting in his door, watch-ing some free man of color at his work or play. If on a voyage he chanced to have a black sailor, invariably he was on chatty, and half-gamesome terms with him. In fact, like most men of a good, blithe heart, Captain Delano took to negroes, not philanthropically, but genially, just as other men to Newfoundland dogs.
>
> (Melville, 2002c, p. 71)

Delano's smug complacency renders him oblivious to the signs of tumult and barely repressed violence surrounding him on all sides. When Babo holds a razor to his Captain's throat, Delano sees this once more as a sign of servile devotion, and "all his old weakness for negroes returned." Indeed, it is only when Delano leaves to return to his ship and Benito Cereno leaps aboard the dinghy with him that the truth of what he has seen is revealed:

> That moment, across the long-benighted mind of Captain Delano, a flash of revelation swept, illuminating in unanticipated clearness his host's whole mysterious demeanor, with every enigmatic event of the day, as well as the entire past voyage of the San Dominick ... Captain Delano, now with the scales dropped from his eyes, saw the negroes, not in misrule, not in tumult, not as if frantically concerned for Don Benito, but with mask torn away, flourishing hatchets and knives, in ferocious piratical revolt.
>
> (Melville, 2002c, p. 71)

Ultimately, however, the slaves' revolt is unsuccessful, and Babo, its leader, is apprehended and brought to trial in Lima. There he remains silent, and is dragged to the scaffold by a mule and beheaded; his body is burned to ashes, but his head is placed on a pole and his defiant gaze con-tinues to meet the eyes of white onlookers. Benito Cereno is unable to emerge from what he calls the shadow of the negro, and shortly thereafter dies of melancholy.

"Benito Cereno" is, in all likelihood, based upon accounts of slave revolts, not only the one which took place on the Spanish slave ship *Amistad* in 1839, but also (as the name of the slave ship San Dominick would strongly suggest) the revolution led by **Toussaint L'Ouverture** against the

French in 1799 in St Domingue which led to Haitian independence. The story is a haunting rendering of the antebellum United States's willed blindness regarding the horrors of slavery and but also its refusal to face the very real possibility of future racialized uprisings and civil strife closer to home.

Emily Dickinson

Melville's canvas was the world. **Emily Dickinson**, on the other hand, appears at first glance to be profoundly rooted in her more circumscribed New England milieu. In one of her poems, she acknowledges that her locality has shaped her poetic vision, stating,

> The Robin's my Criterion for Tune –
> Because I grow – where Robins do –

Indeed, she adds, "The ode familiar – rules the Noon." But with the elegant irony that characterizes her verse, she highlights the underlying paradox:

> Because I see – New Englandly –
> The Queen, discerns like me –
> Provincially –
>
> (Dickinson, 1997, pp. 15–16)

It is precisely because the poet is able to see through the prism of a particular place and culture that she, like the Queen, is capable of discernment on a far grander scale. Emily Dickinson's poetry is anything but provincial in nature.

Dickinson was born in Amherst, Massachusetts, into a close-knit New England family. Her father was a prominent local citizen, one of the founders of Amherst College, who was active in local and national politics; her brother Austin lived next door after his marriage to Dickinson's lifelong friend Susan Gilbert. Her relationship with her mother was a complicated one; in a letter to her mentor **Thomas Higginson**, she wrote, "I never had a mother." Dickinson lived most of her life with her parents and her sister Lavinia in Amherst, and attended Mount Holyoke Female Seminary briefly, but returned home for reasons that have never been determined; some critics have suggested that in the Calvinist atmosphere of the Seminary, she had refused to conform to the religious expectations of the institution and had affirmed that she had no hope of faith. Once home, she was a voracious reader. Interestingly, one of the texts she read was Emerson's "Self-Reliance." Critic Judith Farr, in her study of Dickinson's poetic *oeuvre*, comments that in her copy of Emerson's text, Dickinson had turned down the pages with the following passages: "My life is for itself and not a spectacle. I much prefer that it should be of a lower strain, so it be genuine and equal, than it should be glittering and unsteady," and "What I must do is all that concerns me, not what people think" (Farr, 1992, p. 46). This doctrine of radical self-sufficiency and intellectual independence would be one of the hallmarks of Dickinson's career.

Much has been made of the fact that Emily Dickinson lived a secluded life. Some suggest that this was the result of a broken heart; others have painted her as a fragile reclusive spinster whose contacts with the outside world were tenuous. Some of these characterizations are clearly the result of critical misogyny. The notion that great art was the product of time spent in isolation is often cited in relation to the work of Nathaniel Hawthorne (who spent a decade in seclusion in his family home in Salem) and Henry David Thoreau, who withdrew to Walden Pond, but these periods of withdrawal are not described in relation to male writers as evidence of emotional fragility.

Dickinson did indeed become increasingly reclusive as her life progressed, but this was certainly not at the expense of the power and beauty of her work or of the depth and passion of her relationships. Studies of her correspondence (and indeed of her poetry) have prompted critics to suggest that she had been in love with members of both sexes. The longest and most ardent of these relationships was with her beloved sister-in-law **Susan Gilbert Dickinson**; she was also involved with **Samuel Bowles**, a married man who was editor of the *Springfield Republican*, and with judge **Otis Lord**, who proposed marriage to her when she was nearly 50. Whether or not these relationships were actually consummated is hard to say. What is certainly the case is that some of Dickinson's poems evoke an ardent physicality:

> Wild Night – Wild Nights!
> Were I with thee
> Wild Nights should be
> Our luxury!

Futile – the Winds –
To a Heart in port –
Done with the Compass –
Done with the Chart!

Rowing in Eden –
Ah, the Sea!
Might I but moor –Tonight –
In Thee!

(Dickinson, 1997, pp. 9–10)

Religion is one of Dickinson's major themes. One of her poems speaks of her joy at discerning the divine presence in nature:

Some keep the Sabbath going to Church –
I keep it, staying at Home –
With a Bobolink for a Chorister –
And an Orchard, for a Dome –

(1997, p. 21)

But as always with Dickinson, there is a darker side. In another poem, she speaks of religious revelation in a disturbing series of images:

He fumbles at your soul
As Players at the Keys
Before they drop full Music on –
He stuns you by degrees –
Prepares your brittle Nature
For the Ethereal Blow
By fainter Hammers – further heard –
Then nearer –Then so slow

After evoking the vision of God as heavenly organist/rapist, followed by the evocation of pounding hammer rhythms, she continues with powerful imagery of lightning bolts and a divine tempest that reinforces the insignificance of the individual and the radically transformative (and sometimes destructive) nature of the divine:

Your Breath has time to straighten –
Your Brain – to bubble Cool –
Deals – One – imperial – Thunderbolt –

That scalps your naked Soul –
When Winds take Forests in their Paws –
The Universe – is still –

(1997, pp. 19–20)

Dickinson did, however, believe in a reality beyond the physical surface of things:

This World is not Conclusion.
A Species stands beyond –
Invisible, as Music –
But positive, as Sound –

Later in the same poem, however, she ridicules the pomposity of organized religion and speaks of its incapacity to heal or assuage the nagging pain that comes from doubt:

Much Gesture, from the Pulpit –
Strong Hallelujahs roll –
Narcotics cannot still the Tooth
That nibbles at the soul –

(1997, p. 37)

In still another poem she describes the Bible as "an antique Volume – / Written by faded Men / At the suggestion of Holy Spectres –. " This, in Dickinson's Calvinist milieu of Amherst, was a revolutionary attitude indeed. Dickinson's true faith was in the act of poetic creation, and it was to this that she turned to address moments of pain and bereavement in her own life. In one of the paradoxes that she so loved, she reminds us that it is the moments of suffering that bring us closest to what is real:

I like a look of Agony,
Because I know it's true –
Men do not sham Convulsion,
Nor simulate, a Throe –

(1997, p. 8)

In another poem, she highlights the paradox that while joy may render us complacent and ineffectual, it is pain that draws forth our inner strength:

Power is only Pain –
Stranded, thro' Discipline,
Till Weights – will hang –
Give Balm – to Giants –
And they'll wilt, like Men –
Give Himmaleh –
They'll Carry – Him!

(1997, p. 11)

Clearly Dickinson knew whereof she spoke. Many of her poems speak of death with disturbing immediacy. Death appears in many guises, characterized as a suitor who takes the poetic subject for a buggy ride ("Because I could not stop for Death – / He kindly stopped for me – "), or as an elopement:

It was a quiet way –
He asked if I was his –
I made no answer of the Tongue –
But answer of the Eyes –
And then He bore me on
Before this mortal noise
With swiftness, as of Chariots
And distance, as of Wheels.

(Dickinson, 1970, p. 480)

Death is seen as a transitional state, a crossing over, though to what is never made quite clear.

Dickinson's poetic style is a radical new departure in many ways. Although at first reading her poetry evokes the familiar rhythms of conventional hymns and ballads, devices such as **slant rhyme**, **enjambment** (going beyond conventional line breaks or endings), and **dashes** often bring the reader up short and force us to pause to unravel meanings. Her attitude toward publication was ambivalent, to say the very least. Only around a dozen of her poems were published in her lifetime, though she had sent some of her poems to editors such as Thomas Wentworth Higginson. To Higginson, she sent a query that balances in tone between the arch and the demure, asking ironically, "Are you too deeply occupied to say if my Verse is alive?" But at the same time she believed deeply in her own artistic vision and actively resisted editorial attempts to bowdlerize her poems or rein in her formal innovations. Declaring "Publication – is the Auction / Of the Mind of Man," her ultimate loyalty was to the purity of her own poetic vision. She transcribed her poems on unlined white paper, sewing them together in 30 carefully ordered groups called fascicles, each consisting of 16 to 24 poems, which were found in a drawer after her death. The posthumous publication of Dickinson's poems is really an extraordinary story, and was brought about by **Mabel Loomis Todd**, the lover of Dickinson's brother Austin. Despite the fact that she only saw Dickinson in her coffin, Todd was aware of her poetic genius. When upon Dickinson's demise her sister Lavinia came across the fascicles of poems, she asked Todd to transcribe some of them. Later, Todd persuaded Dickinson's mentor Thomas Higginson to publish two posthumous volumes of poetry, which she and Higginson edited. It is disconcerting to think how easily Dickinson's poems could have been lost to posterity had it not been for Todd's timely intervention. Emily Dickinson's poetry has the contained passion and elegance of a Bach fugue, and she is without a doubt one of the greatest poets that America has ever produced.

Walt Whitman

In his 1844 essay **"The Poet,"** **Ralph Waldo Emerson** had spoken of the poet and of the function of poetry. Describing the poet as "the sayer, the namer" who represents Beauty, and poetry as a "metre-making argument," he describes his vain search among his fellow citizens for a poet capable of knowing the value of American materials. Nevertheless, he declares with confidence, "America is a poem in our eyes; its ample geography dazzles the imagination and it will not wait long for metres." (Emerson, 1983, p. 465).

Only 11 years later, such a poet burst upon the American literary scene. **Walt Whitman** emerged at a moment when America was increasingly divided over issues related to slavery, women's rights, immigration, and territorial expansion. He had worked as a printer's apprentice and as a teacher in the Long Island schools, and as a journalist in popular newspapers such as the *Aurora* and the Brooklyn *Daily Eagle*. His book of poems *Leaves of Grass*, published in 1855 at his own expense, was by any standard a revolutionary departure. The daguerreotype image of the poet that precedes the title page illustrates this, depicting Whitman in workingman's clothing with his hand placed jauntily on his hip, hat cocked aslant, shirt collar unbuttoned. In his Preface, he sets out his poetic manifesto,

Figure 7.1   Walt Whitman, *Leaves of Grass*. Image of author on page facing title page.

proclaiming, "The United States themselves are essentially the greatest poem. In the history of the earth hitherto the largest and most stirring appear tame and orderly to their ampler largeness and stir." He goes on to declare that the American poet is to be commensurate not only with the American people but with American nature, as he "incarnates its geography and natural life and rivers and lakes." For Whitman, the American poet is a seer, an individual, "commensurate with a people," but marked by generosity and a lack of elitist pomposity, as well as by an openness to competitors (Whitman, 1973, pp. 711, 713).

In **"Song of Myself,"** he proclaims his own status as America's representative poet:

> Walt Whitman, a kosmos, of Manhattan the son,
> Turbulent, fleshy, sensual, eating, drinking and breeding,
> No sentimentalist, no stander above men and women or apart from them

No more modest than immodest.
Unscrew the locks from the doors!
Unscrew the doors themselves from the jambs!

(Whitman, 1973, p. 52)

And unscrew them he did, with a vengeance. Whitman speaks with jubilant openness of sexuality, not only between men and women but in relationships between members of the same sex:

I mind how we lay in June, such a transparent summer morning;
You settled your head athwart my hips and gently turned over upon me,
And parted the shirt from my bosom-bone, and plunged your tongue to
    my barestript heart,
And reached till you felt my beard, and reached till you held my feet.

(1973, p. 33)

The poetic subject/voyeur observes and celebrates Americans of all social classes, from trappers to boatsmen to female factory workers to young mothers to runaway slaves:

The runaway slave came to my house and stopped outside
I heard his motions crackling the twigs of the woodpile,
Through the swung half-door of the kitchen I saw him limpsey and weak,
And went where he sat on a log, and led him in and assured him [...]
And remember perfectly well his revolving eyes and his awkwardness,
And remember putting plasters on the galls of his neck and ankles.

(1973, pp. 37–8)

Whitman's poetic revolution was one not only of content but of form. His use of free verse was a radical departure from the mincing prissy couplets of many of his predecessors. Another (often parodied) characteristic of his poems is the Whitmanian catalogue, a series of dazzling starbursts of metaphors on a common theme.

A child said, What is the grass? Fetching it to me with full hands;

How could I answer the child? ... I do not know what it is any more than he.

I guess it must be the flag of my disposition, out of hopeful green stuff woven.
Or I guess it is the handkerchief of the Lord,

A scented gift and remembrancer designedly dropped,
Bearing the owner's name someway in the corners, that we may see
        and remark, and say Whose?
[...]
And now it seems to me the beautiful uncut hair of graves.

Tenderly will I use you curling grass
It may be you transpire from the breasts of young men,
It may be if I had known them I would have loved them;
It may be you are from old people and from women, and from
        offspring taken soon out of their mothers' laps,
And here you are the mothers' laps.

                                                    (1973, pp. 33–4)

Here Whitman successively unfurls a series of arresting images of the "uniform hieroglyphic" of the grass: green flags of hope, a coquettish divine souvenir, and – in an unforgettable metaphor which would all too soon convert itself into grim reality as the storm clouds of America's approaching Civil War grew thicker – the uncut hair of graves. But Whitman's optimism and vitality, even when faced with the apparent finality of death, impel him to decipher the hieroglyphic of the grass in life-affirming terms:

What do you think has become of the young and old men?
And what do you think has become of the women and children?

They are alive and well somewhere;
The smallest sprout shows there is really no death,
And if ever there was it led forward life, and does not wait at the end to
    arrest it,
And ceased the moment life appeared.
All goes onward and outward ... and nothing collapses,
And to die is different from what any one supposed, and luckier.

                                                    (1973, pp. 34–5)

It has often been stated that Whitman and his poetry are a bundle of contradictions. Although in many ways he is the last writer on earth that one would associate with Puritanism, his vision of America as the "greatest poem," a country like no other that is destined to be an example to all other nations, is a secularized version of American exceptionalist rhetoric. Similarly, the notion of the poet as exemplary individual has certain resonances of the Puritan doctrine of **exemplary selfhood**, except that here the role of the poet is not as moral exemplar or defender of religious faith, but rather as a heroic, larger than life individual who embodies on behalf of his countrymen the quest for Beauty and poetic truth. And of course his links to Transcendentalism and Emersonian thought are obvious, with his notion of Nature as a hieroglyph of the Divine. It is true that the yoking of Whitman's exacerbated individualism, on the one hand, and the notion that he speaks on behalf of the widest possible range of his fellow citizens on the other, seems contradictory. However, if we consider Whitman as a product of Jacksonian republicanism (with a small "r"), some of these contradictions begin to make sense. Shira Wolosky (2004) argues convincingly that Whitman's art is deeply informed by Jacksonian politics, particularly the liberal-republican structure of political representation, in which presidential authority is derived from its capacity to represent the entire electorate – precisely the constituency that Whitman's poetic persona claims to embody.

The outbreak of the **Civil War** in 1861 was devastating for Whitman (as indeed it was for his fellow citizens, both North and South). In his self-assigned role as **"Wound Dresser,"** taking comfort and succor to the wounded and dying soldiers in Washington hospitals, he was directly confronted with the carnage of the war, as we see in an unbearably poignant poem titled **"Reconciliation,"** written in 1865:

Word over all, beautiful as the sky
Beautiful that war and all its deeds or carnage must in time be utterly
    lost,
That the hands of the sisters Death and Night incessantly softly wash
    again, and ever again, this soil'd world;
For my enemy is dead, a man divine as myself is dead,
I look where he lies white-faced and still in the coffin – I draw near,
Bend down and touch lightly with my lips the white face in the coffin.
(Whitman, 1973, p. 321)

The following chapter traces the growing tensions that led to a war that would tear America apart.

Chapter 8

A House Divided:
Abolitionism, the Women's Movement, and the Civil War

Introduction

Edgar Allan Poe's short story **"The Fall of the House of Usher"** was first published in 1839, more than 20 years before the outbreak of the American Civil War. In it, he describes a gloomy mansion inhabited by the last remnants of an aristocracy doomed to extinction. Roderick Usher is described as follows:

> A cadaverousness of complexion; an eye large, liquid, and luminous beyond comparison; lips somewhat thin and very pallid, but of a surpassingly beautiful curve; a nose of a delicate Hebrew model, but with a breadth of nostril unusual in similar formations; a finely moulded chin, speaking, in its want of prominence, of a want of moral energy; hair of a more than web-like softness and tenuity; these features, with an inordinate expansion above the regions of the temple, made up altogether a countenance not easily to be forgotten.
>
> (Poe, 1908, p. 132)

Some critics have suggested that the phrase "breadth of nostril" may be a coded allusion to racial ambiguity. Roderick's sister Madeline is on the verge of death, and the reader is given only a glimpse of her as she crosses the room in which Roderick and the unnamed narrator are conversing. Shortly after, she succumbs, and is placed in her coffin. Roderick, however, is aware that she has been entombed alive. A gust of wind blows the door of the chamber open:

> without those doors there did stand the lofty and enshrouded figure of the Lady Madeline of Usher. There was blood upon her white robes, and the

evidence of some bitter struggle upon every portion of her emaciated frame. For a moment she remained trembling and reeling to and fro upon the threshold, then, with a low moaning cry, fell heavily inward upon the person of her brother, and in her violent and now final death-agonies, bore him to the floor a corpse, and a victim to the terrors he had anticipated.

(Poe, 1908, p. 144)

The description of the demise of Roderick and Madeline Usher is disturbingly sexual in nature. It is followed by the collapse of the mansion, as the fissure which extended from top to bottom of the façade cracks open wide, causing the house to fall into the stagnant tarn which surrounds it.

Abolitionism

These images, of the house divided which is doomed to collapse into a fragmented ruin, and of siblings bound by complex emotions of love and hatred, engaged in fratricidal conflict, are haunting metaphors for the United States in the years preceding the Civil War. As the century progressed, the cracks in the national façade widened; the issue of whether strong central government should prevail or whether power should be devolved to the individual states took on regional overtones related to the question of slavery and abolition. The North, with an economic base of trade and small farming, was more open to abolitionist ideas. The Southern elites, however, felt that the abolition of slavery would sound the death knell for their economy, founded on the large-scale cultivation of cotton, which required the extensive use of slave labor. Regional animosity was exacerbated when new territories petitioned to join the Union, making it imperative to determine whether they would be admitted as free states or slave states, thus potentially altering the precarious balance of legislative power in Congress.

The Missouri Compromise and the Nullification Controversy

In 1819, when Missouri petitioned to join the Union as a slave state, Northerners objected. After extensive debate in Congress, a compromise was reached. According to the **Missouri Compromise**, as it came to be known, slavery would be excluded in the future from all parts of the Louisiana Purchase north of the latitude 36°30', but would be allowed in

Missouri; and Maine would be admitted to the Union as a free state. The elderly **Thomas Jefferson**, writing from his Monticello estate, viewed developments with a sense of deep foreboding, stating: "this momentous question, like a fire bell in the night, awakened and filled me with terror. I considered it at once as the knell of the Union."

Jefferson's fire bell in the night tolled once more for the Union at the time of the **Nullification Controversy**. When a new tax was proposed which would levy heavy duties on British imports, Southern planters, who depended on British markets for their cotton. feared that this would provoke British retaliation. Thus the **"Tariff of Abominations,"** as it was called, was declared null and void by South Carolina, who invoked the concept of state sovereignty. After President **Andrew Jackson** declared this treasonous and threatened to march on Charleston, a compromise was finally reached in the form of an agreement to impose a much lighter tariff. Nonetheless, the notion that each state could, within its own borders and at its own will, disregard national legislation was symptomatic of the extreme fragility of anything resembling national consensus.

The abolitionists

In the meantime, the abolitionist movement gained impetus in the North. A leading African-American abolitionist, the free man of color **David Walker**, published his ***Appeal to the Colored Citizens of the World*** (1829), calling in eloquent terms upon his fellow African-Americans to resist oppression:

> at the close of the first Revolution in this country with Great Britain, there were but thirteen States in the Union, now there are twenty-four, most of which are slave-holding States, and the whites are dragging us around in chains and hand-cuffs to their new States and Territories to work their mines and farms to enrich them and their children, and millions of them believing firmly that we being a little darker than they, were made by our creator to be an inheritance to them and their children forever – the same as a parcel of brutes ... Are we MEN! – I ask you, O my brethren! Are we MEN! Did our creator make us to be slaves to dust and ashes like our-selves? Are they not dying worms as well as we? Have they not to make their appearance before the tribunal of heaven, to answer for the deeds done in the body, as well as we? Have we any other master but Jesus Christ alone?

> (Walker, 1830)

The watershed year of 1831 saw both the foundation of the crusading abolitionist newspaper *The Liberator*, edited by **William Lloyd Garrison** and the armed slave revolt led in Virginia by **Nat Turner**. Turner's forces (consisting of approximately 50 slaves) left a bloody trail in their wake, killing at least 55 whites. After evading capture for some weeks, Turner was captured and executed; over 50 of the rebels were executed as well, and many innocent African-Americans were subjected to mob violence. In Turner's rebellion, the nightmare of every Southern slaveholder was made manifest. North–South polarization on the issue of slavery was further exacerbated, with some abolitionists hailing Nat Turner as a prophetic, Moses-like hero attempting to lead his people from bondage, while Southerners viewed him as a fiend in human form.

Frederick Douglass

A literary genre which proved to be one of the most powerful weapons in the arsenal of abolitionist rhetoric was the **slave narrative**, an account of the lived experience of slaves, usually relating the escape of a slave from bondage in the South in order to take refuge in the North. In most cases, these texts are preceded by a **legitimizing narrative** (written by a white abolitionist) attesting to their veracity and authenticity. Without a doubt, slave narratives offer us some of the most gripping reads to be found in American nineteenth-century literature, combining human drama, adventure, tales of deliverance from suffering and violence, and genuine pathos. Much of their rhetorical force comes from their status as testimony to actual events as lived by the tellers, and from the fact that they appealed to the common humanity of their slave authors and their white abolitionist readers. One of the most widely read slave narratives was that of Frederick Douglass.

Frederick Douglass was born a slave on a plantation on the eastern shore of Maryland. His original name was Frederick Augustus Washington Bailey; on attaining his freedom, he changed it to Douglass, partly in homage to one of Sir Walter Scott's protagonists, Lord James Douglas in *The Lady of the Lake*, and partly in order to escape detection by bounty hunters who sought to recapture him. He describes his origins and early years, stating that he has no accurate knowledge of his own age, adding that the lack of information about his origins was a source of distress to him even as a child:

A want of information concerning my own was a source of unhappiness to me even during childhood. The white children could tell their ages. I could not tell why I ought to be deprived of the same privilege. I was not allowed to make any inquiries of my master concerning it. He deemed all such inquiries on the part of a slave improper and impertinent, and evidence of a restless spirit. The nearest estimate I can give makes me now between twenty-seven and twenty-eight years of age. I come to this, from hearing my master say, some time during 1835, I was about seventeen years old ....

Douglass refers to his own mixed-race background.

My mother was named Harriet Bailey. She was the daughter of Isaac and Betsey Bailey, both colored, and quite dark. My mother was of a darker complexion than either my grandmother or grandfather ... My father was a white man. He was admitted to be such by all I ever heard speak of my parentage. The opinion was also whispered that my master was my father; but of the correctness of this opinion, I know nothing; the means of knowing was withheld from me.

(Douglass, 1997, p. 12)

In subsequent years, the young Frederick only saw his mother four or five times; she died when he was only seven. Shortly thereafter, he was sent to the household of his master's brother, Hugh Auld, where Mrs Auld began to teach him how to read until her husband forbade her to continue. Douglass was, however, not only intelligent but resourceful, and he devised ways to learn to read and write. After this, he was sent back to Thomas Auld's plantation and handed over to Edward Covey, a brutal and devious man who had acquired a considerable reputation as a "slave-breaker." There Douglass received regular beatings and was made to work from dawn to dusk. He relates not only his own sufferings but those of his fellow slaves, particularly one woman called Caroline whom Covey had bought as a "breeder," locking her up every night for a year with a married man he had hired from another farmer. The unfortunate Caroline gave birth to twins at the end of the year, and Douglass comments that Covey and his wife saw the children as an addition to their wealth.

The Auld plantation overlooked the Chesapeake Bay. On occasion, Frederick Douglass would stand on the banks and look at the fleets of sailing ships from every part of the world, reflecting on the contrast between the freedom the ships epitomized for him and his own bondage. Addressing the ships, he begins to plan his escape to freedom:

You are loosed from your moorings, and are free; I am fast in my chains, and am a slave! You move merrily before the gentle gale, and I sadly before the bloody whip! You are freedom's swift-winged angels, that fly round the world; I am confined in bands of iron! O that I were free! O, that I were on one of your gallant decks, and under your protecting wing! Alas! betwixt me and you, the turbid waters roll. Go on, go on. O that I could also go! Could I but swim! If I could fly! O, why was I born a man, of whom to make a brute! The glad ship is gone; she hides in the dim distance. I am left in the hottest hell of unending slavery. O God, save me! God, deliver me! Let me be free! Is there any God? Why am I a slave?

(Douglass, 1997, p. 46)

Douglass decides to flee, resolving that death is preferable to continued bondage. He is aware that only a hundred miles to the North he will cross the border into a free state:

I will take to the water. This very bay shall yet bear me into freedom. The steamboats steered in a northeast course from North Point. I will do the same; and when I get to the head of the bay, I will turn my canoe adrift, and walk straight through Delaware into Pennsylvania. When I get there, I shall not be required to have a pass; I can travel without being disturbed. Let but the first opportunity offer, and, come what will, I am off.

(Douglass, 1997, p. 46)

And off he was, escaping not long thereafter. On reaching the North, Douglass worked initially at odd jobs and then became a minister; later he became involved in abolitionist activities. In 1841, he addressed an anti-slavery convention, and the crusading editor of *The Liberator*, William Lloyd Garrison, was in the audience. Garrison immediately realized that Douglass's personal testimony of his life as a slave had an extraordinary impact on audiences, and Douglass became a regular fixture on the lecture circuit. The relationship between Douglass and his white abolitionist mentors, however, was not always an easy one, and it was sometimes felt that the elegance and fluency of Douglass's prose called the credibility of his account into question; on one occasion, it was even suggested that Douglass introduce some quaint plantation expressions into his speeches. In 1845 Douglass's **Narrative** was published, with a preface by Garrison, and became an immediate best seller, with editions in Ireland, England, Germany, and France; British abolitionists purchased Douglass's freedom in 1846. Increasingly, Douglass came to believe that African-Americans should control their own representations and be their own advocates; Garrison felt differently, and the two parted with some acrimony. After the Civil War, Douglass went on to a distinguished diplomatic career, first as chargé d'affaires in Santo Domingo and then minister to Haiti.

Les Cenelles

Another landmark for African-Americans was the publication in 1845 of what has been termed the first anthology of African-American poetry by 18 New Orleans Francophone poets. Most of the mixed-race contributors to **Les Cenelles** had been educated in France; many were the offspring of white men and their African-American mistresses. The decision to publish an anthology of poetry in antebellum Louisiana by Creoles of color was a brave one indeed, doubly so given that legislation existed which prohibited the writing or publishing of any matter tending to cause discontent among the free people of color, or insubordination among the slaves, with penalties of life imprisonment with hard labor or death. Perhaps due to this, the contributions to *Les Cenelles* follow for the most part accepted models of French romanticism, and many on the surface at least deal with conventional themes of love, death, and melancholy. For obvious reasons, though, *Les Cenelles* had to tread carefully. **Armand Lanusse**, the compiler of the collection, obliquely sets out in his Introduction his reasons for publishing the volume, stating "a good education is a shield against the hostile, malicious slurs cast upon us" (Lanusse, 2003, p. 13, my translation), underlining the implicit notion that cultural achievement and the existence of an educated elite refute accusations of cultural inferiority. What is notable, however, is that their cultural and stylistic frames of reference are clearly located not in Africa, but France.

Armand Lanusse, the editor of the volume *Les Cenelles*, embodies the conflicts and contradictions which characterized many of these poets: he was light-skinned enough to pass for white had he so wished, and indeed he fought in the Civil War on the side of the South with the Confederate Louisiana Native Guards. However, he dedicated his life to the defense of education for Creoles of color. **Camille Thierry**, probably the most gifted of these poets, was the son of a Frenchman from Bordeaux and a free woman of color. **Pierre Dalcour** was the offspring of two free people of color and was educated in France; he returned to New Orleans but was disillusioned by the racism he encountered, ultimately returning to France. **Victor Séjour**, another contributor, was the offspring of a well-to-do free man of color and a mixed-race mother; his father had emigrated from St Domingue to New Orleans after the revolt of 1792. Later, in France, Séjour served as private secretary to Napoleon III. Dalcour and Séjour ultimately achieved a degree of literary fame in France, where they were part of Parisian literary circles that included figures such as Cyrille Bissette, Alexandre Dumas, and Alphonse Lamartine.

The Woman Question

Slaves were not the only group to feel that they had been denied the most basic freedoms. Obviously, one cannot compare the lot of nineteenth-century women (difficult though it was in many cases) with the horrors of slavery. Nonetheless, and although there were crucial differences in their status, it is true that neither women nor slaves could vote, nor were they free agents in economic terms. In many ways, the significant involvement of American women in abolitionist movements was responsible for their growing awareness of the limitations of their own existence.

The discourse of domesticity

Fanny Fern, one of the "d – d mob of scribbling women" whose consider-able popular and commercial success had caused Nathaniel Hawthorne to despair, once commented on the considerable gap between lofty Revolutionary rhetoric about freedom and individual rights and the practi-cal everyday reality of most women's lives. Writing on the Fourth of July, in a short article ironically titled **"Independence,"** she comments in breezy journalistic style:

> Well – I don't feel patriotic. Perhaps I might if they would stop that deafen-ing racket. Washington was very well, if he *couldn't* spell, and I'm glad we are all free; but as a woman – I shouldn't know it, didn't some orator tell me. Can I go out of an evening without a hat at my side? Can I go out with one on my head without danger of a station-house? Can I clap my hands at some public speaker when I am nearly bursting with delight? Can I signify the contrary when my hair stands on end with vexation?
>
> (Fern, 1859)

Some women viewed the home as the space of morality and conscience, the appropriate site for the exercise of redemptive female authority. For others, however, domestic space was constraining and claustrophobic, and there was a drive to exercise political and economic authority in the wider world beyond the home.

For obvious reasons, it would be an error to affirm that nineteenth-century American women were completely lacking in power and agency. One useful distinction in this regard is that between power and authority. *Power* can be defined as the ability to act effectively on persons or things. *Authority*, however, is the socially validated right to make a particular decision and command obedience, and usually involves a hierarchical chain of command.[1] The complex issues of power and authority were at the forefront of debates regarding the role of American women in the nineteenth century, for while women did exercise a degree of power, they were rarely to be found in positions of authority.

Linda Kerber, in her seminal study *Women of the Republic*, suggests that women in post-Revolutionary America attempted to reconcile the paucity of opportunities for women to engage in political activity with the notion of **civic virtue** as a foundational value of the Republic. For Kerber, the discourse of **Republican Motherhood** enabled women to incorporate political values into domestic life, with mothers educating future (male) citizens and shaping their moral choices, thus participating indirectly in national life through their husbands, brothers, and sons (Kerber, 1980, pp. 7–12, 35–6).

One constantly encounters in writing of the period the metaphor of the domestic sphere, both in the writing of the period and in recent historiography, to describe the complex reality of gender relations in nineteenth-century America. Barbara Welter (1966), in an influential essay, "The Cult of True Womanhood", analyzes the discourse of separate spheres. She characterizes the four cardinal virtues ascribed to women in popular writing of the period as domesticity, piety, purity, and submissiveness; the notion of separate space was viewed as a negative phenomenon which helped maintain women's subordinate status. Carroll Smith-Rosenberg, however, offers a very different interpretation in "The Female World of Love and Ritual," arguing that in the nineteenth century there existed a distinctive women's culture offering mutual support (in childbirth and reciprocal childcare, for example) and shared emotional ties. What is clear, however, is that the involvement of many American women in the struggle for the abolition of slavery gave rise to increased political awareness about

---

[1]   See Rosaldo (1974) for a lucid discussion of power and gender roles.

the limitations of their own situation. Women, like slaves, were denied the right to vote or to participate openly in politics; often men controlled the property their wives had inherited from their own families.

A compelling example of the ways in which the campaign for women's rights and the crusade to abolish slavery coincided and collided is offered by the debate between **Catherine Beecher**, a prominent educator (and the sister of **Harriet Beecher Stowe**), and **Angelina Grimké**, who along with her older sister Sarah would become known as one of the earliest advocates of equal rights for women. The Grimkés were the daughters of John Faucheraud Grimké, a South Carolina slaveowner and Chief Justice of the South Carolina Supreme Court. Although Sarah had wished to become an attorney, her father refused to countenance the idea. When he became ill, Sarah accompanied him to Philadelphia for medical treatment and while there became a Quaker. After her father's death, she moved in 1821 to Philadelphia, and eight years later Angelina, who had also converted to Quakerism, joined her there. The two women were staunchly against slavery, in part because of the brutality they had witnessed on their family's plantation, and they became involved in abolitionist activities. Angelina wrote a letter to the prominent abolitionist William Lloyd Garrison declaring her support for his opinions, and Garrison promptly published her letter without consulting her in the abolitionist newspaper *The Liberator*, with her name attached. In many quarters this was greeted as an outrageous intrusion into the masculine public sphere. A pastoral letter (widely assumed to be aimed at the Grimkés) was subsequently published in the *New England Spectator* and read aloud from Congregationalist pulpits, in which the ministers thundered, "A woman's power is in her dependence, flowing from the consciousness of that weakness which God has given her for protection." They added that when a woman dared to disregard this alleged "weakness" and "assumes the place and tone of a man as a public reformer," she consequently was not entitled to male "care and protection" and had exposed herself to "shame and dishonor" (quoted in Henry, 1997; see also Ceplair, 1989, p. 303).

Angelina Grimké's *Appeal to the Christian Women of the South* (1836) is essentially couched in religious and theological terms. She argues that slavery is sinful, and that the crusade for its abolition is tantamount to the crusade against sin. This astutely uses the authority of biblical references to legitimize women's political involvement in the crusade against slavery, characterizing it as a deeply moral course of action which women are indeed obliged as Christians to carry out. This promptly stirred up a bit of a hornet's nest. Grimké's fellow Quakers were not happy with her stance and expressed their condemnation in meeting. Other prominent women found Grimké's initially involuntary projection into the public realm distressing. One such was Catherine Beecher, a prominent educationalist.

In 1837 Beecher published a text titled **"An Essay on Slavery and Abolitionism, with Reference to the Duty of American Females,"** directly addressed to Grimké. In her preface, Beecher states that the essay had begun as a letter to a personal friend, whose intellectual and moral standing she acknowledges, and whom she addresses as "my dear Friend." Her central argument (which echoes the earlier pastoral condemnation of Grimké's activities) is that Grimké's entry into the public sphere of political debate was not only indecorous and inappropriate but ultimately ineffective. Maintaining that men could enter into public debate, appeal to public sentiment, or "drive by physical force," she describes what she sees as the appropriate constraints on the exercise of power by women:

> But all the power, and all the conquests that are lawful to woman, are those only which appeal to the kindly, generous, peaceful and benevolent principles ... Woman is to win every thing by peace and love; by making herself so much respected, esteemed and loved, that to yield to her opinions and to gratify her wishes, will be the free-will offering of the heart. But this is to be all accomplished in the domestic and social circle ....

The public sphere, however, was a different matter:

> But the moment woman begins to feel the promptings of ambition, or the thirst for power, her ægis of defence is gone. All the sacred protection of religion, all the generous promptings of chivalry, all the poetry of romantic gallantry, depend upon woman's retaining her place as dependent and defenceless, and making no claims, and maintaining no right but what are the gifts of honour, rectitude and love.
>
> (Beecher, 1837)

Here again we encounter the characterization of the domestic realm as the proper space for the exercise of female influence. It is directly implied that by acting outside her "proper" sphere, a woman forfeits the right to respect and protection from men. Later, Beecher argues that political activities such as petitions to Congress are completely outside the sphere of "female duty," adding that well-educated women can exercise power by influencing men rather than by direct action. However, she suggests that it would be disastrous for women if education caused them to challenge male prerogatives and surrender their "graceful and dignified retirement and submission" to men. She then states baldly:

> An ignorant, a narrow-minded, or a stupid woman, cannot feel nor understand the rationality, the propriety, of the beauty of this relation; and she it is, that will be most likely to carry her measures by tormenting, when she cannot please, or by petulant complaints or obtrusive interference, in matters which are out of her sphere, and which she cannot comprehend.
>
> (Beecher, 1837)

Here the constraints that the discourse of separate spheres placed upon women is set forth very directly. In this perspective, any woman like Grimké who did not submit to male authority and who chose to debate political issues outside the confines of the home was "ignorant," "narrow-minded," or "stupid," incapable of understanding matters which fell outside her domestic sphere. Beecher's essay concludes with a comment that slavery can only be ended by calm, rational Christian discussion of the issue, which would enable females to wield a "wise and appropriate influence." In short, women could wield limited power, but authority was firmly placed in the hands of men.

Angelina Grimké riposted with a series of letters to Beecher published weekly in the abolitionist newspapers, in which she responds to the accusations against her. In Letter XII, **"Human Rights not Founded on Sex"** (1837), she sets forth in passionate terms the analogies she has drawn between the crusade to abolish slavery and the campaign for women's rights:

> The investigation of the rights of the slave has led me to a better understanding of my own. I have found the Anti-Slavery cause to be the high school of morals in our land – the school in which human rights are more fully investigated, and better understood and taught, than in any other. Here a great fundamental principle is uplifted and illuminated, and from this central light, rays innumerable stream all around. Human beings have rights, because they are moral beings: the rights of all men grow out of their moral nature; and as all men have the same moral nature, they have essentially the same rights ... Now if rights are founded in the nature of our moral being, then the mere circumstance of sex does not give to man higher rights and responsibilities, than to woman.
>
> (Grimké, 1838, p. 115)

She then concludes that her belief is that whatever it is morally right for man to do is morally right for women as well, since one's duties are not linked to sexual difference but rather from our relationships, our capacities, and the historical period in which we live. After this, Grimké denounces the infantilization of women, "taught to lean upon an arm of flesh," to be pampered like a spoiled child or converted into a domestic drudge. This, she alleges, has given man a charter to exercise tyranny, selfishness, lust, and brutal violence. She then turns on its head Beecher's accusations of stupidity, ignorance, or narrow-mindedness, declaring that only a narrow-minded view of human rights and responsibilities could induce someone to accept this view of subordination of one human being to another. She concludes with the following ringing appeal to a different vision of gender relations for the future:

> Sure I am, that the signs of the times clearly indicate a vast and rapid change in public sentiment, on this subject. Sure I am that she [Woman] is not to be, as she has been, "a mere second-hand agent" in the regeneration of a fallen world, but the acknowledged equal and co-worker with man in this glorious work.
>
> (Grimké, 1838, p. 121)

The "vast and rapid change in public sentiment" envisaged by Grimké and her sister Sarah was not long in making itself felt even more forcefully. **Elizabeth Cady Stanton**, who later would play a key role in the **Seneca Falls** conference on women's rights, was also actively involved in the crusade to abolish slavery. Her husband **Henry Brewster Stanton** was deeply committed to the abolitionist cause, and the young couple spent their honeymoon in England with the intention of attending the World Anti-Slavery convention. There, Elizabeth Cady Stanton met other female activists such as **Lucretia Mott**, a Quaker minister from Pennsylvania. On the first day of the Convention, however, a decision was taken not to seat female delegates. This caused outrage, and Stanton and Mott resolved to organize a meeting in the United States with the sole purpose of discussing women's rights.

This convention was held in 1848 in Seneca Falls, New York, attracting approximately three hundred delegates. One hundred of the delegates (including 32 men, one of whom was Frederick Douglass) signed a document titled **"Declaration of Sentiments."** Its rhetoric is almost identical to that of the **Declaration of Independence**. After stating the "self-evident" truth that all men and women are created equal, with the inalienable right to life, liberty, and the pursuit of happiness, it adds:

> The history of mankind is a history of repeated injuries and usurpations on the part of man toward women, having in direct object the establishment of an absolute tyranny over her. To prove this, let facts be submitted to a candid world:
>
> He has never permitted her to exercise her inalienable right to the elective franchise.
>
> He has compelled her to submit to laws, in the formation of which she had no voice.
>
> He has withheld from her rights which are given to the most ignorant and degraded men – both natives and foreigners.
>
> Having deprived her of this first right of a citizen, the elective franchise, thereby leaving her without representation in the halls of legislation, he has oppressed her on all sides.
>
> He has made her, if married, in the eye of the law, civilly dead.
>
> He has taken from her all right in property, even to the wages she earns.
>
> He has made her, morally, an irresponsible being, as she can commit many crimes with impunity, provided they be done in the presence of her husband. In the covenant of marriage, she is compelled to promise obedience to her husband, he becoming, to all intents and purposes, her master – the law giving him power to deprive her of her liberty, and to administer chastisement.[2]

A long litany of grievances ensues, skillfully using almost the exact wording to be found at many junctures of the Declaration of Independence but substituting "man" for the figure of the allegedly despotic monarch George III, thus highlighting the discrepancy between the promises of equality enshrined in the Declaration and the lived reality of half of the citizens of the early Republic. This rhetorical tactic proved gratifyingly effective to a certain extent. As a consequence of Seneca Falls and its mobilization of public opinion, legislation was passed protecting married women's earnings as well as their right to manage their own property. Not until 1920, however, did American women achieve the right to vote.

---

[2] http://usinfo.org/docs/democracy/17.htm, accessed August 9, 2009.

The Prelude to the Civil War

The 1850 Compromise and the Fugitive Slave Law

Only two years after Seneca Falls, another uneasy legislative compromise was brokered in Congress when California applied to join the Union. In the terms of the **1850 Compromise**, California was admitted as a free state; New Mexico and Utah were to be organized as territories, without resolving the issue of slavery; the slave trade in the District of Columbia was abolished, and a new Fugitive Slave Law would replace that of 1793. According to the provisions of the **1850 Fugitive Slave Law**, slaveholders were allowed to recapture runaway slaves, even in free states; public officers were compelled not only to assist but to call on bystanders to apprehend runaways; fines and six months imprisonment were the sentences for those helping slaves or trying to rescue them; runaways were forbidden to testify in their own defense (thus encouraging the capture of free people of color). This law would have far-reaching consequences for people like Frederick Douglass, who left the country to avoid apprehension and a return to slavery.

African-American novelists

In addition to slave narratives and poetry, African-Americans made their presence felt as novelists. In 1853, **William Wells Brown** published his novel *Clotel: or, The President's Daughter: A Narrative* in London. Brown had escaped from slavery, and his own legal status in the US was that of property; British abolitionists purchased his freedom in 1853. His novel tells the story of Thomas Jefferson's alleged slave mistress **Sally Hemings**, his daughters and granddaughters, challenging official patriotic narratives about the Founding Fathers and using a pastiche of sentimental and politicized discourses. **Harriet Wilson**'s novel *Our Nig* appeared in 1859. Blending conventions of the slave narrative and the sentimental novel, it tells the story of Frado, a mixed-race girl who is abandoned by her white mother upon the death of her African-American father and grows up as a servant to a white family in Massachusetts.

Another African-American writer, **Frances Harper**, first became known for her poetry, although she would go on to publish her best-known long work, *Iola Leroy*, long after the Civil War. One poem, **"The Slave Mother,"** offers a poignant image of a mother who is about to be parted from her child:

> She is a mother, pale with fear,
> Her boy clings to her side,
> And in her kirtle vainly tries
> His trembling form to hide.[3]

This image of a child being taken away from his mother also appears in the writing of Harriet Beecher Stowe.

Harriet Beecher Stowe

The Fugitive Slave Law was one of the factors that impelled **Harriet Beecher Stowe** to write her novel *Uncle Tom's Cabin.* Stowe was the daughter and sister of clergymen, and married another, Calvin Stowe. Her husband was a professor at Lane Theological Seminary, in Cincinnati, directly across the river from Kentucky, a slave state. There, Stowe encountered not only a vocal and militant abolitionist movement, but also runaway slaves as well as the bounty hunters who attempted to bear them back into captivity. Harriet Beecher Stowe was a mother of six, running a household on a clergyman's salary, and her life was full to overflowing with domestic obligations. She nonetheless taught children who had escaped with their parents from slavery in a school run by the Beecher family. Her personal nadir came when she lost one of her children to cholera; this brought home to her the suffering of slave mothers when they were parted from their children. In 1850, she and her family moved to Maine, where her husband had joined the faculty of Bowdoin College. After the passage of the Fugitive Slave Law, on receiving a letter from her abolitionist sister-in-law suggesting that she write something to alert public opinion to the evils of slavery, she threw herself into the writing of **Uncle Tom's Cabin**, which would become the best-selling book in nineteenth-century America after the Bible.

Most of us are familiar with the story. A Kentucky landowner, Arthur Shelby, is forced because of debts to save his farm by selling off some of his slaves: Uncle Tom, a benign and kindly man with a wife and children; Eliza, his wife's light-skinned maidservant, and Eliza's child. Eliza overhears the plan, and escapes with her son. Stowe appeals directly to the maternal sensibilities of her female readers, asking them how they would feel if their own children were torn away from them by a brutal trafficker

---

[3]   http://www.pbs.org/wgbh/amex/lincolns/filmmore/ps_harper.html, accessed November 4, 2009.

in human beings, and how quickly they would be prompted to escape. Pursued by slave traders, Eliza flees with her child in her arms across floes of ice over the Ohio River:

> A thousand lives seemed to be concentrated in that one moment to Eliza. Her room opened by a side door to the river. She caught her child, and sprang down the steps towards it. The trader caught a full glimpse of her just as she was disappearing down the bank; and throwing himself from his horse, and calling loudly on Sam and Andy, he was after her like a hound after a deer. In that dizzy moment her feet to her scarce seemed to touch the ground, and a moment brought her to the water's edge. Right on behind they came; and, nerved with strength such as God gives only to the desperate, with one wild cry and flying leap, she vaulted sheer over the turbid current by the shore, on to the raft of ice beyond. It was a desperate leap – impossible to anything but madness and despair; and Haley, Sam, and Andy, instinctively cried out, and lifted up their hands, as she did it.
>
> The huge green fragment of ice on which she alighted pitched and creaked as her weight came on it, but she staid there not a moment. With wild cries and desperate energy she leaped to another and still another cake; stumbling – leaping – slipping – springing upwards again! Her shoes are gone – her stockings cut from her feet – while blood marked every step; but she saw nothing, felt nothing, till dimly, as in a dream, she saw the Ohio side, and a man helping her up the bank.
>
> (Stowe, 1994, p. 52)

Later, Eliza is reunited with her husband George in Canada.

The saintly Uncle Tom is not so fortunate. He is sold down the river to Louisiana, first to the relatively benevolent master Augustine St. Clare in New Orleans. The members of the St. Clare ménage are a representative sample of attitudes toward slavery. St. Clare is relatively benevolent but negligent and lacking in will; his indolent wife is remarkably unpleasant and despotic. St. Clare's Northern cousin Ophelia is in favor of the principle of abolition, but is repelled by African-Americans in the flesh. Uncle Tom forms a particularly strong bond of affection with Eva, St. Clare's youngest child.

But when St. Clare dies, Uncle Tom is sold on to one of the most unpleasant villains in literature, Simon Legree, allegedly based on the sadistic Cane River planter Robert McAlpin who is said to have burned slaves alive. Legree's mixed-race mistress, Cassy, is replaced as the object of his attentions by a young slave called Emmeline; the two desperate women join forces and play upon Legree's superstition in order to escape from his violence and abuse. Stowe tells us that some years before, a female slave had been confined to a garret in the plantation house for several weeks, and ultimately died there. It is implied that she was beaten to death; the slaves (and Legree) believe that the place is haunted, and it is said that the sounds of cursing and blows, together with wails of pain and despair, can still be heard. The two women escape; but rather than fleeing through the swamp, they double back and hide in the garret, where they had stashed provisions. Legree, when he hears their movements, is convinced that his past sins have come back to haunt him. Uncle Tom dies nobly from the wounds inflicted by a savage beating, and Legree drinks himself to death; the two women escape to the North. George Shelby, the son of Tom's former owners, arrives to buy his freedom, but it is too late. The novel ends as he returns to Kentucky and sets all his slaves free.

For present-day readers, some facets of the novel can appear problematic. Stowe's direct appeal to the sentiment of readers can often seem cloying, and her racial attitudes often impress us as actively offensive, with African-Americans characterized as primitive and childlike, so loyal to their masters that they are willing to submit to hideous mistreatment and violence. The very name of the noble, Christ-like slave, Uncle Tom, has become a term of opprobrium for many African-Americans in our own time. The novelist **James Baldwin**, in a seminal essay titled **"Everybody's Protest Novel"** (1949), calls our attention to the fact that only the mixed-race characters such as Eliza and George are able to escape, while the darker Uncle Tom is condemned to death.

In the nineteenth century, however, Stowe's use of the conventions of domestic melodrama in order to show how slavery tore families apart was highly effective in mobilizing public sentiment in favor of abolition. It is said that **President Lincoln**, on being introduced to Mrs Stowe, commented, "So this is the little lady who started this big war." (Stowe, 1911, p. 203). The book first appeared in serialized form in the antislavery periodical *The National Era*; 300,000 copies were sold in the United States alone in the year following its publication. In 1852, it was published in London, and 200,000 copies were sold. It was translated into most major languages. In recent decades, the novel has undergone a major critical reassessment. It is clear that Stowe's brilliant rhetorical strategy of using the discourse of sentiment in order to tap into nineteenth-century America's most deeply cherished beliefs in the sacred character of the family and of the domestic sphere and of the possibility of redemption through Christian love and forgiveness enabled her to create a novel that not only moved millions of readers but also brought about major social change.

The Dred Scott decision

Despite the enthusiastic reception of Stowe's novel, however, the lot of African-Americans steadily grew worse in antebellum America. In 1857 Dred Scott, a Missouri slave, petitioned for his freedom on the grounds that he and his wife Harriet, though slaves, had lived in states and territories where slavery was illegal. In this landmark case, **Dred Scott vs. Sanford**, the Supreme Court ruled seven to two against Scott's petition, stating that neither he nor any other person of African ancestry could claim to be a US citizen, and thus Scott was ineligible to bring suit in federal court.

Harper's Ferry and John Brown's raid

In October 1859, the tension was ratcheted up even further when the abolitionist **John Brown** and a group of armed followers seized the United States Armory and Arsenal at **Harper's Ferry**, in the hope of prompting a slave insurrection. The revolt was unsuccessful, and Brown was wounded, captured, tried, and condemned to death. **Henry David Thoreau** had met Brown when the latter had visited Concord in order to raise funds to buy arms on behalf of anti-slavery forces in Kansas. In a passionate essay titled **"A Plea for Captain John Brown,"** Thoreau sets aside his earlier arguments in favor of passive resistance, arguing that Brown's forces were small in number but prepared to sacrifice their lives in a noble cause. Later, Thoreau acknowledges that in some situations violence may be the only way of effecting change. With Brown's execution, political and geographical polarization in the nation became exacerbated even further. For abolitionists, Brown became a martyr. Southerners felt that Harper's Ferry presaged other similar attempts by abolitionists to arm the slaves, prompting them to reestablish local militias; they characterized the raid as an outcome of the Republican Party's platform.

Harriet Jacobs

For women the horrors of slavery were compounded by the constant threat (and in many cases, the grim reality) of sexual exploitation. One such woman was **Harriet Jacobs,** whose *narrative,* published in 1861 on the eve of the Civil War, bears witness to her desperate attempts to avoid the repeated attempts of her master to force her to be his concubine. As Jacobs relates it, the first years of her life were relatively happy despite her status as a slave; her mistress was benevolent and kind, and taught her to read and sew. However, upon her mistress's death, 12-year-old Harriet was bequeathed in inheritance to her benefactor's niece, who was only three years old. This meant that Jacobs was actually in thrall to the child's father, a Dr Norcom.

As Harriet Jacobs reached puberty, Norcom began a relentless campaign of sexual harassment, whispering "foul words" in her ear. She staunchly resisted his advances, and asked his permission to marry a free man of color. This was refused. In desperation, and to avoid being forced into concubinage by Norcom, Jacobs became involved with a white lawyer, and had two children by him; her reasoning was that her white lover would buy her and her children and set them free. The notion of bearing a child out of wedlock, however, and indeed of openly discussing matters related to sexuality, violated many powerful taboos in nineteenth-century America, and Jacobs was aware that a frank discussion of these issues could potentially alienate abolitionist readers. Using the conventions of sentimental writing, she addresses the reader directly:

> O, ye happy women, whose purity has been sheltered from childhood, who have been free to choose the objects of your affection, whose homes are protected by law, do not judge the poor desolate slave girl too severely! If slavery had been abolished, I, also, could have married the man of my choice; I could have had a home shielded by the laws; and I should have been spared the painful task of confessing what I am now about to relate; but all my prospects had been blighted by slavery. I wanted to keep myself pure; and, under the most adverse circumstances, I tried hard to preserve my self-respect; but I was struggling alone in the powerful grasp of the demon Slavery; and the monster proved too strong for me. I felt as if I was forsaken by God and man; as if all my efforts must be frustrated; and I became reckless in my despair.
>
> (Jacobs, 1987, p. 54)

Jacobs casts slavery as an institution which foments sexual immorality, and appeals to the solidarity of white female readers by contrasting their own sheltered upbringing with her own plight. Norcom, however, refused to sell her, and continued in his pursuit. When she learned that he was

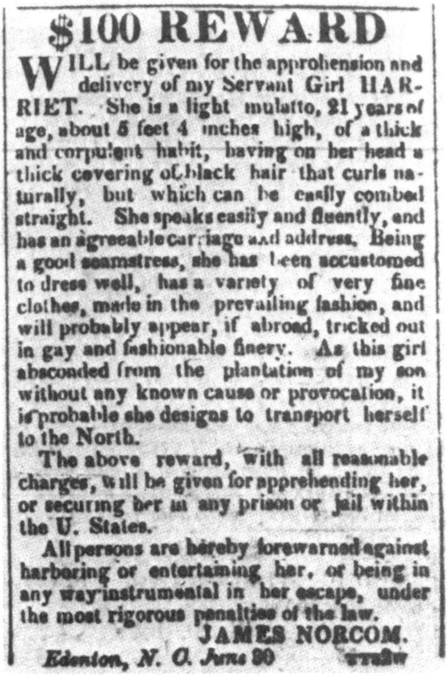

$100 REWARD

WILL be given for the apprehension and delivery of my Servant Girl HARRIET. She is a light mulatto, 21 years of age, about 5 feet 4 inches high, of a thick and corpulent habit, having on her head a thick covering of black hair that curls naturally, but which can be easily combed straight. She speaks easily and fluently, and has an agreeable carriage and address. Being a good seamstress, she has been accustomed to dress well, has a variety of very fine clothes, made in the prevailing fashion, and will probably appear, if abroad, tricked out in gay and fashionable finery. As this girl absconded from the plantation of my son without any known cause or provocation, it is probable she designs to transport herself to the North.

The above reward, with all reasonable charges, will be given for apprehending her, or securing her in any prison or jail within the U. States.

All persons are hereby forewarned against harboring or entertaining her, or being in any way instrumental in her escape, under the most rigorous penalties of the law.

JAMES NORCOM.

Edenton, N. C. June 30 ttw3w

Figure 8.1 Advertisement for the capture of Harriet Jacobs. From *The American Beacon*, July 4, 1835. Courtesy of the North Carolina Office of Archives and History, Raleigh, North Carolina.

building a house where he was preparing to install her, she escaped, first concealed by neighbors and then hiding in a crawlspace in her beloved grandmother's house, to which her Uncle Philip had prepared a concealed trapdoor. This space was seven feet wide, nine feet long, and three feet high, lacking light or air. There she remained for seven years, emerging only at night for brief periods of exercise. Norcom, convinced that she had escaped to the North, placed notices in Northern newspapers offering a reward for her recapture.

In the meantime, Jacobs's children had been bought by their father, and she was occasionally able to catch a glimpse of them from her garret through a peephole she had made.

> I suffered for air even more than for light. But I was not comfortless. I heard the voices of my children. There was joy and there was sadness in

the sound. It made my tears flow. How I longed to speak to them! I was eager to look on their faces; but there was no hole, no crack, through which I could peep. This continued darkness was oppressive. It seemed horrible to sit or lie in a cramped position day after day, without one gleam of light.

(Jacobs, 1987, p. 114)

Appalling though her situation was, Jacobs stoutly maintains that it was preferable to her lot as a slave. This poignant description of a woman who can only look at her children from a distance and who has effectively preferred the fate of living entombment to that of sexual exploitation and slavery would resonate powerfully with female readers.

Finally, in 1842, Jacobs was able to escape to the North, where she became involved in the abolitionist movement. Early in 1861, just before the Civil War broke out, her narrative was published in New York; in order to avoid recapture, Jacobs changed her name to Linda Brent, while Norcom is referred to as Dr Flint. The book was edited by **Lydia Maria Child**, who was well aware of the controversial nature of Jacobs's subject matter. In her Introduction, Child acknowledges that she will be accused of indecorum, but staunchly states that she presents these pages to the public "for the sake of my sisters in bondage who are suffering wrongs so foul, that our ears are too delicate to listen to them" (Child, 1987).

In the meantime, Dr Norcom had died, but his descendents continued to pursue Jacobs as part of their inheritance from his estate; given the provisions of the Fugitive Slave Law, they were within their rights in doing so. Ultimately, Jacobs and her children were purchased from them by her employer, a Mrs Willis, and at last freed. Jacobs speaks of her gratitude to Mrs Willis for the gift of her freedom, but also of her outrage on contemplating her own Bill of Sale and verifying that she, as a human being, was considered an article of merchandise in the city of New York.

Abraham Lincoln's election and the outbreak of the Civil War

With the election of the Republican candidate **Abraham Lincoln** to the Presidency in November 1860, the die was well and truly cast. Southerners viewed his election as a provocation to their region, and in December the South Carolina legislature formally revoked the state's ratification of the Constitution. In the ensuing weeks, several other states (Alabama, Mississippi, Louisiana, Texas, Florida, and Georgia, all major producers of cotton) joined South Carolina in seceding from the Union, and in February

1861 they met in Montgomery, Alabama to form the **Confederate States of America**. Although the Constitution of the Confederacy resembled that of the United States in many aspects, it emphasized the primacy of states' rights, described as the "sovereign and independent character" of each state, and guaranteed the preservation of slavery. At the same time, however, and probably in an attempt to gain support from Britain (where a powerful abolitionist movement existed alongside equally powerful textile manufacturing interests), the legality of the international slave trade was denied.

When the Federal garrison of Fort Sumter in Charleston, South Carolina, required reinforcements and supplies, Lincoln declared his determination "to hold, occupy and possess" federal property. The Confederacy took this as a declaration of war, and its President, **Jefferson Davis** made the decision to attack this symbol of Northern authority. On April 12, 1861, the Confederate forces fired on **Fort Sumter**. Lincoln called for volunteers to put an end to the rebellion, and in response Virginia, Arkansas, North Carolina, and Tennessee renounced the Union and joined the Confederacy. The Civil War had begun.

Initially, both sides were convinced that the war would be short. In this, they were sadly mistaken. Both in absolute terms and in terms of the proportion of the number of casualties to the overall population, it remains the bloodiest war in American history, with approximately 359,000 Union soldiers and 258,000 Confederate troops dead either of injuries on the battlefield or in military hospitals (Brogan, 1999, p. 345). The extraordinarily high mortality rates were due in part to the grim juxtaposition of obsolete military tactics (cavalry charges, major battles with floods of troops facing each other in waves of frontal assaults) and new technology, particularly repeating rifles and expanding minié bullets, resulted in slaughter on a massive scale. In addition, many soldiers had come from the country and had not been exposed to childhood diseases such as measles and mumps; many were laid low with these illnesses as well as malaria, typhoid, and dysentery. If they were lucky enough to survive the battles, they were often faced with insalubrious conditions and lack of food in prisoner of war camps such as Andersonville and Libby. The grim names of places where the main battles were fought over the next four years, and the carnage which took place, evoke Jefferson's image of the bell tolling in the night: **Bull Run** (3,000 casualties), **Shiloh** (23,000), **Antietam** (21,000), **Fredericksburg** (15,000). One of the most gripping portrayals of the war's terrible human cost is **Walt Whitman**'s description, in **"A March in the Ranks Hard-Prest,"** of the dying men in a hospital which had been hastily improvised in a church:

... crowds, groups of forms vaguely I see on the floor, some in the pews laid down,

At my feet more distinctly a soldier, a mere lad, in danger of bleeding to death, (he is shot in the abdomen,)

I stanch the blood temporarily, (the youngster's face is white as a lily,)

Then before I depart I sweep my eyes o'er the scene fain to absorb it all,

Faces, varieties, postures beyond description, most in obscurity, some of them dead,

Surgeons operating, attendants holding lights, the smell of ether, the odor of blood,

The crowd, O the crowd of the bloody forms, the yard outside also fill'd,

Some on the bare ground, some on planks or stretchers, some in the death-spasm sweating,

An occasional scream or cry, the doctor's shouted orders or calls,

The glisten of the little steel instruments catching the glint of the torches,

These I resume as I chant, I see again the forms, I smell the odor,

Then hear outside the orders given, Fall in, my men, fall in;

But first I bend to the dying lad, his eyes open, a half-smile gives he me,

Then the eyes close, calmly close, and I speed forth to the darkness,

Resuming, marching, ever in darkness marching, or in the ranks,

The unknown road still marching.

(Whitman, 1973, pp. 305–6)

The chiaroscuro imagery of the wounded men amid the glint of surgical tools and the stench of blood, and the contrast between the moving moment of shared tenderness and compassion shared with the dying boy and the literal and metaphorical darkness that awaits the poet outside in a world of barked orders and of massed troops marching down an unknown road, convey the sense of national tragedy and pointless human waste with extraordinary force.

A key moment in the conflict came in 1863 when Lincoln issued the **Emancipation Proclamation**. With it, he struck a blow at the heart of the Southern system. Although initially it affected slavery only in the Confederacy, it signaled an important change in military tactics, with the use of armed African-American troops. This hardened Southern opposition even more. Jefferson Davis is said to have denounced the policy as "the most execrable measure recorded in the history of man." But the lack of industry in the South proved ultimately to be fatal, as did the centrifugal nature of power in a system based upon states' rights rather than centralized policy, and the surrender on April 9, 1865 at **Appomatox** Courthouse of the Confederate forces under **General Robert E. Lee** to those of the Union **General Ulysses S. Grant** signaled the end of the war.

Abraham Lincoln's central preoccupation, even over and above the issue of slavery, was to preserve the unity of the American nation. The war had taken a fearful personal toll on him, and this was compounded by the death of his son Willie from malaria. A week after Appomattox, on the evening of April 14, he and his wife went to the theatre to see the play *Our American Cousin*. There, a Southern sympathizer called **John Wilkes Booth** entered the presidential box, shot Lincoln in the head, and leapt onto the stage, shouting "*Sic semper tyrannis!*" (Thus always to tyrants!). The President was taken to a nearby house, and died the following morning. Booth was subsequently captured and shot while resisting arrest.

Lincoln's death was a tragedy for both North and South. He had favored a policy of reconciliation, and his demise left profound wounds in the national consciousness. The subsequent outpouring of grief was astonishing in its intensity; millions lined the roads to salute his coffin as the funeral train passed through hundreds of towns on its final journey back to Lincoln's native Illinois. Once again, it was the poet Walt Whitman who captured the despair of the nation and portrayed its lacerating grief, in his elegy **"Memories of President Lincoln: When Lilacs Last in the Dooryard Bloomed"**:

> Coffin that passes through lanes and streets,
> Through day and night with the great cloud darkening the land,
> With the pomp of the inloop'd flags with the cities draped in black,
> With the show of the States themselves as of crape-veil'd women standing,
> With processions long and winding and the flambeaus of the night,
> With the countless torches lit, with the silent sea of faces and the unbared heads,
> With the waiting depot, the arriving coffin, and the sombre faces,
> With dirges through the night, with the thousand voices rising strong and solemn,
> With all the mournful voices of the dirges, pour'd around the coffin,
> The dim-lit churches and the shuddering organs – where amid these you journey,
> With the tolling tolling bells' perpetual clang,
> Here, coffin that slowly passes,
> I give you my sprig of lilac.

(Whitman, 1973, pp. 330–1)

Bibliography

Rolena Adorno and Patrick Pautz, ed. and trans., *The Narrative of Cabeza de Vaca* (Lincoln: University of Nebraska Press, 2003).

Paula Gunn Allen, ed., *Studies in American Indian Literature* (New York: Modern Language Association of America, 1993a).

Paula Gunn Allen, "Teaching American Indian Oral Literatures," in Paula Gunn Allen, ed., *Studies in American Indian Literature* (New York: Modern Language Association of America, 1993b), pp. 33–51.

William Apess, *On Our Own Ground: The Complete Writings of William Apess, a Pequot*, ed. Barry O'Connell (Amherst: University of Massachusetts Press, 1992).

Abraham Arias-Larreta, *Pre-Columbian Masterpieces* (Kansas City, MO: Editorial Indoamérica, 1967).

James Baldwin, "Everybody's Protest Novel," *Partisan Review*, 16 (June 1949), pp. 578–85.

Brian Barbour, ed., *Benjamin Franklin: A Collection of Critical Essays* (Englewood Cliffs, NJ: Prentice Hall, 1979).

Catherine Beecher, "An Essay on Slavery and Abolitionism," (1837), www.gutenberg.org/files/26123/26123-8.txt, accessed February 2, 2009.

Sacvan Bercovitch, *The Puritan Origins of the American Self* (New Haven, CT: Yale University Press, 1977).

Sacvan Bercovitch, *The American Jeremiad* (Madison: University of Wisconsin Press, 1978).

Sacvan Bercovitch, ed., *The Cambridge History of American Literature* (Cambridge, UK: Cambridge University Press, 1994).

John Bierhorst, ed., *Four Masterworks of American Indian Literature* (Tucson: University of Arizona Press, 1974).

Robin Blackburn, *The Making of New World Slavery from the Baroque to the Modern, 1492–1800* (London: Verso, 1998).

William Bradford, *Bradford's History of Plimoth Plantation* (Boston: Wright and Potter, 1901).

Anne Bradstreet, *The Tenth Muse, Lately Sprung up in America* (London: Stephen Bowtell, 1650).

Anne Bradstreet, *Several Poems* (Boston: John Foster, 1678)

Hugh Brogan, *The Penguin History of the USA*, 2nd edn (London: Penguin, 1999).

William Byrd, *The Secret Diary of William Byrd of Westover*, ed. Louis Wright and Maria Tinly (Richmond, VA: Dietz Press, 1941).

Colin Calloway, ed., *The World Turned Upside Down: Indian Voices from Early America* (Boston: Bedford Books, 1994).

Vincent Carretta, *Equiano, the African: Biography of a Self-Made Man* (London and New York: Penguin, 2007).

Michael P. Carroll, "The Trickster as Selfish-Buffoon and Culture Hero," *Ethos*, 12, no. 2 (Summer 1984), pp. 105–31.

Susan Castillo, *Colonial Encounters in New World Writing: Performing America, 1500–1786* (London: Routledge, 2005).

Susan Castillo and Ivy Schweitzer, eds., *The Literatures of Colonial America: An Anthology* (Oxford: Blackwell, 2001).

Larry Ceplair, ed., *The Public Years of Sarah and Angelina Grimké* (New York: Columbia University Press, 1989).

Lydia Maria Child, Introduction to Harriet Jacobs, *Incidents in the Life of a Slave Girl, Written by Herself*, ed. Jean Fagan Yellin (Cambridge, MA: Harvard University Press, 1987).

Sir Edward Coke, *The First Part of the Institute of the Law of England*, 4th edn (London, 1739).

James Fenimore Cooper, *The Deerslayer*, ed. Robert Clark (London: J. M. Dent, 1993).

James Fenimore Cooper, *The Pioneers*, in *Cooper: The Leatherstocking Tales I* (New York: Library of America, 1985).

John Cotton, *The Whole Book of Psalmes, Faithfully Translated into English Metre* (Cambridge, MA, 1640).

J. Hector St. John de Crèvecoeur, *Letters From an American Farmer* (Philadelphia: Matthew Carey, 1793).

Philip Curtin, *The Rise and Fall of the Atlantic Complex: Essays in Atlantic History* (New York and Cambridge, UK: Cambridge University Press, 1998).

Cathy Davidson, *Revolution and the Word: The Rise of the Novel in America* (Oxford: Oxford University Press, 1986).

Bernal Díaz del Castillo, "History of the Conquest of New Spain," trans. Susan Castillo, in Susan Castillo and Ivy Schweitzer, *The Literatures of Colonial America: An Anthology* (Oxford: Blackwell, 2001), pp. 40–62.

Emily Dickinson, *The Complete Poems of Emily Dickinson*, ed. Thomas H. Johnson (London: Faber & Faber, 1970).

Emily Dickinson, *Selected Poems*, ed. Helen McNeil (London: J. M. Dent, 1997).

Wai Chee Dimock, *Empire for Liberty: Melville and the Poetics of Individualism* (Princeton, NJ: Princeton University Press, 1991).

Henry Dobyns, *Their Number Become Thinned: Native American Population Dynamics in Eastern North America* (Knoxville: University of Tennessee Press, 1983).

Frederick Douglass, *Narrative of the Life of Frederick Douglass, an American Slave, Written by Himself*, ed. William L. Andrews and William S. McFeely (New York: Norton, 1997).

Alan Dundes, "Earth-Diver: Creation of the Mythopoeic Male," *American Anthropologist New Series*, 64, no. 5, part I (October 1962), pp. 1032–51.

Emory Elliott, "New England Puritan Literature," in Sacvan Bercovitch, ed., *The Cambridge History of American Literature*, vol. 1 (Cambridge, UK: Cambridge University Press, 1994), pp. 171–306.

Ralph Waldo Emerson, *Emerson: Essays and Lectures*, ed. Joel Porte (New York: Library of America, 1983).

Olaudah Equiano, *The Interesting Narrative of the Life of Olaudah Equiano, or Gustavus Vassa, The African, Written by Himself*, ed. Werner Sollors (New York: Norton, 2001).

Betsy Erkkila, "Phillis Wheatley and the Black American Revolution," in *A Mixed Race: Ethnicity in Early America*, ed. Frank Shuffleton (New York: Oxford University Press, 1993), pp. 225–40.

Betsy Erkkila, "The Poetics of Whiteness: Poe and the Racial Imaginary," in *Romancing the Shadow: Poe and Race*, ed. Gerald Kennedy and Liliane Weissberg (Oxford: Oxford University Press, 2001), pp. 41–74.

Judith Farr, *The Passion of Emily Dickinson* (Cambridge, MA: Harvard University Press, 1992).

Fanny Fern, "Independence," *New York Ledger*, June 10, 1859.

Tara Fitzpatrick, "The Figure of Captivity: The Cultural Work of the Puritan Captivity Narrative," *American Literary History*, 3, no. 1 (Spring, 1991), pp 1–26; www.jstor.org/stable/489730, accessed August 3, 2008.

Benjamin Franklin, *The Autobiography of Benjamin Franklin* (London: Central School of Arts and Crafts, 1910, private edn).

Margaret Fuller, *Woman in the Nineteenth Century*, ed. Larry J. Reynolds (New York: Norton, 1998).

Edwin Gaustad, *Liberty of Conscience: Roger Williams in America* (Grand Rapids, MI: William B. Eerdmans, 1991).

Antonello Gerbi, *The Dispute of the New World: The History of a Polemic, 1750–1900*, trans. Jeremy Moyle (Pittsburgh, PA: University of Pittsburgh Press, 1973).

Paul Giles, *Transatlantic Insurrections: British Culture and the Formation of American Literature, 1730–1860* (Philadelphia: University of Pennsylvania Press, 2001).

Paul Giles, *Atlantic Republic: The American Tradition in English Literature* (Oxford: Oxford University Press, 2009).

Frederic Gleach, *Powhatan's World and Colonial Virginia: A Conflict of Cultures* (Lincoln: University of Nebraska Press, 1997).

Richard Gray, *A History of American Literature* (Oxford: Blackwell, 2004).

Michael Green and Theda Purdue, *The Cherokee Nation and the Trail of Tears* (New York: Viking, 2007).

Jack Greene, "An Uneasy Connection: An Analysis of the Preconditions of the American Revolution," in *Essays on the American Revolution*, ed. Stephen Kurtz and James H. Hutson (Chapel Hill: University of North Carolina Press, 1973), pp. 32–80.

Angelina Grimké, *Letters to C. H. Beecher, in Reply to an Essay on Slavery and Abolition Addressed to A. E. G.* (Boston: I. Knapp, 1838). Available at http://utc.iath.virginia.edu/saxon/servlet/SaxonServlet?source=utc/xml/pretexts/abolitn/abesaegb.xml&style=utc/xsl/utc.xsl&n1=5&clear-stylesheet-cache=y, accessed November 2, 2009.

Sandra Gustafson, *Eloquence is Power: Oratory and Performance in Early America* (Williamsburg, VA: Omohundro Institute, 1999).

Patricia Harrington, "Mother of Death, Mother of Rebirth: The Virgin of Guadalupe," *Journal of the American Academy of Religion*, 56, no. 1 (1988), pp. 25–50.

Nathaniel Hawthorne, *Nathaniel Hawthorne, Selected Tales and Sketches*, ed. Michael Colacurcio (Harmondsworth, UK: Penguin, 1987).

Nathaniel Hawthorne, *The Scarlet Letter*, ed. Seymour Gross, Sculley Bradley, Richmond Croom Beatty, and E. Hudson Long (New York: Norton, 1988).

Nathaniel Hawthorne, *The Blithedale Romance* (Oxford: Oxford University Press, 1991).

Katherine Henry, "Angelina Grimké's Rhetoric of Exposure," *American Quarterly*, 49, no. 2 (June 1997), pp. 328–55. Available at www.jstor.org/pss/30041584, accessed February 2, 2009.

David Humphreys, Joel Barlow, John Trumbull, and Lemuel Hopkins, *The Anarchiad*, ed. Luther Riggs (New Haven, CT: Stafford, 1861).

Rhys Isaac, "Books and the Social Authority of Learning: The Case of Mid-Eighteenth-Century Virginia," in *Printing and Society in Early America*, eds. William Joyce, David Hall, and Richard Brown (Worcester, MA: American Antiquarian Society, 1988), pp. 228–49.

Thomas Ingersoll, "'Releese us out of this Cruell Bondegg': An Appeal from Virginia in 1723," *William & Mary Quarterly*, 3rd series, LI, no. 4, October 1994, pp. 777–82.

Harriet Jacobs, *Incidents in the Life of a Slave Girl, Written by Herself*, ed. Jean Fagan Yellin (Cambridge, MA: Harvard University Press, 1987).

Thomas Jefferson, *Notes on the State of Virginia*, ed. Frank Shuffleton (New York: Penguin, 1999).

Myra Jehlen, ed., *Herman Melville: A Collection of Critical Essays* (Englewood Cliffs, NJ: Prentice-Hall, 1994).

John Jennings, "The Poor Unhappy Transported Felon's Sorrowful Account of his Fourteen Years Transportation at Virginia in America," *Virginia Historical Magazine*, 56 (1948), pp. 180–94.

Carol Karlsen, *The Devil in the Shape of a Woman: Witchcraft in Colonial New England* (New York: Norton, 1999).

Gerald Kennedy and Liliane Weissberg, eds., *Romancing the Shadow: Poe and Race* (Oxford: Oxford University Press, 2001).

Linda Kerber, *Women of the Republic: Intellect and Ideology in Revolutionary America* (Chapel Hill: University of North Carolina Press, 1980).

Lyle Koehler, *A Search for Power: The "Weaker Sex" in Seventeenth-Century New England* (Chicago: University of Chicago Press, 1980).

Alfred Kroeber, "Cultural and Natural Areas of Native North America," *University of California Publications in American Archaeology and Ethnology*, 38 (1963), pp. 1–242.

Alfred Krupat, *The Turn to the Native: Studies in Criticism and Culture* (Lincoln and London: Nebraska University Press, 1996).

Karen Kupperman, *The Jamestown Project* (Cambridge, MA: Harvard University Press, 2007).

Stephen Kurtz and James H. Hutson, eds., *Essays on the American Revolution* (Chapel Hill: University of North Carolina Press, 1973).

Amy Schrager Lang, *Prophetic Woman: Anne Hutchinson and the Problem of Dissent in the Literature of New England* (Berkeley: University of California Press, 1987).

Armand Lanusse, *Les Cenelles: Choix de poesies indigènes* (Shreveport, LA: Les Cahiers du Tintamarre, 2003).

Edward Larkin, Introduction to Thomas Paine's *Common Sense* (Toronto: Broadview, 2004).

D. H. Lawrence, *Studies in Classic American Literature* (London: Penguin, 1977).

Walter A. McDougall, *Promised Land, Crusader State: The American Encounter with the World Since 1778* (New York: Houghton Mifflin, 1997).

F. O. Mattheissen, *American Renaissance: Art and Expression in the Age of Emerson and Whitman* (Oxford: Oxford University Press, 1941).

James R. Mellow, *Nathaniel Hawthorne in His Times* (Boston: Houghton Mifflin, 1980).

Herman Melville, *Typee* (London: Humphrey Milford, 1924).

Herman Melville, *Moby-Dick*, ed. Hershel Parker and Harrison Hayford (New York: Norton, 2002a).

Herman Melville, *Bartleby the Scrivener*, in *Melville's Short Novels*, ed. Dan McCall (New York: Norton, 2002b).

Herman Melville, *Benito Cereno*, in *Melville's Short Novels*, ed. Dan McCall (New York: Norton, 2002c).

Perry Miller, *Errand into the Wilderness* (Cambridge, MA: Belknap Press), 1956.

Frank Moore, ed., *Songs and Ballads of the American Revolution* (New York: D. Appleton, 1856).

Toni Morrison, *Playing in the Dark: Whiteness and the Literary Imagination* (London: Pan, 1993).

Thomas Morton, *New English Canaan, or New Canaan* (London: Charles Greene, 1637).

Frank L. Mott, *Golden Multitudes* (New York: Macmillan, 1947).

David Murray, "Using Roger Williams' Key into America," *Symbiosis: A Journal of Anglo-American Literary Relations*, 1, no. 2 (October 1997), pp. 237–53.

David Murray, "Translation and Mediation," in *The Cambridge Companion to Native American Literature*, eds. Joy Porter and K. Roemer (Cambridge, UK: Cambridge University Press, 2005), pp. 69–83.

Edmund Nequatewa, *Truth of a Hopi* (Flagstaff, AZ: Northland Publishing, 1994).

Mary Beth Norton, *In the Devil's Snare: The Salem Witchcraft Crisis of 1692* (New York: Vintage, 2002).

John O'Sullivan, "The Great Nation of Futurity," *The United States Magazine and Democratic Review* 6 (November 1839).

Anthony Pagden, *Peoples and Empires* (New York: Modern Library, 2003).

Thomas Paine, *Common Sense*, ed. Edward Larkin (Toronto: Broadview, 2004).

Susan Scott Parrish, *American Curiosity: Cultures of Natural History in the Colonial British Atlantic World* (Chapel Hill: University of North Carolina Press, 2006).

Cornelius de Pauw, *Recherches philosophiques sur les américains*, vol. 2 (Berlin: G. J. Decker, 1768).

Roy Harvey Pearce, ed., *Whitman: A Collection of Critical Essays* (Englewood Cliffs, NJ: Prentice-Hall, 1962).

Donald Pease, *The American Renaissance Reconsidered* (Baltimore: Johns Hopkins University Press, 1985).

Gaspar Pérez de Villagrá, *Historia de la Nueva Mexico*, trans. and ed. M. Eincinias, A. Rodríguez, and J. Sánchez (Albuquerque: University of New Mexico Press, 1992).

Edgar Allan Poe, "The Fall of the House of Usher," in *Tales of Mystery and Imagination* (Dent: London, 1908), pp. 128–44.

Edgar Allan Poe, *The Narrative of Arthur Gordon Pym and Related Tales* (Oxford: Oxford University Press, 1994).

Joy Porter, "Historical and Cultural Contexts," in *The Cambridge Companion to Native American Literature*, eds. Joy Porter and K. Roemer (Cambridge, UK: Cambridge University Press, 2005), pp. 39–68.

Joy Porter and K. Roemer, eds., *The Cambridge Companion to Native American Literature* (Cambridge, UK: Cambridge University Press, 2005).

Mary Louise Pratt, *Imperial Eyes: Travel Writing and Transculturation* (London and New York: Routledge, 1992).

Gladys Reichard, "Literary Types and Dissemination of Myths," *Journal of American Folklore*, 34, no. 133 (1921), pp. 269–307.

Michelle Rosaldo, "Woman, Culture and Society: A Theoretical Overview," in *Woman, Culture and Society*, ed. Michelle Rosaldo and Louise Lamphere (Stanford, CA: Stanford University Press, 1974), pp. 17–42.

John Carlos Rowe, *At Emerson's Tomb: The Politics of Classic American Literature* (New York: Columbia University Press, 1997).

Mary Rowlandson, *A True History of the Captivity and Restoration of Mrs. Mary Rowlandson, a Minister's Wife in New-England* (London, 1682).

Gordon Sayre, *Les Sauvages Américains: Representations of Native Americans in French and English Colonial Literature* (Chapel Hill: University of North Carolina Press, 1997).

Gordon Sayre, *The Indian Chief as Tragic Hero: Native Resistance and the Literatures of America, from Moctezuma to Tecumseh* (Chapel Hill: University of North Carolina Press, 2009).

Ivy Schweitzer, *The Work of Self-Representation: Lyric Poetry in Colonial New England* (Chapel Hill: University of North Carolina Press, 1991).

Richard B. Sewall, ed., *Emily Dickinson: A Collection of Critical Essays* (Englewood Cliffs, NJ: Prentice-Hall, 1964).

Samuel Sewall, *The Diary of Samuel Sewall, 1674–1729*, vol. 2, ed. M. Halsey Thomas (New York: Farrar, Strauss, & Giroux, 1973).

Carole Shammas, "The Origins of Transatlantic Colonization," in *A Companion to Colonial America*, ed. Daniel Vickers (Oxford: Blackwell, 2006), pp. 25–43.

Richard Slotkin, *Regeneration Through Violence: The Mythology of the American Frontier, 1600–1800* (Middletown, CT: Wesleyan University Press, 1973).

John Smith, *The Generall Historie of Virginia, New England, and the Summer Isles* (1629).

Carroll Smith-Rosenberg, "The Female World of Love and Ritual: Relations between Women in Nineteenth-Century America," *Signs*, 1 (Autumn, 1975), pp. 1–29.

Charles Edward Stowe, *Harriet Beecher Stowe: The Story of Her Life* (London: Nisbet & Co., 1911).

Harriet Beecher Stowe, *Uncle Tom's Cabin*, ed. Elizabeth Ammons (New York: Norton, 1994).

Edward Taylor, *The Poetical Works of Edward Taylor*, ed. Thomas Johnson (Princeton, NJ: Princeton University Press, 1966).

Stith Thompson, ed., *Tales of the North American Indians* (Mineola, NY: Dover Publications, 1929).

Henry David Thoreau, *Walden and Resistance to Civil Government*, 2nd edn, ed. William Rossi (New York: Norton, 1966).

Russell Thornton, "Health, Disease, and Demography," in Philip J. Deloria and Neal Salisbury, eds., *A Companion to American Indian History* (Oxford: Blackwell, 2004), pp. 68–84.

Teresa Toulouse, *The Captive's Position: Female Narrative, Male Identity, and Royal Authority in Colonial New England* (Philadelphia: University of Pennsylvania Press, 2006).

Hamilton Tyler, *Pueblo Gods and Myths* (Norman: University of Oklahoma Press, 1964).

Royall Tyler, *The Contrast* (New York: The Dunlap Society, 1887).

John Underhill, *Newes from America* (London: Peter Cole, 1638).

El Inca Garcilaso de la Vega, *Comentarios reales de los Incas*, vol. I, ed. Angel Rosenblatt (Buenos Aires: Emece Editores, 1943).

Daniel Vickers, ed., *A Companion to Colonial America* (Oxford: Blackwell, 2006).

David Walker, *Appeal: In Four Articles, Together with a Preamble to the Colored Citizens of the World, but in Particular, and Very Expressly, to the United States of America* (Boston: D. Walker, 1830).

James D. Wallace, "Hawthorne and the Scribbling Women Reconsidered," *American Literature*, 62, no. 2 (June 1990), pp. 211–26.

Immanuel Wallerstein, *World-Systems Analysis: An Introduction* (Durham, NC and London: Duke University Press, 2004).

Jace Weaver, Craig S. Womack, and Robert Warrior, *American Indian Literary Nationalism* (Albuquerque: University of New Mexico Press, 2006).

Max Weber, "The Spirit of Capitalism," in *Benjamin Franklin: A Collection of Critical Essays*, ed. Brian Barbour (Englewood Cliffs: Prentice Hall, 1979), pp. 14–19.

Albert K. Weinberg, *Manifest Destiny: A Study of Nationalist Expansionism in American History* (Baltimore: Johns Hopkins University Press, 1935).

Barbara Welter, "The Cult of True Womanhood: 1820 to 1860," *American Quarterly*, 18 (Summer 1966), pp. 151–74.

Phillis Wheatley, *Memoir and Poems of Phillis Wheatley, A Native African and a Slave*, 3rd edn (Boston: Isaac Knapp, 1838).

Walt Whitman, *Leaves of Grass*, ed. Sculley Bradley and Harold W. Blodgett (New York: Norton, 1973).

Michael Wigglesworth, *The Day of Doom; Or a Description of the Great and Last Judgement* (London, 1666).

Roger Williams, *Key into the Language of America*, John Teunissen and Evelyn J. Hinz, eds. (Detroit: Wayne State University Press, 1973).

John Winthrop, *A Journal of the Transactions and Occurrences in the Settlement of Massachusetts and the other New-England Colonies, from the year 1630 to 1644* (Hartford, CT: Printed by Elisha Babcock, 1790).

John Winthrop, *History of New England 1630–1649*, vol. II, ed. James Hosmer (New York: Scribners, 1908).

Shira Wolosky, "Walt Whitman: The Office of the Poet," in Sacvan Bercovitch, ed., *The Cambridge History of American Literature*, vol. IV (Cambridge, UK: Cambridge University Press, 2004), pp. 362–426.

John Woolman, *Some Considerations on the Keeping of Negroes* (1754).

Howard Zinn, *A People's History of the United States* (New York: Harper, 2003).

Alonso de Zorita, *Life and Labor in Ancient Mexico* (New Brunswick: Rutgers University Press, 1963).

Index